TUSCALOOSA

200 YEARS IN THE MAKING

MARGARET CAMMER FURMAN, STATE CAPITOL, TUSCALOOSA, c. 1840s
(Courtesy The University of Alabama Libraries Special Collections)

PERKINS AND COBBS GENERAL MERCHANDISE, NORTH SIDE OF BROAD STREET, TUSCALOOSA, c. 1855
(Private collection. Courtesy Cowan's Auctions, Inc., Cincinnati, Ohio)

TUSCALOOSA

200 YEARS IN THE MAKING

G. WARD HUBBS

THE UNIVERSITY OF ALABAMA PRESS
Tuscaloosa

The University of Alabama Press
Tuscaloosa, Alabama 35487-0380
uapress.ua.edu

Typeface: Sabon and Myriad Pro Condensed

Manufactured in China

Cover images: (*inset*) Greensboro Avenue, Tuscaloosa, 1939 (Courtesy Tuscaloosa Preservation Society); (*background*) Map of Tuscaloosa from John La Tourette's 1838 Map of the State of Alabama (Courtesy The University of Alabama Libraries Special Collections)

Cover and interior design: Robin McDonald

Cataloging-in-Publication data is available from the Library of Congress.

ISBN: 978-0-8173-5944-7
E-ISBN: 978-0-8173-9233-8

TUSCA2OOSA BICENTENNIAL

PAT, CANADIAN BY BIRTH, TUSCALOOSAN BY CHOICE.

For you, of course.

MRS. JULIAN C. PERKINS AND THREE UNIDENTIFIED INDIVIDUALS SITTING ON A PARK BENCH, c. 1890

(Courtesy The University of Alabama Libraries Special Collections)

AN UNIDENTIFIED TUSCALOOSAN, c. 1890
(Courtesy The University of Alabama Libraries Special Collections)

WHAT WOULD IT BE TO US, could we have thus before us now, the faithful representation of the great and the good, whose faces will never more be seen on earth!

— P. H. May, editor of the *Tuscaloosa Flag of the Union*, 1841

VIEW OF LOCK NO. 1, BLACK WARRIOR RIVER, c. 1890
(Courtesy The University of Alabama Libraries Special Collections)

Contents

Acknowledgments

ANY THANKS I OFFER WILL NECESSARILY FALL SHORT. Nonetheless, I will try.

The members of the Tuscaloosa Bicentennial Commission, especially Cathy Randall and Kari Frederickson, were not just firmly behind this project, they sought me out to write it in the first place. After that, Editor-in-Chief Daniel Waterman and his assistant Kristen Hop at the University of Alabama Press worked hard in seeing it to completion. Robin McDonald did his usual extraordinary work designing the book.

Those at the Hoole Special Collections Library, especially Kevin Ray, Marina Klaric, and Lorraine Madway, did exceptional work in finding the many photographs from their exceptional collection of Tuscaloosa materials. Scotty Kirkland and Meredith McDonough at the Alabama Department of Archives and History assisted me with their usual enthusiasm. Kathryn H. Braund at Auburn University explained that Chief Yoholo-Micco's speech in the statehouse, despite my initial skepticism, had all the earmarks of the real thing. Frances Robb, Alabama's peerless authority on early photography, helped me in describing several of the photographs and suggested the great portrait of William Henry Sheppard that she donated to the Hoole Special Collections Library. The *Tuscaloosa News* has served this town well for over a century now, as this book has demonstrated; in keeping with their legacy, the current staff stepped in once again to allow the use of their photographs, especially in the final chapter. My sincerest thanks to all of you.

Several Tuscaloosans—all dear friends—generously read the manuscript and then offered valuable suggestions. These begin with the respected South-

Edwin C., Julian H., and Brook K. Perkins swimming in Swift Creek, c. 1890. (Courtesy The University of Alabama Libraries Special Collections)

ern historians at the University of Alabama, Kari Frederickson and Paul M. Pruitt Jr. Thomas Sawallis interrupted a very busy schedule to give his fine eye to what I had thought was my final draft. Tuscaloosans are indeed fortunate to have Robert O. Mellown, without whose research and writing the significance of Tuscaloosa's architecture would never be known. Not only did he check over what I wrote, but Robert never hesitated to answer my obscure questions or offer the use of his fifteen linear feet of collected materials on Tuscaloosa. Similarly, Christopher Lyle McIlwain Sr., generously presented me with the materials he collected on Tuscaloosa during his twenty years of research for Civil War Alabama; I and others are having to reinterpret those years as a result of his innovative and thorough work. As always, Lawrence Frederick Kohl gave me his wise and much valued counsel.

Pamela Sawallis has been much more than my friend and colleague at Birmingham-Southern College. I have come to rely on her rare gift of knowing exactly where a small change—perhaps a different word, restructured sentence, or added paragraph—would make a world of difference. This can be rather humbling.

And James N. Ezell, a Tuscaloosa historian in his own right, not only gave me access to his own considerable research, but spent hours—perhaps days—tracking down hundreds of minute facts that made the manuscript far richer. He then read and critiqued it.

I am immensely grateful to all of you.

And I am grateful to those Tuscaloosans—from 1819 to today, known and unknown—whose collective efforts gave us the opportunity to create lives well lived.

Twice As Nice
Consignment Shop

Six Decisions

Opposite page: The town clock is a reminder that in Tuscaloosa the past still lives with today. (Courtesy Robin McDonald)

"I STEPPED INTO A PAST," wrote Carl Carmer of his half-dozen years in Tuscaloosa, "that lives and is concurrent with today." In the 1920s when the native New Yorker came to teach in the University of Alabama's Department of English, he found the languid town exotic. He would try to make sense of his life in the "river-bordered town" when he returned to the North by writing an odd sort of literary guide, *Stars Fell on Alabama*, which has become a minor classic. He failed. The best he could do was to "remember my life in Tuscaloosa as an unreality stumbled upon long ago."

We must give Carmer credit for grasping that he had somehow "stumbled upon" a town where time operates in unfamiliar ways. "Tuscaloosa lives a life of its own," he wrote. It is "an enchanted life in an age other than ours." But that was as far as he got. Carmer couldn't make sense of that "age other than ours," that "past that lives and is concurrent with today." Perhaps we expect too much of poets. Had he invested the effort to look into what Tuscaloosans had been doing during the century before he arrived, however, Carmer would not have remained so bewildered. He would have instead found the Druid City to be less baffling, and immensely more interesting, than the "strange country" that so intrigued him.

To begin with, Carmer would have discovered that the Tuscaloosa of his day was the product of a few pivotal decisions. Some of these decisions Tuscaloosans made on their own; others were made for them. Some were made quickly; others took decades. Some met with near universal approval; others were bitterly divisive. Some were made by Tuscaloosans unaware that they were even making a decision. No matter, each changed the town entirely.

Stars Fell on Alabama, Carl Carmer's memoir of his six years in Alabama while teaching English at the university, paints an affectionate but unflinching portait of the state. (Courtesy The University of Alabama Libraries Special Collections)

Those key decisions began in 1825 when the state legislature chose the frontier village along the Black Warrior River as the next state capital. The construction boom had hardly ended when the legislature moved the government again, this time to Montgomery. Tuscaloosans were left with vestiges of glory and little else. The 1861 decision for Alabama to secede from the Union led directly to the town's invasion during the waning days of the Civil War. But Robert E. Lee's surrender at Appomattox would not bring peace as a bitterly divided citizenry tore their social fabric apart. In a concerted effort to reignite Tuscaloosa's failed economy, town boosters meanwhile worked to attract industry and to turn their old town into a modern city—with unforeseen consequences. Even as Carmer published *Stars Fell on Alabama* in 1934, radio was opening a wider world to Tuscaloosans, and their world would only continue to expand when they went off to fight in the Second World War. Exposure to new people and new ideas, aided by television, would bring the issue of racial division to a head and increase the effectiveness of the civil rights movement. And years later, many of these combined efforts would pay off with the establishment of a huge plant to manufacture one of the world's finest automobiles.

Several of these decisions were local versions of bigger changes going on across the country. But *changes* understates the matter. *Revolutions* is closer to the mark. The secession of the Southern states and creation of the Confederacy was certainly revolutionary, as was the resulting end of slavery and granting of voting rights to black Americans. The introduction of modern domestic inventions—electric lights, telephones, water systems, automobiles, and such—has been called the Second Industrial Revolution. The civil rights movement wrought social upheavals that are still ongoing. All of these were no less revolutionary, in different ways, than America's War of Independence.

The fact that these revolutions, from secession through the civil rights movement, were also taking place nationally does not make Tuscaloosa into a smaller version of the country. Nor does the fact that other towns across America also experienced these same revolutions mean that all their stories are the same. Each town dealt with these revolutions in its own way. That is because a town, or a community, is not a place. A town *occurs* in a place, but it is not the place itself. The history of a town is thus the story of how a people—by way of their aspirations, their ordeals, their divisions, their failures, their successes—built their community. Each town is different because its people dealt with challenges in their own distinctive way. Each town creates its own personality.

Although many towns face similar challenges, each must also face unique challenges and events. Tuscaloosa has had its share of these—from the coming of the state's capital, to its invasion and burning during the Civil War, to the significant roles it played during the Second World War and the civil rights movement. Out of these, Tuscaloosans fashioned their own distinguishing responses that further shaped the town's personality. But one event looms large.

On April 27, 2011, Tuscaloosa was hit by a massive tornado that caused widespread destruction and took many lives. The immediate and lasting result was an outpouring of aid from all over the country. (Courtesy Robin McDonald)

When an April 2011 tornado destroyed an eighth of Tuscaloosa and claimed the lives of fifty-three Tuscaloosans, all sorts of people—whether complete strangers or close friends—immediately began helping each other. They worked through the night, the next day, and the next week. They worked for months and sometimes years afterward. And not just those living within the city's limits. Folks came to help from all over Alabama, from all over the nation, and even from foreign countries. They arrived in their pickup trucks loaded with canned goods, bottles of water, and much-needed bags of ice. They brought their chainsaws and hammers. Some showed up empty-handed and asked where to start. They came to clear the rubble, repair the damage, and rebuild what was gone. They also came to put their arms around the shoulders of those who hurt.

Those volunteers made their decision immediately, with hardly a thought. Why? Helping others in need is what good people do—certainly. But people also came by the tens of thousands because they believed that the tornado had done more than wreck homes and businesses. The tornado had threatened something special that was worth their efforts to restore. Those volunteers may not have been able to say exactly what that something special was, but they knew that it had something to do with Tuscaloosans and not just damaged buildings. And surely those volunteers felt something akin to what someone in 1906 called the Tuscaloosa Idea: that indefinable something that keeps luring folk back to the banks of the Black Warrior.

The town clock stands prominently at the intersection of University Boulevard and Greensboro Avenue, the city's center since its incorporation in 1819. That town clock does more than tell the time. It reminds us that this moment in Tuscaloosa is the product of all those moments that came before. The town clock reminds us that, in the words of Carl Carmer, the past lives with today in Tuscaloosa.

Tuscaloosans secure the state capital... only to lose it

Opposite page: Legislators met in the Alabama statehouse, designed by William Nichols, when Tuscaloosa served as the state's capital, from 1825 to 1847. Engraving from Amaud P. Pfister's "The Alabama March." (Courtesy Alabama Department of Archives and History)

AS 1819 WAS DRAWING TO A CLOSE so was Alabama's territorial stage. On December 13, the legislature decided to incorporate the frontier village at the Falls of the Black Warrior. The next day, Alabama would join the Union as the twenty-second state.

Confusion abounded. To begin with, the legislators had jumped the gun by deeming themselves the General Assembly of the *State* of Alabama—it was still the *Territory* of Alabama. Then came the problem of spelling—sometimes *Tuscaloosa* and at other times *Tuskaloosa*—within the same document. No matter the spelling, the name had never been in doubt. Following the reports from Hernando de Soto's ill-fated 1540 expedition, the European mapmakers charged with tracing his route placed the Indian towns he described prominently on their maps. They had no way of knowing that the European diseases his men unknowingly introduced had drastically reduced the native population, perhaps by as much as 90 percent. The towns were gone, but the names stayed. The location of Chief Tuscaloosa's town moved about on the maps as subsequent explorers failed to find it. The name finally stayed put at the end of an extensive series of shoals where the Black Warrior River left the Appalachian Mountains' foothills.

Richard Breckenridge found "as handsome a situation for a town as I ever saw," upon reaching those shoals on August 27, 1816. He noted

N. Currier's Lith. N.Y. W. K. Hewitt. on Stone

THE ALABAMA STATE MARCH,

COMPOSED AND RESPECTFULLY DEDICATED TO

HIS EXCELLENCY, ARTHUR P. BAGBY,

Governor of the State of Alabama.

BY

AMAUD P. PFISTER

OF

TUSCALOOSA. ALA.

NEW YORK.
Published by GEIB & WALKER *23 Maiden Lane.*

"some excellent land and some good springs." Only four days later, a merchant arrived with his load of sugar, coffee, rum, wine, dry goods, and a thousand oranges. James Crump had left Mobile twenty days earlier by boat, making his way against the current. He sold the dry goods and rum at the village before transferring his remaining wares to a couple of wagons and heading up the road to Huntsville, which he reached 120 miles and eight days later. Only a half-dozen oranges spoiled.

American settlers had only started coming to what they called the Falls of the Black Warrior a few months before Breckenridge and Crump's 1816 stopovers. The Treaty of Fort Stephens, signed that October with the Choctaws, would legitimize the settlers' intrusion into the Tombigbee and Black Warrior River valleys. Questions

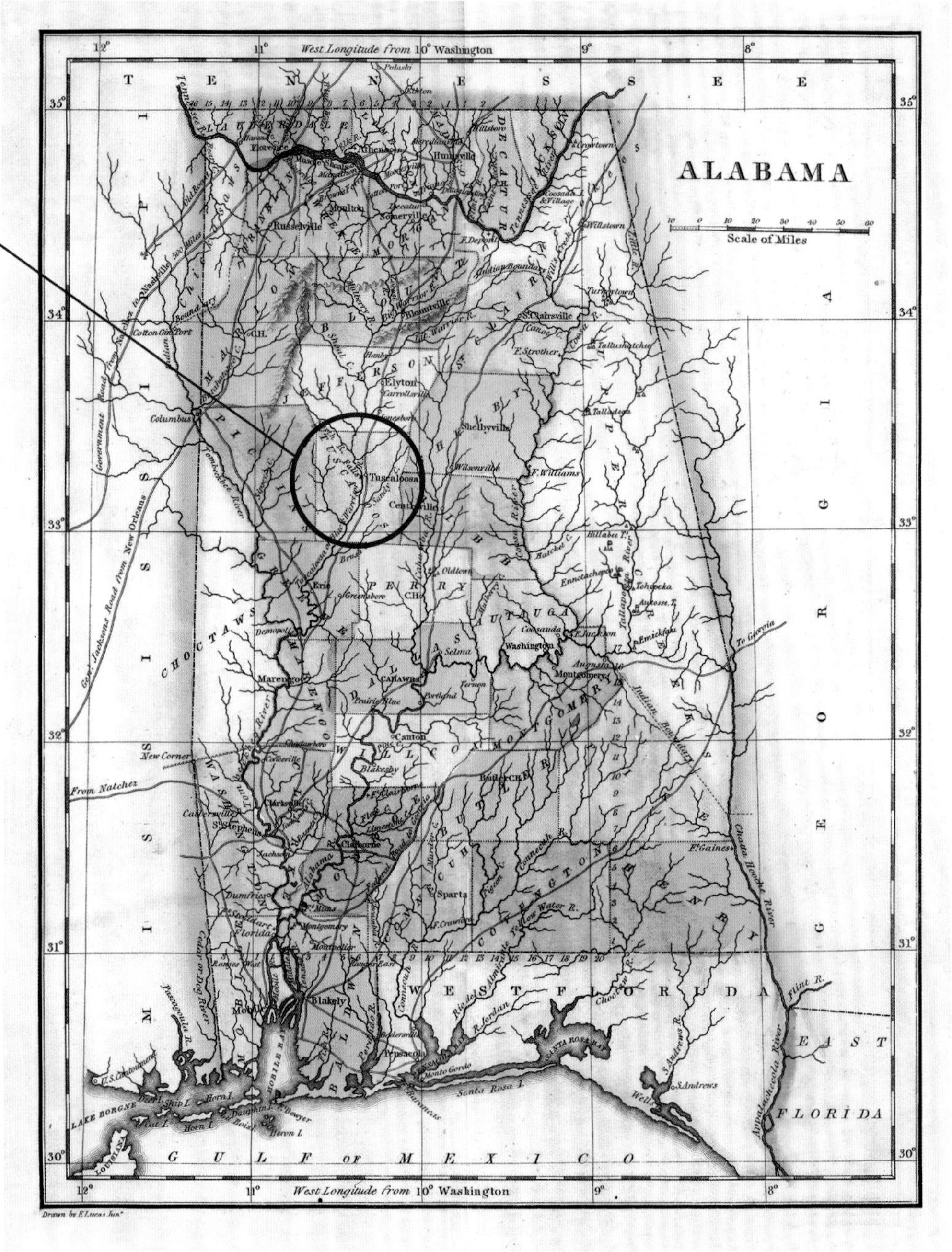

Early travelers between north and south Alabama nearly all came through Tuscaloosa, at the Falls of the Black Warrior River, seen here in the 1822 map drawn by Lucas and Turner. (Courtesy The University of Alabama Libraries Special Collections)

about land ownership would continue—but no longer with the Indians.

Breckenridge reached the falls from the north, tromping down the Huntsville Road beneath a nearly unbroken canopy of enormous longleaf pines. Unlike most mature forests, which were hardwood, the South's frequent lightning strikes ignited the underbrush and hardwood seedlings but left the fire-resistant longleaf pines to thrive. The resulting trees were spaced so far apart that early settlers reported not needing roads to drive their wagons through the forests. There were exceptions. Northeast of the falls in higher country and especially on the northern slopes—where the ground never quite dried out enough for regular fires to start—the longleaf pines disappeared, replaced by a hardwood forest primarily of oaks, hickory, sweetgum, chestnut, and beech. Within the forests lived all sorts of wild animals from elk and deer to wolves and bears. Huge wild swine, the descendants of de Soto's roving pantry, wandered at their leisure. None of the settlers knew then that beneath the forest northeast of the falls lay the enormous Warrior Coal Field along with deposits of limestone and iron ore.

The Black Warrior River that Crump managed to negotiate began high on the South Cumberland Plateau as nameless streams became the Mulberry and Locust Forks. These in turn merged to become the Black Warrior proper, which flowed southwest through the Appalachian foothills, gaining momentum and size as it was fed by more creeks and streams. The river passed through a magnificent series of shoals, stretching for miles, where exquisite spider lilies grew. After the last of these, the river entered the coastal plain and began meandering lazily through softer sediments until it emptied into the Tombigbee River, where Demopolis would be founded by French exiles. Along both banks of that route from the falls to Demopolis grew a nearly continuous band of native cane, or bamboo. This thirty-foot "magnificent reed," in the words of one visitor, kept the water "perfectly clear" by holding back the soil. The "Nile of the Western Country," as a promotional piece labeled the Black Warrior in 1818,

British naval officer Capt. Basil Hall made this sketch of a road through the "Pine Barrens" on a trip across Alabama in the 1820s. An immense longleaf pine forest surrounded the village of Tuscaloosa. (Courtesy Alabama Department of Archives and History)

The shoals of the Black Warrior are seen here during the summer. The stone pillars supported several nineteenth-century bridges. (Courtesy The University of Alabama Libraries Special Collections)

THE ACTUAL FALLS OF THE BLACK WARRIOR *were a couple of miles upstream, where the water poured over a ledge stretching from bank to bank. The ceaseless sound it created could be heard throughout Tuscaloosa and prompted many to try their hands at describing its intoxicating sight and sound. "Hark!" wrote one captivated by its beauty in 1835, the "faint roar of its waters dashing over the numerous ledges of sandstone, shelving and irregular, which fill up its bed here for miles. The sound comes up, sudden and fitful, on the night winds like the echo of distant music to the ear—now quick and loud like a smothered blast; now soft and faint, and slow—now gradually dying away; even mournful and plaintive, but never ceasing, the varying sound."*

stretched 169 miles from its beginnings in the foothills to its end at the Tombigbee.

Although known as the Falls of the Black Warrior, the actual waterfall was a ledge of several feet in height stretching from bank to bank perhaps two miles upriver from the settlement. The river plunging over the shelf there produced a soft roar that could be heard for several miles. The sound breaks "the silence of the primeval woods which overshadow them, even yet," one Tuscaloosan would write years later. Its "ceaseless monotone, not unlike the moan of pines shaken by the winds...floats...by night like an echo from the past, and a voice of the ever ongoing present, blended in one stream of sound." The constant voice of the falls stood out because about the only other sounds were the chirps of birds as they soared in the skies or perched in the trees. And not just the familiar birds of today—the region was home to the now-extinct ivory-billed woodpecker and passenger pigeon.

The first settlers came to the falls for several reasons. The flat land on the south side was high enough above the river to escape its periodic floods, and the soil could easily grow corn and cotton. Well over a hundred native species of fish—an important food source—could be found in the river. Perhaps most important, anyone traveling between north and south Alabama had to pass through their settlement, the state's most inland port. Crump was just the first of thousands—and probably tens of thousands—who over the next several decades would have to transfer from horse to boat, or vice versa, at the falls.

Judging by the number of people who were arriving, many voiced the same opinion as one young man who wrote back home that "this section of the country promises to be very agreeable." Only six months after Breckinridge and Crump arrived, boats were traveling regularly to the falls with settlers and goods. During the spring of 1818, Tennesseans arrived daily by way of the Huntsville Road—so many, according to one of them, that the "small log cabin village" they found upon arrival would grow within a few months "to be a considerable town." Indeed, the inhabitants numbered some three hundred earlier that year, and by September the population had doubled to six hundred.

Perhaps Tuscaloosa was a "considerable town" to the Tennesseans, but it was little more than a crude frontier village to one New Englander. "What they call their *houses*," he wrote in a long and detailed letter to his wife back home, "are either the most despicable rough dirty & uncomfortable rolling log Cabins, or less durable & more mean buildings." Those "mean buildings" were built of clapboard sawn with a whipsaw and nailed in place—when nails were to be had. The New Englander searched for words to express how bad things were, almost repeating himself a few pages later: "They all live in dirty, small Sod & mud Cabins, or in those of a more mean construction, & are generally almost destitute of all the Comforts & conveniences of Life." Few buildings had even a single pane of glass. Some had no floors but dirt; others used split timbers laid directly on the ground; while still others were raised on pilings high enough for hogs, dogs, cats, and fowl to retreat beneath to escape bad weather. "I have sometimes been very much anoyed," the correspondent continued, "by the growling, squealing, barking, squalling & cackling of those animals und[er] the floor where I slept." His room had no ceiling; and the roof, like the floors, was of split oak timbers "thro which the Rains at times pour, *litterally*, in *Streams*." He could only keep his door shut by setting a chair against it. The detached kitchen was simply the "filthiest Place you can conceive of"—and he was describing Charles Lewin's establishment, "which is the best tavern in this place & where I have the best accommodation the Establishment affords."

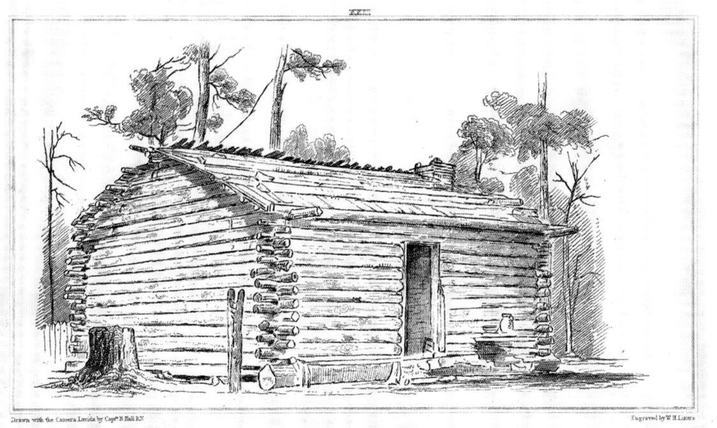

An example of "the most despicable rough dirty & uncomfortable rolling log Cabins," drawn by Capt. Basil Hall on his trip across Georgia and Alabama in the 1820s. (Courtesy Alabama Department of Archives and History)

By 1821, when the New Englander was complaining, Tuscaloosa had grown to about twenty stores, mostly small shanties lined up along a single street. Prices were notoriously high: flour at $25 a barrel; 62½ cents a pound for coffee, 37½ cents a pound for bacon; and beef was simply unavailable. Most of the meat seems to have come from fishing, as it may have throughout much of the nineteenth century. The streets were in such bad repair that the four or five residents who kept coaches could not use them. Shoes were caked in mud. The Baptists and Methodists both had houses of worship, but they were of the same poor construction as the cabins and were "generally left open for hogs &c to enter at pleasure." In fact, a sow had recently given birth to six or seven piglets under the coarse square box that served as the Methodist minister's pulpit. Despite the difficulties in transportation, someone had managed to get a billiard table all the way to the falls. First things first.

These settlers were technically squatters. They could not own their own property because the land was still in a legal morass that went back almost three years before statehood. On the same day in March 1817 that the Territory of Alabama was carved out of the Territory of Mississippi, Congress passed another act reserving up to ten prospective townsites for public land sales. The territorial government then reserved section twenty-two south of the Black Warrior for what would officially become Tuscaloosa in late 1819. But meanwhile, Congress threw a wrench into the works by subsidizing the Connecticut Asylum for the Education and Instruction of Deaf and Dumb Persons by granting the institution up to thirty-six square miles of public land. William H. Ely, a retired businessman who was active in promoting the Connecticut Asylum, was appointed its commissioner and charged with selecting and selling the tracts. He made his way to Alabama, where public land was abundant.

Ely first reached Tuscaloosa in mid-1820, only six months after its incorporation. He, too, recognized that the small but growing settlement was "destined at no distant period to be a place of considerable Importance," so he chose four and a half sections of land for the Connecticut Asylum on the west and south sides of the section set aside for the Tuscaloosa townsite. With the river to the north, this left the only public land to the east, but at least clear title was available. Ely then sold the land he had selected to a group of local investors, who proceeded to subdivide and resell it to individuals. They incorporated the western tract separately as the "lower part of the Town of Tuskaloosa," and the new residents were soon erecting businesses, a dozen or so storehouses, a hotel, and substantial houses. Lawyers moved to the "*New* Town" after a jail and handsome brick courthouse were built. That did not last long, however. Newtown merged with Tuscaloosa within a few years, and in 1842 a tornado wiped away much of the once thriving west end of Tuscaloosa.

Many of these "barberous People," Ely wrote back home indignantly, "are incensed against me." He seemed surprised that Tuscaloosans would resent an outsider dropping in, choosing the best lands, and then making them pay for what they had presumed was their own. When they let him know of their displeasure, he began leaving his room only when armed. Staying confined, he admitted, taxed severely "my health & spirits & render me quite unhappy."

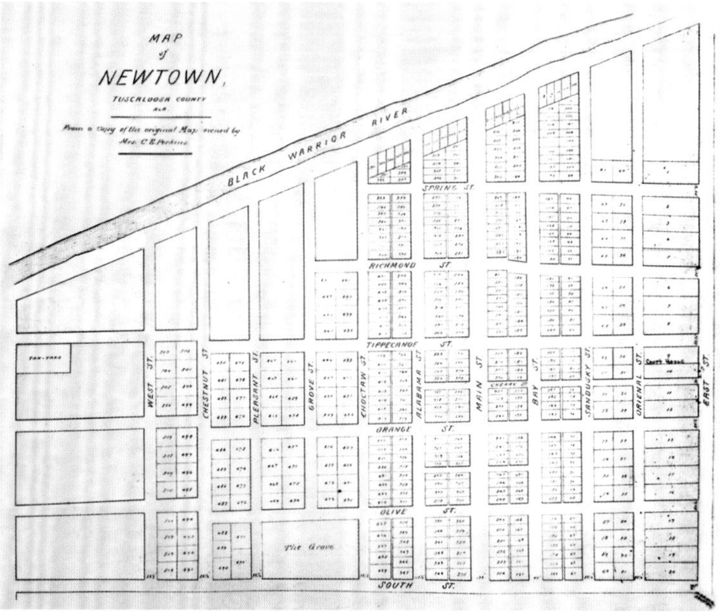

An early copy of a map of Newtown, built on the land chosen by William H. Ely. The site of the courthouse can be seen on the far right side of the map. (Courtesy Alabama Department of Archives and History)

So it was hardly surprising that Ely had little positive to say about Tuscaloosans. They paid little attention to religion, he charged. Flagrant crimes were frequent, and the guilty regularly escaped. Tuscaloosans were heard to utter gross and excessive profanity, even in front of their ministers. Everyone drank alcohol excessively (confirmed by Crump's having sold all his rum before continuing to Huntsville). Much of the population was "extreemly indolent, either too proud, or too lazy to work, or even think, they disipate their time & money, & would their morals if they had any, without enjoyment, lounging about Taverns, Stores, tipling and gambling houses, or in making & attending horse hunting or fighting." Their government, habits, and manners he found "more Mobocratic than I have ever anywhere else met with." Ely concluded that they were "a very avaricious People. *Money* is their God, & *Cotton* the *Idol* of their devotions." In this respect they differed scarcely from all those others who had caught Alabama Fever. As one put it simply, "I came here to make money."

Few stayed long at all. The vast majority were gone within two or three years. Gideon Lincecum, for example, set out from Eatonton, Georgia, in March 1818, "determined to seek a home in the wilderness." Six weeks later he arrived at the falls, where he made eight dollars a day sawing lumber with a whipsaw. But he was gone in November after hearing of even more desirable lands farther west. Lincecum had stayed in Tuscaloosa a little over six months.

Without a stable population, without enduring institutions, with no one to vouch for one's reputation, with rootless strangers coming and going in search of their main chance, with no loyalties except to oneself—in short, without much—Tuscaloosans of that era made poor material for creating communities. The Falls of the Black Warrior was just another outpost along the line where "barberous People" stopped awhile before moving on. Building a community requires better material than that.

THEY BLAMED IT ON THE RAIN. The state senate's Seat of Government Committee reported that Cahawba, the capital since 1820, was "liable to be inundated by the waters of both the Cahawba and Alabama rivers," making it at times "impracticable to reach the State House without a conveyance by water." As if that were not enough, the justices had been "reluctant to perform the hazardous duty of holding the Supreme Court" during June for fear of yellow fever. Flooding and disease may have been the pretext for moving the capital, and certainly those were concerns, but other issues—politics in particular—had been festering for years.

William Wyatt Bibb served as the territorial governor of Alabama, and was elected as Alabama's first governor following statehood. (Courtesy Alabama Department of Archives and History)

The maneuvering had started in 1818 when the territorial legislature met in St. Stephens. Those living in the Tennessee Valley wanted the capital in Huntsville, but they lacked the votes. The legislators from the Tennessee Valley could, however, make common cause with the residents along the Tombigbee and Black Warrior in west Alabama to make Tuscaloosa the capital since it was where the Huntsville Road met the riverboats. But wily Governor William Wyatt Bibb preempted their action by convincing the federal government into donating the land at the confluence of the Cahaba and Alabama Rivers, which was easily reached by his supporters living along those rivers. (The Creek Nation in east Alabama did not figure into the considerations.) Cahawba would be Alabama's capital. The representatives from the Tennessee Valley were to be placated by having Huntsville named the temporary seat of government while Cahawba was readied.

The residents of north Alabama were not pleased. Those who favored Tuscaloosa wrote a provision into the state constitution calling for the 1825 legislature to reconsider the permanent site without the governor's concurrence. Despite some likely irregular voting in Jefferson County, which prompted a challenge, on December 13, 1825—exactly six years to the day after its incorporation—Tuscaloosa became the state's new capital. South Alabamians could get there by steamboat and north Alabamians by horse, buggy, or wagon.

That still did not make traversing the young state any easier. The Black Warrior was only deep enough for boats during the winter months, and mountains and rivers restricted the number of major roads to three: The Natchez Trace, which ran from Nashville to Natchez, cut across the state's northwestern corner. The Federal Road began in Athens, Georgia, went through the Creek Nation to the territorial capital of Fort Stephens, and ended in New Orleans. And the Valley Road ran along the western side of the Appalachians from Knoxville to Huntsville; from there, the Huntsville Road, as the Valley Road was known in Alabama, continued through the mountains until it entered Tuscaloosa and became Broad Street (now University Boulevard), the town's main thoroughfare, which paralleled the river. New roads—the 1819 Byler Road north from Tuscaloosa to the Muscle Shoals, an 1821 road south from Tuscaloosa through Greensboro, and a later one from east Alabama through Tuscaloosa to Fort Tombigbee—kept Tuscaloosa at the center of things. Nonetheless, the Huntsville Road would remain the principal route between north and south Alabama.

The difficulties encountered by a young woman traveling south down the Byler Road from LaGrange, Alabama, to Tuscaloosa in 1833 were probably typical.

Juliet Coleman and her party encountered only miserable log cabins and taverns the entire way. One night they were offered beds in a one-room hut already occupied by bear hunters and mountaineers. They chose instead to camp out in the woods. "I assure you I thought of home as the wind howled round the tents and the large fires roared & blazed to keep off the wild beasts," she wrote. "I knew we were in a wilderness of more than a hundred miles extent where were plenty of panthers and bears and wolves"—a fact corroborated by a tavern keeper she met who had himself killed sixteen panthers. After nine days and 160 miles, Coleman finally reached the Black Warrior.

The settlement there, on the north side of the falls, was then known as Kentuck. (No one knows the origin of the name, but David Crockett, who had been in Alabama during the Creek War, named his Tennessee homestead Kentuck.) The commercial district, if it could be called that, consisted of a cotton warehouse, a cash store, and perhaps a few other rough buildings. "The whole place did not extend fifty yards from the river," according to E. A. Powell, who had spent time there as a young man not long before Coleman arrived. Beyond the commercial district stood the vast stretches of dense cane that stretched along the river. Kentuck's reputation was that of "a gambling Hell," recalled Powell, where certain Tuscaloosans could prey on the innocent. "The misguided countryman who would allow himself to be drawn into its coils very generally found out that the old saw of 'the more you lay down the less you pick up,' was true." Sometime in the mid to late 1830s, the name Kentuck would be dropped. Some favored using North Tuscaloosa. Others, probably steamboat pilots, preferred North Port. That name stuck, and by 1841 the settlement had a post office under that name. A decade later, Northport would be described as a third the size of Tuscaloosa and, in the words of one local, "shockingly improved, so much so as to support three Churches & do about half as much Business as Tusca."

Coleman and her party were ferried across the Black Warrior into Tuscaloosa. Had she made her journey south a year later, in 1834, she might have arrived in time to cross over an imposing bridge. As one contemporary described it, "This Bridge is the largest wood one I have ever seen. It is fully 350 yds long. Roofed over; & a dark & dismal place it is to cross through on a dark night." Its great length resulted from having to be high enough to survive floods and to reach the main part of town. Once believed to be the work of the great bridge-builder Horace King (who would rebuild it in the 1870s), the Tuscaloosa bridge was actually built by Seth King—sometimes Horace's rival, at other times a financier, but no blood relation. The toll bridge's $30,000 cost was enormous for the time, but the expense was justified. The first bridge over the Black Warrior marked the beginning of several major investments in bridge construction by the entrepreneur Robert Jemison Jr.

Those coming to Tuscaloosa by river had a much easier time of it than Juliet Coleman. Only eleven years after Robert Fulton began American commercial steamboat travel in 1807, frontiersmen built and launched the woefully underpowered *Alabama* at the territorial capital of St. Stephens. And only two years after that, in May 1820, Tuscaloosans heard for the first time the toot of a steamboat whistle. The *Tensa* had arrived after a nineteen-day journey upriver from Blakely on the eastern shore of Mobile Bay. "Extatic," proclaimed the newspapers. "Tuscaloosans marveled over the physical survival of the *Tensa*," which had suffered no damage "ascending the long, serpentine, and (by boats of her class) hitherto unexplored Black Warrior," and in doing so demonstrated that the steamboat was to the "incalculable . . . advantage of Tuscaloosa, and the country around and above."

The maneuverability and agility of these side-wheelers with their shallow drafts made them well suited for the snag-filled Alabama rivers. While steamboats started small at about 72 tons (the carrying capacity of the *Cotton Plant*, a contemporary of the *Tensa*), within twenty years the 320-ton *Tuscaloosa* would be plying the Black Warrior. Even so, these side-wheelers would be dwarfed by the enormous plodding sternwheelers that came later.

WHETHER THEY TREKKED through the wilderness or jumped off a newly docked side-wheeler, few who arrived during the late 1820s were prepared for what they saw and heard.

Tuscaloosa was a beehive of activity. Refined and tasteful structures were going up where William Ely had once suffered to stay in rude huts. Hammers and saws competed with the birds to be heard above the dull roar of the falls. Workmen yelled

Tuscaloosa's first bridge, built in 1834 by Seth King, as depicted from the Northport side by Margaret Cammer Furman. (Courtesy The University of Alabama Libraries Special Collections)

to one another to keep their efforts coordinated. Chisels could sometimes be heard carving large stones into fancy shapes. The rutted mud paths were giving way to graded streets. And the sounds of carriage wheels were starting to compete with the oinking pigs that still wandered about. People scurried to purchase their goods from the new businesses that had just opened. A fine amateur band blared out music upon occasion. Many towns grew quickly during the early years of Alabama's statehood, but not like this. Simon Suggs, the fictional backwoods confidence man, listed some of the "strange sights" he encountered on his first visit to Tuscaloosa: the windows of the apothecary shining forth in a "blaze of varied light," prints and advertising cards at the bookseller's shop. Suggs only felt comfortable when walking into the local groceries, as saloons were known at the time.

The spark behind all the activity was, of course, the arrival of the state government. High among the priorities of the first legislators to meet in Tuscaloosa was the creation of a stunning visual expression of their new state's hopes and aspirations. Great architecture would thus become an important feature of Tuscaloosa's capital days—beginning with a new statehouse. A committee soon recommended for the site what was known as Childress' Hill, high above the river at the western end of Broad Street. After completing its own design, the committee hired William Nichols to superintend construction. At least they made one wise choice.

The English-born Nichols was among the finest architects in the nation and certainly the finest in the South. He had already served as the state architect of North Carolina, where he had been quite active designing public buildings, especially at the University of North Carolina. While there, he also designed a number of important homes. His skills and talents were exactly what the frontier town needed. And Tuscaloosa had what Nichols wanted: a blank slate on which to create his best work. Only a few months before his arrival in the spring of 1827, one Tuscaloosan had written back to his mother in Maine that there "is no magnificence here. The country is new and [even] the planters live in log houses." That would completely change in a few short years.

The architect immediately recognized that the committee's design simply would not do. (One contemporary described it as having "more the appearance of a dutch barn or a cotton factory than a State Capitol.") Nichols submitted an entirely new plan within the appropriated $40,000 budget, but the committee rejected it as too small. His revision was a quarter larger, cost $15,000 more, and resembled his work on the North Carolina capitol.

This final plan was a cruciform (i.e., four major sections projecting out from a

Fast light-draft sidewheelers were well suited for navigating Alabama's sometimes treacherous rivers. (Courtesy Alabama Department of Archives and History)

Opposite page: In 1829, Alabama's legislators met for the first time in the new statehouse designed by William Nichols. This photograph, taken when the building housed Central Alabama Female College, shows the main entrance on the east side of the building. (Courtesy The University of Alabama Libraries Special Collections)

central space). The capitol's ground-floor level was surrounded by walls of roughly textured sandstone. The walls above, encompassing the two main floors, were of brick painted grey to imitate granite. Rising in the middle of it all was a large and graceful classical dome surmounted by a ten-foot lantern, or windowed cupola, which was itself domed. On the capitol's north and south porticoes, Nichols introduced Doric columns carved from solid sandstone blocks. Indeed, classical details were used throughout the building. Nichols had managed to fulfill everyone's expectations with this proposal not only by increasing its size but by linking Alabama's vision for itself to the ancient ideals of Greek democracy. His revised plan was approved by the general assembly in late 1827, and construction began almost immediately.

When, in November 1829, the legislators met officially for the first time in the unfinished statehouse, they entered by stepping through a small central arch below the massive gabled east front. A little beyond the vestibule they entered the rotunda. Straight across to the west was the supreme court. The offices of various officials, including the governor, were in the north and south wings to the right and left.

Climbing the stairs to the main floor, the representatives turned south to enter their rectangular hall, a room clearly inspired by the House Chamber in the nation's capitol. There they faced the speaker's rostrum flanked by Ionic columns and a frieze appropriately inscribed *Pro Patria* (For Country). Visitors looked down from a gallery supported by eight large Ionic columns arranged in a semi-ellipsis. The representatives' counterparts, the state senators, met in the north wing. Their hall was also rectangular, but this time twelve Corinthian columns were arranged in the room's center to support the visitors' gallery. The president of the senate sat below "rich crimson damask curtains, disposed in folds and hanging festoons from the beak of [a] golden spread Eagle." From the shallow domed ceiling hung a "splendid Chandelier, designed to light up the whole chamber."

But it was the capitol's rotunda that took everyone's breath away. Standing on the ground floor and looking up, Alabamians first saw the second-floor gallery. Sixteen feet above that were massive Corinthian pilasters. And at the top was a beautiful dome with a surface of elegant sunken panels. What made it all especially dramatic was the sun beaming through the wide round hole in the dome's peak, ninety feet above the ground floor. The rain was kept out by the lantern.

Governor Gabriel Moore could not contain his enthusiasm when he spoke to the first legislators to convene there. Alabama had been "a mere wilderness, the resort of savages and wild beasts only," but in just a few short years the new state had a new capitol, "inferior to none in elegance, in Taste, or in usefulness." Another observer voiced the same sentiments in judging the Nichols statehouse "quite as elegant as might be expected from an infant state like ours, and at this early period of her history—not quite out of her *teens*." Yet another contemporary described it as "one of the most beautiful, chaste and delicate specimens of Grecian architecture to be found in our country."

Those politicians needed places to stay when they came to Tuscaloosa, and the innkeepers responded magnificently. The legislature had met in the Bell Tavern while planning their stone and brick capitol.

And the state's de facto governor's house was Barnett's Tavern whenever Governor John Gayle was in town, as the state neither built nor acquired an official residence for the governor. Mrs. Gayle found the rooms "tolerably comfortable" but the food unacceptable. "I could not have bel[ie]ved, if I had not seen it, what fare is put before the boarders; and so much want of cleanliness!"

Other politicians found their experiences in Tuscaloosa hotels to be of an entirely different character. Charles Lewin had been the proprietor of Tuscaloosa's best tavern in 1821, the same one that William Ely had found so offensive. Six years later, after Tuscaloosa had become the state capital and Lewin the owner of a newly built brick hotel in Newtown, he decided to give a great feast for the legislators. Mrs. Lewin, known to be a "queen of the kitchen," must have done the cooking, for the legislators were extremely pleased, announcing in the newspaper that the Lewins' "entirely *gratuitous* act" had afforded the politicians "*satisfaction* and *pleasure*." So much *satisfaction* and *pleasure* that Lewin subsequently learned that those same legislators had elected him a member of the state bank's board of directors—purely by coincidence, of course. As one who knew him put it, tongue firmly in cheek: the short man was "fat, jolly and ponderous, weighing, perhaps, 200 pounds. He was genial and clever, how else could he have been elected a bank director?" Soon citizens were rushing to Tuscaloosa to stay at Lewin's hotel and—once again, purely by coincidence—asking Lewin's help in securing loans from the state bank. The proprietors at Tuscaloosa's four other main hotels followed Lewin's example, and in short order they too were elected bank directors. In fact, every prominent Tuscaloosa innkeeper soon was numbered among the sixty-seven bank directors elected annually by the legislators. Tuscaloosa's hotels filled to capacity with loan seekers. Contemporaries would blame the poor loans, especially those secured by the innkeeper/bank directors, for the failure of the Bank of the State of Alabama following the Panic of 1837.

Those same hotels, inns, or taverns (the terms were used more or less interchangeably) probably had more artisans boarding there than politicians and loan seekers. In 1830, when the building boom hit full stride, skilled craftsmen comprised nearly 30 percent of all men employed in Tuscaloosa, by far the largest category. Some whom Nichols particularly trusted came with him from North Carolina, such as John Robb, who seemed to have served as his chief stonemason. But when Robb could not handle all the work, Nichols placed advertisements in Tennessee, Kentucky, and Ohio newspapers for more artisans. The chance to work on such fine buildings attracted some from even farther afield. The staircases were built by a carpenter from Connecticut. The bulk of the craftsmen, however, were locals. The contractor William Morton Jr., for example, formed and fired the bricks in Kentuck. Tuscaloosa carpenter Henry A. Sossaman, along with his partner Mr. Brown, built the roof and wooden dome. The pair would later work together on many other Tuscaloosa buildings.

Most of the workmen remain nameless today, especially the many slaves owned by contractors. One slave whose name we do know was George Hamer, who years later recounted whipsawing logs for the

Mary C. Barry is believed to have painted these pictures of her Newtown home and its garden, probably first laid out in the 1820s or '30s by the home's builder and first owner, Major Hardin Perkins. In Barry's painting of the garden, the back of her home is on the right. (Courtesy Tuscaloosa County Preservation Society)

structural timbers used in the statehouse. Townspeople would sometimes apprentice their slaves to the contractors in order to improve their skills. Edmond S. Farish, who contracted for the carpentry and joinery in the house chamber, was known to take on townspeople's slaves as apprentices. He also apprenticed four boys newly released from slavery with a contract requiring Farish to teach them "his own trade as far as their capacities [would] receive, treat them with humanity—feed and clothe them well i.e. Comfortably," and at the age of twenty-one "give them a decent suit of Sunday clothes and five dollars in money and a written recom-

Inset from John La Tourette's 1838 Map of the State of Alabama (Courtesy The University of Alabama Libraries Special Collections)

mendation of good character." Few if any of Tuscaloosa's great structures could have been built without these unrecognized bound workers.

Tuscaloosa benefited greatly from the work of free black artisans, chief among them Solomon Perteet, a plasterer from Georgia who first came to Tuscaloosa during the building boom of the 1820s. His work on the statehouse lasted until at least 1841, when he was called in to do repairs. Other free blacks included James Abbott, who made his way shaving and cutting hair. Barbering was a profession dominated by free blacks in the South and, in a town like Tuscaloosa with many public men coming and going, it could be especially lucrative. Ned Berry was also in a good position to use his wagon and four strong horses to carry goods and passengers to and from the steamboats. The 1830 census listed twenty-two free

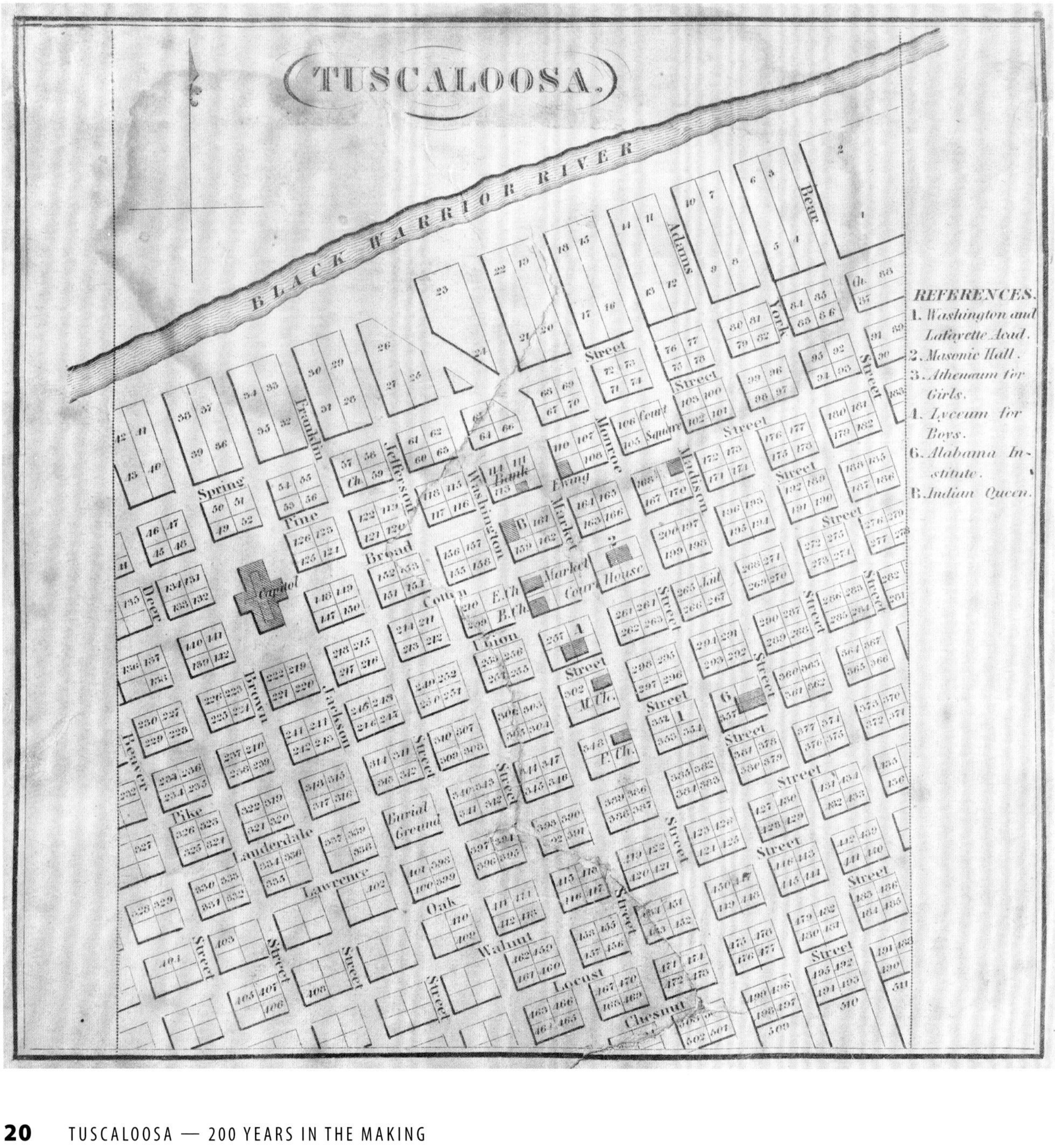

Tuscaloosa's first residence to be built in the Classical Revival style, the Dearing House, was probably designed by William Nichols. It now serves as the University Club. (From *The City of Tuskaloosa, Its Many Advantages*... [Cincinnati: Keating, 1887])

blacks, a number that grew to at least sixty over the next decade.

Tuscaloosa's free blacks were in a unique position—tasting freedom but never truly enjoying it—that forced them to work the system in inventive ways. Jack Winn was born a slave but worked in a blacksmith shop across the river. By hiring out his and his son's off time, Winn accumulated enough money to purchase first his own freedom for $2,000, then his wife's, and eventually their children's. The African-born Fanny Gould somehow managed to sell enough of her gingerbread to purchase her husband for $400; she then hired him out as an expert bricklayer for a dollar a day (which *she* received) plus board. But the efforts of Winn and Gould paled beside those of Solomon Perteet. No doubt in response to his petition and their familiarity with him as the capitol's plasterer, the legislature authorized Perteet in 1829 to release his wife and her son from slavery after he posted a bond of $1,200. Two years later he purchased the teamster Ned Berry for $700, recording his intention to free Berry once Perteet had been reimbursed the $700. Perteet purchased Gideon Berry, probably Ned's son, in 1840 and transferred the title to Ned upon payment of another $700. Enterprising and prosperous free blacks often tried to purchase family and friends in order to prevent their being sold away.

Solomon Perteet was able to make these purchases because he was wealthy. Parlaying his success as a plasterer, he began investing in real estate. He purchased 80 acres of land in 1830, 200 acres in 1836, and another 193 acres the next year. He was also buying lots in town, which he began selling off when their value appreci-

Christ Episcopal Church, originally designed by William Nichols, was the site of the 1831 dedication ceremonies for the University of Alabama. (Courtesy The University of Alabama Libraries Special Collections)

ated a few years later. During the 1840s he began lending money and was prosperous enough to withstand the loss of $17,000 from standing security for a white man who apparently skipped town without paying. Upon his death in 1863, Perteet was able to bequeath $8,000 to one of his daughters with the bulk of his estate going to his wife, Lucinda. He was buried prominently in Greenwood Cemetery. But Perteet was truly exceptional. The rest of Tuscaloosa's free black community continued to live on a precarious middle ground.

The artisans who dominated Tuscaloosa's professions in the early 1830s were putting their skills to use on more than the statehouse, of course. They built a town hall/market and courthouse, both in the Federal style, a block south of Broad Street on opposite corners of Market Street (which became known as Greensboro Street further south in the residential district). Nichols may have designed the town hall/market but almost certainly had a hand in designing Tuscaloosa's first home in the Classical Revival style. Many of those coming in the wake of the government's arrival were wealthy, unlike the original settlers, and wanted only the best. Steamboat captain and entrepreneur James Hunter Dearing was one of those new residents. Rather than building in the restrained and refined red brick Federal style, the architect chose to announce Dearing's success with six massive Ionic columns to front his home at the end of Broad Street directly facing the capitol nearly a mile to the west. The walls were stuccoed and painted white to resemble the marble of Grecian temples. His brother Alexander Buonaparte Dearing would build an even more imposing Classical Revival home a few years later near the south end of East Margin Street (which in 1887 would become Queen City Street).

Nichols surely designed Christ Church, Alabama's second oldest Episcopal house of worship. In form and proportions, it represented the architect at the top of his form. The recessed entrance along one gable end was flanked by two Ionic columns. The nave was illuminated by five Roman arched windows with recessed panels on either side. The result was a simple elegance. Christ Church was deceptively small. Yet it was large enough to hold the most important event to occur during Tuscaloosa's years as the state's capital: the 1831 dedication ceremonies of the University of Alabama.

The legislators had chosen, after much deliberation, to locate the university on a large plot a mile to the east of the Tuscaloosa townsite. Here was good flat land with ample springs and the Huntsville Road running right through it. To prevent "immoral persons" from settling adjacent

The University of Alabama, an architectural masterpiece (Courtesy The University of Alabama Libraries Special Collections)

to their "Seminary of Learning," an additional fifty acres were added as a buffer.

The University of Alabama campus may have been the finest work Nichols created in his long career. He had been given the commission in 1828 after his plans for the capitol had been accepted. And like the capitol, he once again developed further his previous North Carolina designs, in this case the university in Chapel Hill. He laid out the Alabama campus buildings in the shape of the Greek letter Π. On the west and east (the left and right legs of the Π) were rows of dormitories. To the north (the top of the Π) were classroom buildings, faculty houses, and the Steward's Hall (now known as the Gorgas House). Nichols called for a mirror campus to be constructed south of the Huntsville Road for the state's medical school; when that did not happen, construction began instead on the President's Mansion in 1839.

The University of Alabama plan differed from the University of North Carolina plan in setting faculty houses alongside the academic buildings in order to bring faculty and students closer. The University of Alabama plan also differed by placing a circular domed building, the Rotunda, in the middle of the Π. The Rotunda succeeded in commanding attention at the center of campus, but that created a problem. Because neither the Roman Pantheon nor the University of Virginia Rotunda, whose design Thomas Jefferson had based on the Pantheon, was meant to be seen from all sides, their unadorned circular walls were interrupted only by grand entrance porticoes. But this would not do for the University of Alabama; so in addition to its own grand entrance portico, Nichols surrounded the Rotunda with twenty-four paired Ionic columns. These added depth, perspective, and interest when seen from any vantage.

Opening the fence gate and walking through the cedar-lined path from the Huntsville Road, visitors passed through

A student's sketch of the Rotunda (Courtesy The University of Alabama Libraries Special Collections)

the Rotunda's portico and vestibule into a perfectly round commencement hall encircled by a colonnade of ornate Corinthian columns. Outside the colonnade Nichols placed a mezzanine, or balcony, for visitors. The university library, located on the top floor, featured custom-made bookshelves that followed the contours of the curving walls. Like the statehouse dome, Nichols incorporated a wide round hole surmounted by a lantern that allowed the same dramatic solar illumination. The interior of the Rotunda may have been a visual delight, but it was an acoustic nightmare. One visitor called it "a whispering gallery which echoes 60 times and very loud." A former student recalled that the least harshness in speaking created such confusion that people three feet apart could not hear each other. Stomping a foot "was like thunder," its reverberations taking a minute or longer to die away.

Nichols had intended his plan for the university as a statement in brick and stone of the state's intention to create enlightened young men who could lead the state and protect their rights. The overall effect, especially for those emerging from the wilderness, was breathtaking. "The buildings here exceed any I have ever seen for a College," Juliet Coleman wrote her mother and sister back in Connecticut, "or even any other except for publick buildings at Washington."

With the completion of the statehouse, Christ Church, the University of Alabama, and a number of undocumented structures, Nichols was done with his major work in Alabama. Tuscaloosans still needed fashionable homes and public buildings. But that work would be left to others. He resigned as state architect and pursued better prospects to the west, first in Louisiana and then Mississippi. He had entered a frontier village in 1827, and a mere six years later he departed one of the South's great showplaces.

WILLIAM NICHOLS ALSO LEFT behind many creative, energetic, and even daring individuals. Much of the talent originated at the university. The first faculty, led by Harvard-educated Alva Woods, had assumed that they would be teaching disciplined young men who needed but a little structure and encouragement to focus on their studies. In addition to being forbidden from the usual fighting, stealing, and carrying of weapons, students were not to play cards, attend public amusements, use profanity, travel into town without authorization, or engage in a long list of other sins. They were expected instead to be at their books when not attending class, eating, or at prayer. To the surprise of only the faculty, it seems, the students were instead constantly rebelling. They once hurled brickbats and fired pistols as they chased President Woods across campus. He and his faculty were gone by 1837, replaced by the Reverend Basil Manly, a Southerner who cultivated a better relationship with the students. With him came a new faculty with entirely different talents and expectations.

Foremost among them was Frederick Augustus Porter Barnard. No member of the University of Alabama faculty would approach F. A. P. Barnard's caliber for decades. To say that he taught the students mathematics and natural philosophy (astronomy, chemistry, and the physical sciences generally) only hints at his intellect and range of interests. "Young, dashing, and handsome," recalled a friend, Barnard "was conceded to be the *best* at whatever he attempted to do; he could turn the best sonnet, write the best love story, take the best daguerreotype picture, charm the most women, catch the most trout, and calculate the most undoubted almanac."

Barnard's intellect and range of interests was matched by his productivity. He designed and oversaw the building of the university's observatory, the first in the South, and equipped it with instruments he ordered from London. He published a mathematics textbook. By swinging a pendulum from inside the statehouse dome, he replicated Léon Foucault's demonstration of the Earth's rotation. (Because bodies in motion do not alter their direction, the pendulum seems to shift its course as the day goes on, when in fact it is the Earth that is moving.) The proud editor of the *Independent Monitor* observed that "every person finds it gratifying to be able to verify so remarkable a phenomenon with his own eyes."

Barnard's most extraordinary contributions while in Tuscaloosa came in the realm of photography. Louis-Jacques Mandé Daguerre announced to a wide-eyed world in early 1839 his new process of capturing images on a silvered copper plate. The shortcoming of Daguerre's process was that the time needed for an exposure was much too long to expect anyone to sit still for a portrait. Barnard, along with his friend the physician William H. Harrington, worked throughout 1840 to come up with a method to reduce the exposure time to a matter of seconds. Barnard's subsequent article in the *American Journal of Science and Art* explaining their process is considered a "milestone in American photographic history" in that it made photography practical, especially portraits. "What must it be to a distant posterity," wrote the editor of the *Tuscaloosa Flag of the Union* three weeks after Barnard and Harrington opened

Frederick A. P. Barnard was Tuscaloosa's foremost intellectual of the 1840s and '50s. (From the *American Journal of Education*, 1859)

Below right: On the back of this, the earliest known photograph taken in Alabama, Mrs. Martin inscribed: "Mrs. Sarah A. Martin Taken in Tuscaloosa Ala. in the year 1840 by Dr. Harrington and Professor Barnard of the University of Alabama, and the first daguerreotype ever taken in Tuscaloosa." The two daguerreotypists captured well her attributes—good wife and mother, warm friend, and faithful Christian—as described by another contemporary. **Above right:** Paired with the portrait of Mrs. Martin is one of her husband, future governor Joshua L. Martin. (Courtesy Alabama Department of Archives and History)

their Tuscaloosa photographic studio, "to dwell upon the very counterparts of those who have their own times glorious! What would it be to us, could we have thus before us now, the faithful representation of the great and the good, whose faces will never more be seen on earth!"

Barnard did not limit himself to the scientific world. He taught himself seven European languages and wrote a book on sign language (he was himself hearing impaired). As an editorialist and poet, Barnard was also included in what came to be known as the Tuscaloosa Bards.

Quite the literary center was emerging in Tuscaloosa during the 1840s and '50s. The state government attracted many professionals, such as journalists, legislators, clergy, and especially lawyers—the very people in the early nineteenth century who most dealt with words. And the University of Alabama's professors and better students were also part of that core of talented Tuscaloosans. These lettered individuals were not hesitant to write, but surely their isolation at the end of a long road and a long river in a frontier state must have spurred them on even more. "Like the sounding of a bell in a vast wilderness," wrote one of the Bards, "we have heard the faint chimes of a scattered few who would awaken us to an elevated devotion."

The Bards were a loose association of perhaps a dozen young authors who wrote poems, articles, works of history, books, and humor. Alexander Beaufort Meek wrote *The Red Eagle: A Poem of the South*, his 1855 Romantic epic poem based upon a real Alabamian, the Creek leader William Weatherford. (Henry Wadsworth Longfellow's epic poem *Song of Hiawatha*, also published in 1855, is based on the cofounder of the Iroquois Confederacy.) John Gorman Barr, by contrast, wrote the sort of humor epitomized later by Mark Twain. His rowdy tales of life in Tuscaloosa, the best of which featured the Irishmen he knew personally, were published in the most widely read national sporting and literary journals of the time. The Bards not only wrote, they even managed to publish Alabama's first literary journal, the short-lived *Southron*, dedicated to the lofty "purpose of promoting the Literature of the South." Altogether, they were enormously productive.

Although the Tuscaloosa Bards never formally organized and the name emerged decades after they were active, other literary associations during the period were highly organized, including the Franklin Institute (begun in 1830), the Lyceum (1831), and the Ciceronian Club (1838). And every student at the university belonged to either the Erosophic or the Philomathic Societies, which were both founded within a year of the university's founding in 1831. Not limited to literature, the societies encouraged well-honed speeches and debates in an age when oratorical skills were greatly valued. Each society not only had its own meeting room and library, but even handed out its own diplomas.

Tuscaloosans, in fact, were joiners. They lived in a newly settled part of the country where "old" meant merely a decade or two, where a good friend today was headed west tomorrow, where all seemed in flux. To take the place of established traditions, to create order in their chaotic world, they established voluntary associations. These they could join or quit as their needs and circumstances changed. Tuscaloosans not only founded literary societies, they also built churches to meet their spiritual needs. Newcomers would join the Masonic lodge to gain immediate entrée into a fraternity of prominent men dedicated to benevolence. When their children needed an education, Tuscaloosans would call for public meetings and raise funds to build their own schools. They would band together to press for such reforms as temperance and Sabbath schools. In all of these enterprises, Tuscaloosans relied on themselves.

Two Baptist ministers had met in early 1818 to organize Tuscaloosa's first church. The congregation called a pastor

JOHN GORMAN BARR, *orphaned in 1835 at the age of twelve, apprenticed himself to a printer before a local merchant sponsored his studies at the University of Alabama. Barr did exceptionally well and stayed after graduation to earn his master's degree and to tutor in mathematics. He then moved into law and politics before leading the Warrior Guards to the Mexican War. Upon his return, the now bewhiskered captain had his photograph taken in uniform, probably by his friend, mentor, and fellow Tuscaloosa Bard, F. A. P. Barnard. Barr edited the local Democratic newspaper and in 1855 published his first piece of Old Southwest humor. In over a dozen of Barr's tales, readers across the country learned of Tuscaloosa's unforgettable characters and the shenanigans they pulled on each other. Barr died on his way to Australia, where he had been appointed consul. He had packed a lot into his thirty-four years. (Courtesy Alabama Department of Archives and History)*

The Central Alabama Female College gained prestige by leasing the former state capitol from the University of Alabama. Above is the school's Alumnae Hall, formerly the chamber of the Alabama House of Representatives. (Courtesy The University of Alabama Libraries Special Collections)

that spring and soon after that built a frame building. The Methodists, who were the more numerous during most of the nineteenth century, followed suit in the summer of 1818, when Ebenezer Hearn preached in a log tavern the first time he came to Tuscaloosa; it did not take long before they, too, had their own church building—presumably without the sow and piglets under the pulpit that had elicited William Ely's complaints. The Presbyterians organized in 1820 and worshipped in the Newtown courthouse until moving into their own church in the main part of town. The Episcopalians established Christ Church in early 1828.

Catholics were already meeting at the village above the falls before incorporation. Their numbers grew steadily over the years, especially with the arrival of a large contingent of Irish immigrants. Their lively Saint Patrick's Day celebrations at local hotels lasted well into the night and made for great reading in the newspapers. This was in no small part due to the many Irish innkeepers who doubled as barkeeps. Despite their prominence and numbers, however, it was not until 1844 that Tuscaloosa received its first priest, and it was not until early 1846 that the first mass was held in the elegant little St. John's Church.

The Masons established their Rising Virtue Lodge in 1819. Freemasonry often preceded the churches on the Alabama frontier because joining a lodge afforded all sorts of practical benefits to people in constant motion in a region without established institutions. The Masons readily gave each other credit in a place where banks were few and swindlers legion. The Masons dispensed charity. And they tried to temper the extremes of American individualism by setting an example of disinterested service, social responsibility, and natural community.

Lacking a public school system (it would take decades to get even the rudiments), Tuscaloosans were again left to their own devices. Itinerant teachers would advertise for students in the newspaper. But parents had no way of verifying the credentials of someone from hundreds of miles away. Something needed to be done.

Churches were the first to establish real schools. The Methodists began in 1828 with Sims Female Academy, perhaps Alabama's first boarding school for girls. Sims was succeeded by the Wesleyan Female Institute in 1834 and twenty years later by the Tuscaloosa Female College. The Presbyterians followed with the Alabama Female Academy (later Institute) in the early 1830s. The Baptists established the Alabama Female Athenæum in 1836 and Alabama Central Female College in 1856. This was the premier women's school in Tuscaloosa in part because they leased the vacated statehouse, adding a dormitory onto the western end. (The college would close when the capitol burned in 1923.) And the Catholics had a short-lived school for girls beginning in 1845.

As Tuscaloosa became more settled, schoolmasters also became more trustworthy. By the late 1840s, Barbara Little and her niece Mary Irving had established a reliable beginning school. "It is safe to say that all Tuscaloosa children passed through this primary school," recalled one graduate. And the Tuscaloosa boys preparing to enter the University of Alabama studied Greek, Latin, and mathematics in Milford Woodruff's school.

Education was part of an even larger nineteenth-century campaign to reform society by first reforming individuals. Many were convinced that the American experiment had freed individuals to do great things, but it had also freed them to do horrible things. Unrestrained and unlettered people were destructive. Only self-disciplined, morally upright, and law-abiding Americans could create a peaceful and ordered republic. Individuals needed education, certainly, but they also needed tools to avoid the temptations—generally alcohol and sloth—that led directly to their ruin. To aid the individual in these endeavors, the reformers joined together to build schools, asylums, and other such institutions while at the same time promoting causes ranging from temperance to the abolition of capital punishment. Tuscaloosans were very much in step with the nation's reform movements.

The Tuscaloosa Society for the Promotion of Temperance was founded in 1829. There can be no evil, they proclaimed, "with which society is cursed, so huge and unmanageable as that which originates from the *use* of ardent spirits." They would have their work cut out for them. In 1843 Brown & Maxwell, perhaps Tuscaloosa's largest supplier of food staples, advertised for sale 210 barrels of whiskey, 30 barrels of brandy, and 100 casks of choice wines. The society's membership was split between those who wanted to reform Tuscaloosa through persuasion and those who wanted new ordinances to restrict the retail sale of liquor. A new and even stricter association, the Young Men's Total Abstinence Society, succeeded the temperance society in 1840. A third group started up in Tuscaloosa two years after that, the Washingtonians, who sought to convert alcoholics by making sober society as appealing as barroom society. The Washingtonians were in turn succeeded by the Sons of Temperance. The slave population even had its own Colored Total Abstinence Society, which was founded in 1839 and had a membership of nearly four hundred by 1851. The temperance movement's high point in Tuscaloosa came with the publication of a pro-temperance newspaper, the *Crystal Fount*, in the early 1850s and the raising of liquor license fees to a staggering $1,000. But when private drinking soared as a result, the measure was repealed; and by the late 1850s fewer citizens were advocating abstinence.

The same impulse that drove temperance—to exercise self-control, to fend off temptation, and ultimately to create a peaceful republic—drove another great reform movement: religious education. To preserve the republic, these reformers believed that citizens needed to adhere to the Scriptures, and that in turn required an educated citizenry. Tuscaloosans once again became heavily involved, this time by joining the American Bible and American Tract Societies and by promoting Sabbath schools. Tuscaloosans established their first Sabbath schools in 1828. Three years later, members of several Protestant denominations pooled their efforts to form the Tuscaloosa Sunday School Union, but in 1832 the Presbyterians went on their own to establish a separate Sabbath school for the children of Tuscaloosa factory workers, enrolling 154 students. In the promotion of religious education, like other reform movements, the success of Tuscaloosa's voluntary associations ebbed and flowed as strong and weak personalities came and went from their ranks.

These same ideals were also behind Tuscaloosa's greatest reform project: the Alabama Insane Hospital. New Englander Dorothea Dix had seen the mentally ill thrown into filthy prison cells and left to freeze in the cold. She started a campaign in 1841 to see that they were instead housed in clean hospitals. Her first success came when the New Jersey legislature decided to build the first modern mental health hospital in Trenton. Dix then went on a tour of Southern states to raise support and money. She stood before the Alabama General Assembly in 1849 to make her case. Her dramatic and convincing speech resulted in an 1852 act establishing the Alabama Insane Hospital that followed her recommendations in every detail. A 320-acre site adjacent to the University of Alabama was chosen to build a state-of-the-art structure that would "command cheerful views."

Dix and the reformers believed that the hospital's design was central to the healing of the patients. Such "an instrument of treatment," in the words of one physician, when located in a pastoral setting, would encourage the mentally ill to become rational and calm. The hospital's central building rose four floors to a dome 150 feet above. On each side stretched three-story transepts stepping back at regular intervals to allow maximum air circulation and sunlight to reach every room. The innovative design ultimately made the entire structure a staggering 780 feet wide. The design called for many conveniences that were new to Tuscaloosa, including large tanks in the dome that served all parts of the hospital with piped hot and cold water. Central steam heating and speaking tubes ran throughout the vast building, and paintings were hung on the walls "to please and tranquilize the mind." But the 1850s would close before the Alabama Insane Hospital was ready for patients.

The craftsmen who built the insane hospital were not the same craftsmen who had built the statehouse and the University of Alabama. Most of them had left two decades before with Nichols or to work on other projects. This sort of mobility was hardly unusual. Coming and going was the norm. Different politicians came and went with every legislative session, but they accounted for just a few of the transients. Starting with the first settlers, Tuscaloosa was often a temporary jumping off point. Gideon Lincecum had already moved six times before he even got to the Falls of the Black Warrior in 1818. From Tuscaloosa he headed for Mississippi and then Texas. After the Confederacy's defeat, he would move again, at the age of seventy-six, to join exiled Confederates in Mexico before finally returning to Texas. Lincecum's mobility may have been a bit extreme—but not by much. In Greensboro, forty miles south of Tuscaloosa, only 10 percent of the population in 1830 still lived in the town ten years later—and Greensboro was a far wealthier and more stable town than Tuscaloosa. Thousands came through Tuscaloosa on their way to somewhere else. One steamboat traveler observed in 1834 a large party of emigrants ferrying across the Black Warrior

by flatboat. "Parties of emigrants, moving to the rich lands recently purchased from the Indians," he wrote back, "are every day passing with their wagons, cattle, and negroes."

The Americans could head into those lands only because the Indians had been forced out. Thousands of Creeks would begin passing through Tuscaloosa in 1835 on their way westward. The Creek Nation had lived apart in the eastern quarter of Alabama until 1832. That year they signed the Treaty of Cusseta, which ceded their Alabama land in exchange for new land in what would eventually become Oklahoma. Because the treaty allowed individual Creeks wanting to remain in Alabama to keep their own individual plots of land, the stage was set for theft. It began when the Alabama General Assembly immediately divided the Creek Nation into nine counties—before the Creeks were given the opportunity to choose their own plots. The skullduggery continued with opportunistic settlers and speculators plying the Creeks with liquor and getting them to sign improper bills of sale. When the federal government threatened to expel the Americans who had entered the Creek Nation illegally, Governor John Gayle asserted Alabama's right to control affairs within its own borders. President Andrew Jackson sent Francis Scott Key to Tuscaloosa to resolve the matter. Tuscaloosans found themselves easily charmed by the author of "The Star-Spangled Banner." But his mission amounted to little because the governor refused to evict the settlers.

Thus the Creeks were left without options and began moving west. When several thousand camped for a few weeks outside of town, it seemed that every Tuscaloosan "turned out to see the Indian youths dash through the streets on their ponies." The edge of the Black Warrior presented quite a contrast, recalled one Tuscaloosan, as "the belles of the little city, arrayed in dainty muslins, and bonneted in the sweet fashions of the time," watched from their buggies as young children were simply tossed into the Black Warrior so that they might learn to swim.

The Alabama Insane Hospital followed closely the architect's conceptual drawing of the ideal hospital, shown here. (From Thomas S. Kirkbride, *On the Construction, Organization, and General Arrangements of Hospitals for the Insane* [Philadelphia: Lindsay & Blakiston, 1854])

Yoholo-Micco led the Creek nation from east Alabama through Tuscaloosa on their way West. (From Thomas L. M'Kenney and James Hall, *The History of the Indian Tribes of North America* [Philadelphia: D. Rice and J. G. Clark,1842])

BECAUSE ONE OF THE TWO ROUTES TO THE WEST *took the Creeks through Tuscaloosa, it was only fitting that their leader would give his farewell in the statehouse. In what could only have been a visually stunning scene filled with incongruities, Yoholo-Micco, also known as Chief Eufaula, sat facing his own warriors and the state's legislators together gathered in the magnificent Hall of Representatives adorned with classical Greek columns. Yoholo-Micco began speaking slowly in his own Mvskoke tongue with an interpreter at his side. "I come brothers, to see the great house of Alabama, and the men that make laws," he began, "and tell them farewell in brotherly kindness before I go to the far west, where my people are now going." As the chief continued in his low and subdued voice, tears started to appear among those assembled. "In these lands of Alabama, which have been my forefather's, where their bones lie buried, I see that the Indian fires are going out—they must soon be extinguished. New fires are lighting in the west—and we will go there." His allusion to fire had symbolic and spiritual meaning to his people. "We will go. We leave behind our good will to the people of Alabama, who build the great houses, and to the men who make the laws." Despite his grave aspect, he ended kindly, "I now bid farewell to you, and wish not only you, but all the people of Alabama, to be happy and prosperous. I leave you in friendship and good will. I have nothing more to say." With the legislators and visitors standing and applauding respectfully, Yoholo-Micco and his warriors left.*

All the people constantly moving to and fro was unsettling. Despite their best efforts—laying out streets and constructing a bridge, erecting beautiful homes and public buildings, establishing voluntary associations—despite it all, Tuscaloosans could not yet call themselves deep-rooted.

THEN THINGS GOT WORSE—much worse. The legislators had blamed the weather, particularly the associated floods and fevers, for the need to move the capital from Cahawba. This time they would not need to assign blame to move the capital from Tuscaloosa.

As settlers rushed in to fill the lands in east Alabama that the Creeks had vacated, the population in west Alabama did not grow at anywhere near the same rate. The result was a major shift in the balance of Alabama's population eastward just as Black Belt cotton began its economic ascendancy. Legislators also began pushing for a north–south rail connection between the Tennessee and the Alabama Rivers. With the votes, wealth, and a presumed new railroad, calls for relocating the seat of government were soon heard from east and south Alabamians. The legislature first passed a constitutional amendment removing the provision that permanently established the capital in Tuscaloosa. Then, in January 1846, the legislature enacted a law stipulating that Tuscaloosa remain the capital until an equivalent statehouse be completed and furnished. And a week after that, the legislature chose to locate that next statehouse in Montgomery. Alabama's capital was destined to return to the banks of the Alabama River.

A third of Tuscaloosa's 4,500 residents left immediately. They did not wait until November 1, 1847, when the construction was finished, the keys turned over, and Montgomery officially succeeded Tuscaloosa as the new seat of government. Despair consumed the Tuscaloosans who remained behind. The loss had "dispirited her inhabitants," observed one visitor only a month after the legislature's vote, "and left her streets nearly as silent as the tombs of the Capulets. . . . Standing in her deserted streets, and viewing the old state house, frowning in gloomy silence on the town she had nurtured and built up, I could not help feeling that sympathy for her fallen fortunes and ruined prospects." Despair turned to anger. "By the vilest machinations of unscrupulous politicians we were deprived of the Capitol," wrote one Tuscaloosan. As a result, "many fortunes which were fairly and honestly linked therewith, have been seriously impaired and deeply injured by this ruthless exercise of power. By it, real estate in Tuscaloosa depreciated some fifty or seventy-five per cent."

Ten years later, Tuscaloosa was still a beautiful town, now familiarly known as the City of Oaks for its tree-lined streets fronting its handsome homes. But the town had aged. "I rambled over all the city," wrote one visitor, "but must confess that it made me feel lonely and sad. The dusty streets, the old, worn out, and dilapidated houses, and fences, presented to me a gloomy appearance." Birds still chirped. The dull roar of the falls still covered the town like a blanket. But the bustle of the carriages, the boys shouting, the horses snorting—the sounds of a living, vibrant town—had grown faint.

The path Tuscaloosans trod from 1819 to 1859 had been tortuous and crooked. In what seemed like no time, they turned their frontier village into a cultured and beautiful state capital. They built schools. They established a literary culture. They promoted moral reforms. And then those efforts all seemed for naught. Prospects did not look promising to Tuscaloosans four decades after incorporation. Little could they suspect that the next few decades would be even more troubling.

THOMAS MAXWELL, *a young Englishman who first arrived in Tuscaloosa on New Year's Day of 1837 found chinaberries growing around his new home. He thought the recently introduced ornamental trees to be "unsightly" and their toxic berries "unwholesome." He was instead rather taken by the majestic oak trees that his neighbors had transplanted from the forest. Maxwell decided to go a step further and planted oaks in the middle of his street. The idea caught on. Before long, the mayor and aldermen were requiring rows of oaks to be planted throughout the town, eventually presenting pedestrians with a welcome "evergreen parasol" on hot summer days and giving Tuscaloosa with a nickname: the City of Oaks, or occasionally, the Oak City. Then someone of a poetic bent remembered that the ancient Celtic religious leaders, the Druids, believed the great oaks there to be sacred. Hence, the Druid City.*

An engraving of oak-tree-lined Broad Street, looking east. (From *The City of Tuskaloosa, Its Many Advantages…* [Cincinnati: Keating, 1887])

Tuscaloosans become citizens of the Confederacy…and reap the whirlwind

Opposite page: Flag of the ironclad CSS *Tuscaloosa*, detail (Courtesy Alabama Department of Archives and History)

THE FIRST WEEK OF THE 1860s opened on a bleak and foreboding note. Nighttime temperatures hovered just above zero. The ice on the ponds was thick enough for skating, if anyone owned skates. The Black Warrior River was running sixty-one feet above the low-water mark—the highest in a decade—cutting off many from the cotton mill and other small industries located along its banks. But more than freezes and floods were on the minds of Tuscaloosans that January. The insane hospital was still empty of patients, for the legislature had not appropriated sufficient funds to finish construction. The Leach & Avery Foundry had burned to the ground, and so had Dr. Snow's mill—both fires thought to be set by an arsonist. And for months the Tuskaloosa and North Port Manufacturing Company, a cotton factory, had been shuttered and put up for sale, leaving many out of work and facing a bitterly cold winter. Thus the Ladies' Benevolent Society sponsored a series of lectures to render "the common necessaries of life to the worthy but suffering poor of the city." They chose for their speaker Landon Cabell Garland, president of the University of Alabama. The peculiar institution was finding its way more and more into

newspaper headlines with each passing year, so it came as no surprise that Garland chose to speak on "African Slavery, as it exists in the Southern States of the American Union."

Slaves had been among Tuscaloosa's first settlers, nearly 30 percent of the county's population in 1820, and their numbers had risen to nearly 44 percent by 1860. Most of that expansion was due to the cotton plantations on the fertile soil to the south and downstream from the falls. Those plantations were getting larger. The most slaves held by one family in 1830 was 101, but by 1860 that figure had more than doubled to 248. A different pattern was seen in the City of Oaks, as carefully reconstructed by historian John W. Quist. In the year 1850, bound Tuscaloosans outnumbered free Tuscaloosans 1,748 to 1,128—a factor of 3 to 2. Of the town's 245 free households (i.e., families or individuals living in a single dwelling), an extraordinary 171, or 70 percent, were known to own slaves (twice the statewide average). This high percentage of slave ownership can be explained by an affluent citizenry and by the many planters who lived in town.

The slave rebellion in the French colony of Santo Domingo, now Haiti, lasted thirteen years and cost hundreds of thousands of lives. (From Hugo Abel, *France militaire: histoire des armées françaises de terre et de mer de 1792 à 1833*. [Paris: Delloye, 1833])

By the time that President Garland delivered his lectures, white Tuscaloosans were pretty much of one mind about slavery. It had not always been so. A wide range of opinions were voiced during the town's first decade. During five weeks in 1824, for example, the editor of the *Tuscaloosa American Mirror* ran advertisements for an abolitionist newspaper, the *Genius of Universal Emancipation*. The purpose of the *Genius*, according to the ad, was to expose "the naked deformity and odious peculiarities of the soul-debasing system of individual oppression" that was at the root of slavery. The *Mirror*'s editor even gave tacit approval to its antislavery message by agreeing to take subscriptions for the *Genius* at his office.

As the 1830s began, some thirty-six men and two women, all of them distinguished, met in the statehouse to organize the Alabama Colonization Society. Among the Tuscaloosans, who numbered half the founders, were the county's largest slaveholder, Congressman R. E. B. Baylor (for whom Baylor University is named), and the Methodist minister. The governor even joined. Discussions about colonization would expose just how confusing life could get when the weft of bound black servitude was woven into the warp of free white mastery.

Colonization's goal was to repatriate black Americans to the west coast of Africa in what would become Liberia. Some wanted every black person living in America to go, while others wanted to limit colonization to the free blacks. These differences reflected the wide range of motivations that drove the colonizationists, which was a great part of its appeal. Many thought that removal was essential to the stability of the nation because they feared a coming race war. Others saw in colonization the opportunity to export democracy and, even more, the opportunity to bring Christianity to the Dark Continent. None could envision blacks and whites living together as equals. A few even supported colonization because they detested slavery. University of Alabama professor Henry Tutwiler, for example, wrote in 1832 that "almost all of the moral and political evil in our Country may be traced to this fruitful source . . . which is fast tending to rend asunder our political fabric." Tutwiler was writing to James G. Birney, a Huntsville resident serving on the University of Alabama's board of trustees and agent of the American Colonization Society. (Birney would go on to become one of America's leading abolitionists, running as the Liberty Party candidate for president in 1840 and again in 1844, when he garnered enough votes in New York to deny Henry Clay the presidency in the three-way race.) Future Tuscaloosan Arthur Hopkins, who was among the charter members of the Alabama Colonization Society, wrote to Birney in 1834 that if I "could better the condition of my slaves by emancipating them, I do not think that I would hesitate to let them go free."

Such talk was rare by then. In August 1831, Nat Turner led a band of fellow slaves on a spree that killed between fifty-five and sixty-five men, women, and children in Southampton County, Virginia. The Turner rebellion awoke fears that stretched back to 1791. That was when a bloody slave revolt broke out in France's most profitable colony, Santo Domingo. The revolution may have ended thirteen years later with the establishment of the free republic of Haiti, but the killing did not. The new Haitian governor-general immediately ordered the massacre of all white French who had been unable to escape. In the end, the lives of between two hundred and three hundred thousand black Haitians and perhaps seventy-five thousand white French had been taken. Some of the Santo Domingo refugees were able to make their way to four townships in the plantation region between Demopolis and Tuscaloosa, warning Alabamians of the consequences of allowing slaves any chance of revolting. Their words seemed to be eerily confirmed by Nat Turner.

The Turner rebellion spurred Tuscaloosans to form extra-legal vigilance committees to scour the mails for abolitionist literature. The slaves' worship services were carefully monitored lest they hear passages of scripture counseling freedom and turn their meetings into forums for insurrection. Nat Turner, after all, had been a deeply religious man who believed God had directed him, as he told his stunned captors in his own fearsome words, to "slay my enemies with their own weapons." Similarly, the Tuscaloosa Temperance Society announced that cheap saloons were where "the slave population was corrupted and made dishonest."

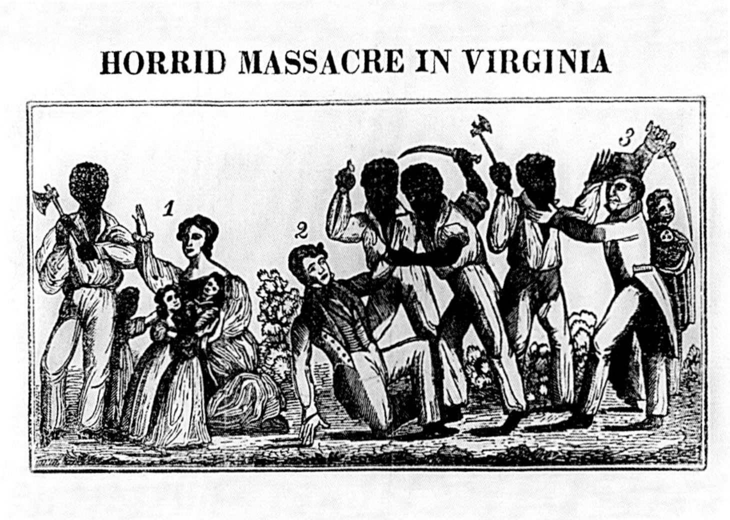

Slave revolts, or the threat of slave revolts, struck mortal fear into white Southerners. Southerners became even more fearful after Nat Turner and his band killed over fifty-five men, women, and children. (From Samuel Warner, *Authentic and Impartial Narrative of the Tragical Scene Which Was Witnessed in Southampton County*, 1831)

Upon hearing of John Brown's raid, Virginians raced to Harper's Ferry to thwart the massive slave rebellion that he had tried to start. Southern states, including Alabama, began to make military preparations. (From *Harper's Weekly*, November 26, 1859)

Certainly reformers were concerned about saving souls and maintaining sobriety. But overhanging it all was the looming threat of another slave rebellion.

Not just the slaves, but the free blacks came under increased surveillance as the years went along. Free blacks were particularly feared, for they gave their enslaved brothers hope. Every time that Solomon Perteet walked the streets of Tuscaloosa, the bound population was reminded that their condition was neither universal nor unchangeable nor natural. In other words, the mere presence of free blacks was a silent encouragement to revolt. That over 85 percent of the Alabama Colonization Society members owned slaves, and often many slaves, suggests that they backed colonization as a means of getting rid of the free blacks in order to remove temptation from their own slaves. The disdain could be seen in the published writings of the humorist John Gorman Barr, who frequently lampooned some of Tuscaloosa's free blacks by name. And letters printed in the newspaper urged the legislature to order the free blacks, many of whom could read, to leave the state because "they secretly poison the ears of our slaves with the incendiary publications of abolitionism." Tuscaloosa's bylaws and ordinances restricting the activities of the free blacks were tightened further during the 1850s. This culminated when Tuscaloosa's aldermen passed an ordinance in early August 1859 requiring all free blacks within the city to register, post security, and not go out at night.

That was just two months before every white Southerner's worst fears were realized. John Brown and his small band, bent on provoking a massive slave rebellion, seized the federal armory and arsenal at Harper's Ferry, in what is now West Virginia. Tuscaloosans grew even more fearful and outraged upon reading in their newspapers that Northern abolitionists had supplied Brown with nearly 200 rifles and 950 pikes before his raid on the arsenal, which itself held an estimated 100,000 rifles and muskets.

Even as Brown was launching his October 1859 raid, the legislature was considering building up the state's military defenses. And two months after the raid, Tuscaloosans were reading Governor A. B. Moore's inaugural address on the front page of their newspapers. He devoted nearly all of his lengthy speech to explaining why the sequence of national events—from the Kansas-Nebraska Act to the Supreme Court's ruling against the slave Dred Scott—were not the political and legal victories that Southerners first thought. Those national events had instead become winning campaign issues for the evil Republicans who would free the slaves to murder their former masters. And what those abolitionists could not effect through Congress, "they intend to accomplish by conspiracy, violence and bloodshed," as the "bloody tragedy at Harper's Ferry" bore witness. Governor Moore's conclusion: "It is, therefore, the duty of the friends of the Constitution . . . to prevent the election of a Black Republican." For their part, Tuscaloosans set about to organize a new militia company to provide "a perfect security against servile insurrection."

So when in the winter of 1860 President Garland gave his orations on "African Slavery, as it exists in the Southern States of the American Union," he was addressing a subject on everyone's minds. His argument began by praising the peculiar institution for providing a sound basis for political, social, and domestic relations. He asserted that slavery was a divinely sanctioned positive benefit to master and slave alike. And he stressed the deep flaws in the antislavery fanatics' appeals to moral conscience. His were hardly new claims, more like the recital of an old and worn-out liturgy. But Garland's words were not meant to break new ground; they were meant to reassure. And his sponsors, the Ladies' Benevolent Society, needed reassurance; an extraordinary 91 percent were linked to slaveholding families.

NO TUSCALOOSANS VOTED for Abraham Lincoln in the November 1860 election. It hardly mattered. Lincoln won a majority in the Electoral College without carrying any Southern state. As required by the previous legislature, Governor Moore scheduled an election for delegates to a state convention to decide whether to take Alabama out of the Union. The governor's rhetoric glossed over the fact that Alabama citizens were deeply divided over what to do. While support for secession in the plantation regions was strong, evidence suggests that a slim majority of Alabama's voters, for varied and complex reasons, favored staying in the Union—at least for the time being. An even larger portion of Alabama's white women, who could not vote, opposed secession. And neither, of

ROBERT JEMISON JR., *future land speculator, entrepreneur, and politician, was a commanding presence in mid-nineteenth century Alabama. Born in Georgia, he reached the Falls of the Black Warrior in the 1830s, and soon his father had a plantation near the village of Kentuck. Upon the death of his father and brother, he gained two plantations totaling over five thousand acres; by 1857, he had added four more plantations. Jemison would hardly limit himself to planting cotton. He hired Seth King to build the first bridge across the Black Warrior (which he charged a toll to use). He built a plank road to the eastern part of the county (once again charging a toll), where he opened coal mines. He was a driving force behind the North East & South West Railroad while at the same time operating a stagecoach line in and out of Tuscaloosa. He brought Dorothea Dix to the state and worked hard to have the Alabama Insane Hospital located in Tuscaloosa. His thriving lumber business profited handsomely from the resulting construction program. As the hospital neared completion in the late 1850s, Jemison began construction on his extraordinary mansion on Greensboro Street. Jemison was one of the county's largest slaveholders, owning at least 114 slaves in 1850. Nonetheless, in 1851 he helped to found the Alabama Colonization Society to establish Liberia as an African colony for black Americans. Jemison remained a Unionist after the election of Abraham Lincoln, believing that secession would hasten the end of slavery. But that left him few options when war broke out, so he threw his lot in with the new government, even representing Alabama in the Confederate Senate. The end of the fighting found Jemison nearly destitute. "I have seen the earnings of a life swept away by a revolution I had no hand in bringing about," he wrote, "the madness & folly of which I did my utmost to prevent." He died in 1871, virtually housebound from multiple ailments. But not long before his death, Jemison had arranged with the black bridge builder Horace King to rebuild the Tuscaloosa bridge destroyed by Croxton's retreating cavalrymen. (Courtesy Alabama Department of Archives and History)*

William Russell Smith was Tuscaloosa's second delegate to Alabama's secession convention. Like Robert Jemison, he was a cooperationist, but their side went down to defeat at the convention. (Courtesy Alabama Department of Archives and History)

course, could any black Alabamian—male or female, free or bound—voice an opinion at the ballot box.

Tuscaloosa was largely a Unionist town. The *Independent Monitor*'s motto, for example, was "Save the Union." Tuscaloosa's two representatives to the convention, who garnered nearly two-thirds of the county's votes, both opposed secession. William Russell Smith was a forty-five-year-old attorney and former Congressman. His counterpart, the fifty-nine-year-old Robert Jemison Jr., was one of the state's leading entrepreneurs and a large slaveholder. They called themselves "cooperationists," arguing that Alabama should only secede in concert with all the other slave states. Their opponents, who urged immediate secession by each state separately, charged—rightly—that because convincing all the slave states to agree to secede together was utterly impossible, cooperation was just another Unionist tactic to forestall secession. Cooperation was, in fact, the same tactic that had been used successfully during another secession crisis a decade earlier. Jemison was just one of many cooperationists who predicted that secession would give the federal government the legal grounds, and ultimately their military the opportunity, to destroy the Constitutionally protected institution of slavery. He would be proven right.

The convention delegates assembled in Montgomery a week into that fateful year of 1861. They asked the Reverend Basil Manly, former University of Alabama president and Tuscaloosa's defeated immediate secessionist candidate, to deliver the opening prayer; and then they elected him the convention's chaplain. It was a small but telling portent of things to come. The immediate secessionists, who held a majority, would defeat the cooperationists' attempts to elect Jemison the convention leader (by a mere eight votes) and on January 11 prevailed in taking Alabama out of the Union. The vote left the two sides bitterly divided. Smith and Jemison claimed that Unionism really represented the majority in the state and demanded that the vote be submitted to the people. The secessionists refused, charging their opponents with treason. Back in Tuscaloosa, the editor of the *Independent Monitor* was enraged, first by the vote to secede and then with the refusal to ask for the voters' sanction. He declared that the people, and not the convention, now had the right to choose the delegates to the Provisional Confederate Congress and, further, that the government they formed should then be submitted to the people to be confirmed or rejected. He vowed "untrammelled and unawed...to fire the people's hearts—to educate the people's minds to know their rights, and to dare to maintain them." But the secessionists in the Alabama convention had already disallowed the people from voting on the decision to secede; they were certainly not about to allow them now to vote on the delegates to the provisional congress or on any new government they would form.

On February 4, 1861, delegates representing six of the seven seceded states met in Montgomery to form a new government. Two weeks later, Manly offered up another opening prayer, this one at the inauguration of Jefferson Davis as the president of the Confederate States of America. Tuscaloosans offered the former statehouse in the vain hope that returning a government to town would restart the economy. But Montgomery would remain the Confederacy's capital for the time being. Then, on April 12, Confederate guns fired on Fort Sumter in Charleston Harbor, South Carolina.

In the North, President Lincoln immediately called for seventy-five thousand militiamen to go into service; he called for an additional forty-two thousand volunteers two weeks later; and Congress authorized an additional half-million volunteers in July.

In the South, four more states seceded and then entered the Confederacy, including the pivotal state of Virginia. Soon clerks in Montgomery were crating the new government's records and sending them to the new capital, Richmond.

And in Tuscaloosa, former cooperationist delegate Robert Jemison quietly withdrew his plans to run for governor on a Unionist ticket, as his backers put on hold any hopes of winning back the state government from the secessionists. He instead joined the government, serving first as a commission broker selling Confederate bonds and securities before being elected to the Confederate Senate. Tuscaloosa's other cooperationist delegate, William

As an immediate secessionist in Unionist Tuscaloosa, Basil Manly, former president of the University of Alabama, failed to win election as a delegate to the secession convention. As consolation, he was elected chaplain of the convention. (Courtesy Alabama Department of Archives and History)

Russell Smith, published a long account of the secession convention's deliberations (in part to show the secessionists' antidemocratic tactics) before bowing like Jemison to his state's decision. Smith raised a regiment of soldiers but entered the Confederate Congress before seeing action.

On May 4, a Friday just weeks after Fort Sumter, Tuscaloosans gathered at the city's wharf. Their long renowned militia company, the Warrior Guards were headed off to war. This was not the first time that Tuscaloosans had bid their Guards farewell. They had once left for the Mexican War and then again for Fort Morgan during the secession crisis. This time their destination was Montgomery. After that, no one knew. Captain Mathews had offered them free passage aboard his new and fast-running steamer, the *Cherokee*. So family and friends said their goodbyes. The young men boarded. The steamer tooted its whistle. Her massive pistons began their methodical hammering. And the *Cherokee* shoved off with Tuscaloosa's most precious cargo. The Warrior Guards would be merged into the

ROBERT EMMET RODES, *the chief engineer of the North East & South West Railroad married into a prominent Tuscaloosa family. The Warrior Guards elected him their captain before they departed from the City of Oaks, and he rose to the rank of colonel of the Fifth Alabama Infantry before the regiment left Montgomery. Rodes would eventually become one of Robert E. Lee's most valued generals. "As if he stepped out from the pages of Beowulf," wrote historian Douglas Southall Freeman, "the tall Rodes stalks through the camps and fights always as if his battle were to decide a great cause." In late 1864, Major General Rodes would be mortally injured by a Union shell fragment near Winchester, Virginia. (Courtesy Alabama Department of Archives and History)*

Fifth Alabama Infantry Regiment in Montgomery and then sent to join the armies gathering for battle in northern Virginia.

The departure of military companies to the front was a glorious affair in some towns—but not in Tuscaloosa. "A more melancholy affair was never witnessed by any one," admitted a well-wisher on the wharf, "every body was in tears, and we imagined that we were at a funeral."

Some put on a brave face. The Warrior Guards are "our town boys, those that we have associated with for years; and feel a deep interest in them." Perhaps "ere many months we may greet them home, and that they shall have acquit[t]ed themselves honorably on the field of Battle."

William Russell Smith, whose sixteen-year-old son had just enlisted, was among those who were not so optimistic. War against the North is no "child's play," he judged sadly. "In the matter of supplies of every description, the North has greatly the advantage. There is scarcely a powder mill in the South!—and no gun factory of any consequence! . . . I fear the worst. The South will never back down now—and the result will be annihilation or victory with us."

Some of those Warrior Guards leaving aboard the *Cherokee* that day would never return. Others would return but not as Warrior Guards. The following January, former *Independent Monitor* editor W. H. Fowler persuaded fifty-two of them to join an artillery battery that he was organizing. (Fowler's Battery, which was reputed to be composed only of former Warrior Guards, would be commended for bravery at the Battle of Chickamauga.) And during the April 1862 military reorganization, the unit was dissolved after the remaining twenty Warrior Guards transferred to another company in the Fifth Alabama.

The new military units from the City of Oaks and the county came with an array of names. The North Port Rifles and the Tuscaloosa Rifles were among the infantry companies organized during that first year. These two united and fought as part of the Eleventh Alabama of the Army of Northern Virginia first under W. H. Fowler (who served in so many capacities during the war that it is hard to keep straight) and then James McMath. Another Tuscaloosa unit, Adams' Company of the Thirty-Sixth Alabama, lost many men at the battles at Chickamauga and Nashville. And then there were the colorfully named Tuscaloosa Plough Boys, who fought at Shiloh and Chickamauga, and the Tuscaloosa Tigers, sent to guard prison camps in North Carolina. An estimated thirty-five hundred men from the county would wear the grey.

TUSCALOOSANS WAVING GOODBYE on the dock expected to read of their sons' adventures in letters home and in the newspaper. None expected that the war would last long or spread much past Virginia, much less reach their homes along the Black Warrior. The City of Oaks was simply too remote. They would be surprised and in short order.

One Tuscaloosan, in fact, was already involved years before the first shot had even been fired. On February 1, 1861, just a few days before the Provisional Confederate Congress convened in Montgomery, Tuscaloosans read in the *Independent Monitor* of a cannon shell invented by their own John B. Read, physician, occasional pharmacist, long-standing surgeon to the university's Corps of Cadets, and inventor. The Read shell allowed the rifling of cannon barrels, thereby vastly increasing their accuracy and distance. In 1856, the same year that Dr. Read registered his patent, he approached Robert Parrott, superintendent of the West Point Foundry, who purchased rights to manufacture the Read shell for the U.S. government. In "dealing with him the South will not be fostering an enemy," concluded the *Monitor*'s editor denying what everyone else feared. Union forces would go on to use the Read shell, conveniently known as the Parrott shell, in their muzzle-loaded Parrott rifles, which ranged from light field pieces to massive ten-inch three-hundred pounders. Confederates fired the projectile out of their formidable Brooke rifled canon; many of these most sophisticated of Southern cannon were made in Selma. The Read shell and its Parrott counterpart are generally acknowledged as the most common projectiles of the war. Dr. Read would attempt repeatedly after hostilities ended to recover lost royalties from the U.S. government, always without success.

Charles Lumsden about 1860 while the university's instructor of military tactics (Courtesy The University of Alabama Libraries Special Collections)

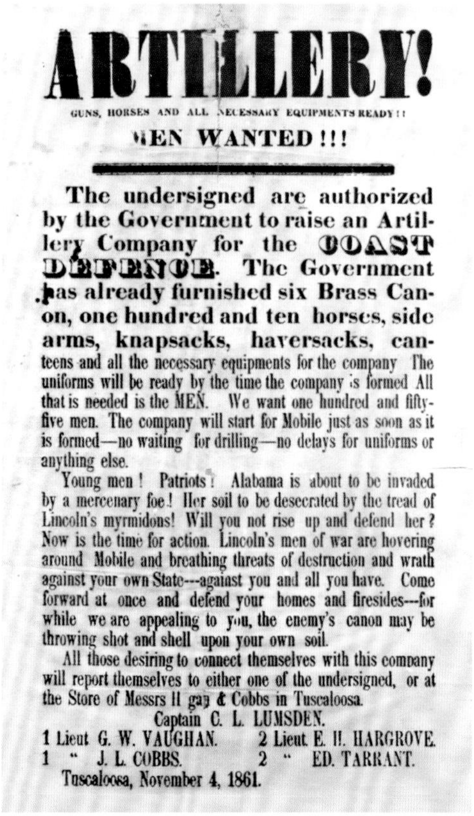

ARTILLERY!

GUNS, HORSES AND ALL NECESSARY EQUIPMENTS READY!!

MEN WANTED!!!

The undersigned are authorized by the Government to raise an Artillery Company for the COAST DEFENCE. The Government has already furnished six Brass Canon, one hundred and ten horses, side arms, knapsacks, haversacks, canteens and all the necessary equipments for the company The uniforms will be ready by the time the company is formed All that is needed is the MEN. We want one hundred and fifty-five men. The company will start for Mobile just as soon as it is formed—no waiting for drilling—no delays for uniforms or anything else.

Young men! Patriots! Alabama is about to be invaded by a mercenary foe! Her soil to be desecrated by the tread of Lincoln's myrmidons! Will you not rise up and defend her? Now is the time for action. Lincoln's men of war are hovering around Mobile and breathing threats of destruction and wrath against your own State---against you and all you have. Come forward at once and defend your homes and firesides---for while we are appealing to you, the enemy's canon may be throwing shot and shell upon your own soil.

All those desiring to connect themselves with this company will report themselves to either one of the undersigned, or at the Store of Messrs H gay & Cobbs in Tuscaloosa.

Captain C. L. LUMSDEN.

1 Lieut G. W. VAUGHAN. 2 Lieut E. H. HARGROVE.
1 " J. L. COBBS. 2 " ED. TARRANT.

Tuscaloosa, November 4, 1861.

Charles Lumsden organized a noted Tuscaloosa artillery unit during the war's first year. Many of his recruits were cadets itching to leave the confines of the University of Alabama and get into the war. (Courtesy The University of Alabama Libraries Special Collections)

Cannon were being made in West Point, in Selma, and even in Tuscaloosa. The Leach & Avery Foundry, which in 1859 had been recognized for making the state's best plows, had been rebuilt after the fire and was churning out weapons of war.

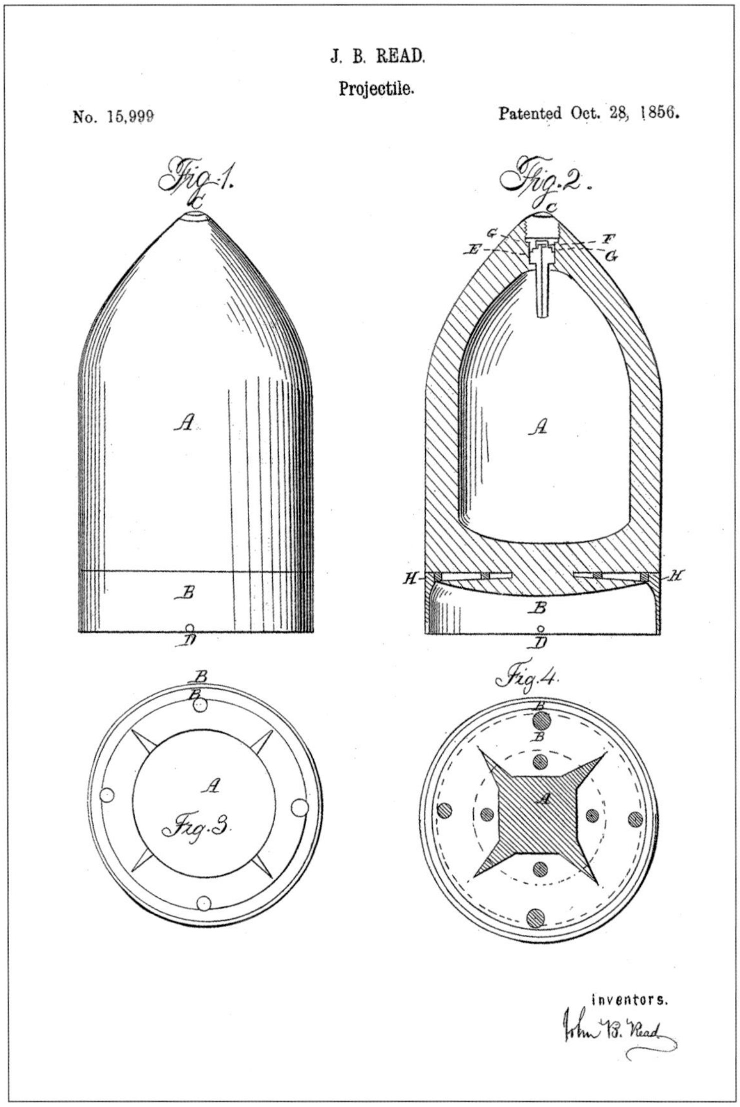

John B. Read of Tuscaloosa received a patent in 1856 for his improved cannon shell. When fired out of a rifled barrel, the shell increased accuracy and distance. The Read shell would be used on both sides during the war. (Reed, John B. Improved Mode of Constructing Projectiles from Cannons. US Patent 15,999, granted October 28, 1856.)

Plowshares into swords, or rather cannon. W. H. Fowler ordered a pair of six-pounders for his battery, and the university soon got its own six-pounders. The foundry was also involved in salvaging the *Cotton Plant*, a steamer that sank in 1824, by using chains pulled by yoked oxen. The workers split the boiler in half lengthwise to make two evaporators for collecting salt, an important nineteenth-century resource used in a variety of ways. Large cypress timbers were clamped to the sides of the evaporators and, with oars and a canvas cover, rowed some 260 miles downstream to the Clarke County salt works.

Tuscaloosans produced other goods for the war effort. Kirkman, Hay & Co. wove coarse cloth for the troops to use, presumably for uniforms. Edward Olmstead's firm in Northport made hats, while Charles Foster's tannery produced shoes. A small factory outside of town made saltpeter, used in explosives.

And Tuscaloosans tried to build an ironclad. The first modern warship, ironclads were essentially steam-powered massed cannon protected by armored plates angled to deflect enemy shells. Carpenters and a sawmill were lined up. The blacksmiths had plenty of iron ore for their forge and needed only a rolling mill. "We expect to hear in a short time that the boat is in process of construction," Alabama newspapers declared in April 1862. But nothing came of it. A gunboat would indeed be built, but not in the City of Oaks. The CSS *Tuscaloosa* would set off later that year from the Selma Ordnance and Naval Foundry and slowly make its way downstream to guard Mobile.

These contributions to the war effort did not intrude significantly into Tuscaloosans' daily lives. The same could not be said for other developments.

Richmond had run out of room for the thousands of prisoners captured at the Battle of First Manassas in July 1861, so Secretary of War Judah Benjamin approached governors to share some of the burden. When Alabama's governor demurred, Benjamin shot back, "I am told you have at Tuscaloosa, the former capital, not only legislative buildings but an insane asylum and a military institute—all unoccupied." Benjamin did not have his facts straight. It hardly mattered. Those veterans of First Manassas were soon on their way, as were some Irish Zouaves from New

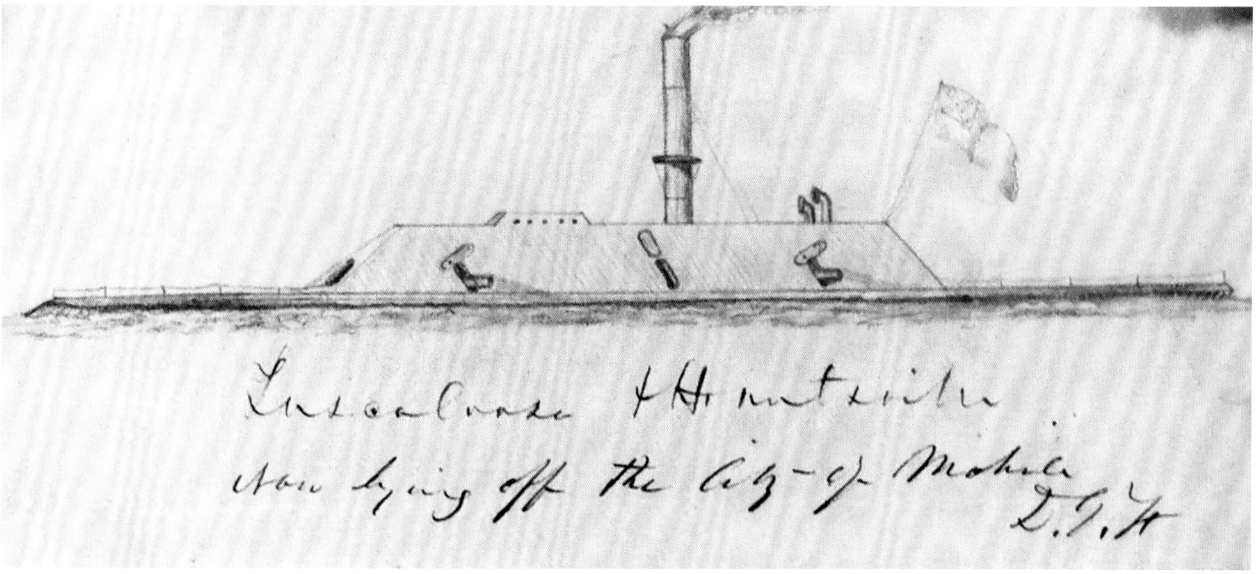

Admiral David Glasgow Farragut sketched the ironclad CSS *Tuscaloosa* during its ineffective defense against the Union fleet in Mobile Bay. (Courtesy National Archives and Records Administration)

TWO CRAFTS BORE THE NAME CSS *TUSCALOOSA*. *The high-seas raider* Tuscaloosa *began as the* Conrad, *a commercial bark captured by the raider CSS* Alabama *in June 1863. Recognizing her potential, the Alabama's captain outfitted the swift ship with two rifled brass 12-pounders, a generous supply of hand weapons and ammunition, and provisions sufficient for a three-month cruise. The* Tuscaloosa, *as she was now named, set off with a fifteen-man crew under Lieutenant J. Low. Her career was short, capturing only one ship before being seized by South African authorities for neutrality violations. Lieutenant Low and his crew left the* Tuscaloosa *and, when no one reclaimed her, the U.S. Navy took possession after the war ended.*

The ironclad Tuscaloosa, *above, was built at the Selma Confederate Naval Works with four-inch armor plating and was outfitted with four smoothbore 32-pounders and a single Brooke rifle, which fired Read shells. Launched in February 1863, the* Tuscaloosa *slowly steamed its way downstream to defend Mobile Bay. During the war's final days, the crew scuttled her in the Spanish River to prevent capture. The wreck was found in May of 1985.*

York captured near Pensacola. Surely someone found it amusing that Irishmen from New York, dressed as French troops in Algeria, captured in Florida, were imprisoned in Alabama. But if so, no one admitted it. Instead, town folk wrote in protest to their fellow Tuscaloosan in the Confederate Senate, Robert Jemison. Their protests mattered not at all. Forty-eight more prisoners arrived in December. And over a hundred more came the following month. But these were not soldiers. These were political prisoners.

After the burning of five railroad bridges and the refusal of many citizens to pledge allegiance to the Confederacy, the military leaders in east Tennessee feared an armed insurgency. They placed Knoxville and the surrounding area under martial law and began rounding up Unionists. When asked what to do, Secretary of War Benjamin replied that the bridge burners were to be tried immediately and, if found guilty, hanged on the spot. The rest of the civilians, who likely could not be convicted in a court, were to be "sent with an armed

Among the first prisoners in Tuscaloosa were civilian Unionists from east Tennessee. (From W. G. Brownlow, *Sketches of the Rise, Progress, and Decline of Secession* [Philadelphia: Childs, 1862])

guard to Tuscaloosa, Ala., there to be kept imprisoned at the depot selected by the Government for prisoners of war. . . . They are all to be held as prisoners of war and held in jail till the end of the war." Unionists—including several physicians, lawyers, preachers, businessmen, and farmers—were on their way within weeks. Among them was Tuscaloosa's most famous political prisoner, Andrew Johnson's son-in-law, Judge David T. Patterson. This violation of the civilians' civil rights shocked even patriotic Southerners. More than that, the political prisoners garnered attention and even sympathy, especially among those with Unionist leanings.

But it was the arrival of the soldiers that created real problems. By December 1861, some five hundred prisoners from First Manassas were crammed into the abandoned paper mill along the river, the venerable Washington Hall at the northeast corner of Broad and Market Streets, and what was known as the Drish Building directly across Market Street from Washington Hall. Another two hundred arrived in March.

The proprietor of Washington Hall did not hesitate to voice his objections to having the center of town turned into a prison. The sergeant in charge, one Henry Wirz, was not known for subtleties. "I'll call out my one hundred and fifty guards and take it by force," he threatened. "If they can't do it, I have five hundred Yankees and they'll *fight like hell*." The prisoners were soon ushered in. Some 155 lived in the dining hall, which had also once served as Tuscaloosa's ballroom and theater. The prisoners slept on the wooden floor. They thought their bones were about to break through their skin until the sergeant supplied them with some promised cots and mattresses. The food they also found less than adequate. "Bread and bacon for breakfast, ditto for supper," wrote a Rhode Islander in his diary. The cornbread was made from "corn and cobs ground together, mixed with water, but no salt, and baked in dripping pans about three inches deep." For Christmas they received a treat of rice and molasses, which they ate off tin plates made by unsoldering their canteens. When one man complained of how little he had to eat, he was put in irons and fed only bread and water.

Sergeant Wirz enforced the strictest discipline. A captain was shackled for talking to prisoners in another room. Five or six others were put in irons for attempting to run away. Three men were confined under ball and chain indefinitely until they divulged the name of a prisoner who hung a small Union flag out the window. When on Washington's birthday the Rhode Island soldiers opened the windows and sang "The Star-Spangled Banner" to an audience of black faces on the street, the Swiss-born Wirz raced up to stop them: "What in Hades you tam fools trying to do? I thought you Rhode Island chaps pretty good fellows but py tam you get no more meat for two, three, four days, do you see?" This may have been the occasion when someone defaced the hotel's portrait of Washington standing beside a grey horse by painting the president's face and hands black. The portrait, which stood on a pillar at the street corner and served as Washington Hall's sign, was presumably discarded; but the pillar on which it stood remained for decades, its original purpose confused or forgotten.

One incident stood out above all others and was recounted in diaries, letters, newspaper articles, and years later in reminiscences. Wirz had printed, but "not generally posted," orders stating that "if prisoners looked out of the windows, that they were to be warned to withdraw, and if they refused, they were to be shot." Redmond McGuire, a newly arrived Wisconsin lad, peered out of a window from his prison room in the Drish Building, "and one of the guards shot his brains out." Then, reported one of his fellow prisoners, Wirz "came up to where we was and cursed and swore that if we didn't quit looking out of the windows that we would all be served the same way." When an older prisoner protested, he was put in irons. And two days later after some new prisoners arrived, two more men—both deaf—were also shot dead peering out windows.

No one quite knew what to make of Wirz. "How we hated that man in Richmond but now he is the best friend we have," wrote one Wisconsin soldier. "We have a Sgt. Wertz over us as big a tyrant as ever ran," another entered into his diary; yet two days later the same prisoner found the tyrant "quite gentlemanly." The Confederate authorities must have been pleased. They promoted him to lieutenant and gave him full command over the Tuscaloosa prisons. After an injury left him in chronic pain, he was again promoted and sent on a diplomatic mission to England and France. Captain Wirz was last as-

Sergeant Henry Wirz, the man in charge of the Tuscaloosa prisons, would eventually be put over the deplorable prison at Andersonville, Georgia. Wirz was a controversial figure. Most Northerners presented him as a vile and malevolent beast; but some, even former prisoners, believed that he had been placed in an untenable situation. Nonetheless, Wirz would be hanged after the war. (From *Harper's Weekly*, September 16, 1865)

Elizabeth Avery Meriwether spent much of the war as a refugee in Tuscaloosa with her three children. She wrote of her adventures in a prize-winning story. (Courtesy Tennessee State Museum, Tennessee Historical Society Collection)

signed to command the new prison camp in Andersonville, Georgia. The uncompromising orders issued from the enigmatic and volatile "Butcher of Andersonville," coupled with the appalling conditions there, resulted in Wirz being sentenced to the gallows—one of the few Confederate soldiers executed for war crimes.

Tuscaloosa's already crowded prisons became overwhelmed after the Battle of Shiloh in early April 1862. A reported five thousand Union prisoners were on their way. Rumors were afloat a month later that 1,200 Federal cavalrymen were heading from Tuscumbia to free what by then was believed to be 2,300 imprisoned in Tuscaloosa.

Authorities began to talk seriously about evacuating the prisoners, and not merely to avert the threatened cavalry raid. Many Confederate officials had been wary of Tuscaloosa's suitability as a prison because "a large number of the people are Union men." Imprisoned Yankee officers were reportedly released on parole only to be invited to oyster saloons and to dine in the private homes of Yankee sympathizers. "Jeff. Davis has gone to Tuscaloosa," the newspapers wrongly reported, because the "Union sentiment is strong and increasing."

Officials had started removing prisoners even before the Shiloh prisoners were expected. Five hundred of those captured at Manassas signed paroles of honor and departed for North Carolina on the first of March. Eleven hundred prisoners left for Knoxville in the middle of May. Some eighteen hundred from the Tuscaloosa and Macon, Georgia, prisons were in Atlanta on their way to Chattanooga the following month. And once the summer of 1862 began, Tuscaloosa had no more prisoners of war.

One reason why Tuscaloosa had made a good site for prisons is that it was one of the more isolated towns in the South, ironic given that it had once been the crossroads of Alabama. By the 1860s, that no longer applied. Without railroads or major east-west wagon roads, 350 miles up a river navigable only half the year, shielded from the north by a mountain range—its isolation was now attractive. Tuscaloosa had served as a good site for prisons and would also serve well for hospitals and as a sanctuary.

Washington Hall was used briefly as a hospital early in the war, and sick and wounded Confederate soldiers were treated at the Indian Queen Hotel throughout the war. In May 1862, the east wing of the insane hospital was filled with soldiers suffering from the measles and camp (typhoid) fever. Local Tuscaloosa women aided at least three physicians in nursing the soldiers. Mrs. Bryce recalled later in life that she lost five of the eighteen men in her ward to camp fever. Some of the five wards each had as many as fifty patients.

And Tuscaloosa's remoteness provided an ideal destination for civilians fleeing from advancing Union forces. The first refugees began arriving after Brigadier General Ulysses S. Grant's forces captured Fort Henry on the Tennessee River in February 1862. Three Union gunboats immediately churned upstream to the Muscle Shoals. The bluecoats occupied Huntsville by April. Those who could left the Tennessee Valley for Tuscaloosa by the Byler and Huntsville Roads. And after the Confederate naval forces guarding Memphis were easily crushed in June, even more refugees headed for Tuscaloosa, just as the last prisoners were leaving.

Among them was Elizabeth Avery Meriwether, wife of a Confederate officer and engineer engaged in building defense works and railroads. Her account of the trek with her sons in a four-wheeled carriage conveyed the sort of trials that many other refugees encountered. Leaving Memphis in December 1862, Mrs. Meriwether witnessed Confederate soldiers eating cornbread with raw bacon, not having the time to even cook it, and sleeping on the wet ground with neither blanket nor fire to warm them. Her third son was born on Christmas Day. It took the four of them until May to finally reach Tuscaloosa. She was, of course, delighted to find a lovely town with wide streets and rows of shade trees. But her ordeal was not over. So many had escaped to the City of Oaks that no rooms were to be had. She finally secured a "little rickety tumble-down house" alongside other "frame shanties occupied by poor refugees." Furniture was not to be had either, but for the generosity of some Tuscaloosans who gave her a mattress, table, and chairs. Then came the problem of food—once again, not to be had. As a soldier's wife, she received a daily allotment from the government of such things as field peas, which she made into soup. And the government provided Confederate officers with tobacco. Her husband, who did not smoke, sent his allowance to his wife in Tuscaloosa, and she bartered it for dairy products.

The most memorable incident during Mrs. Meriwether's time in Tuscaloosa was her encounter with her neighbor John R. Drish, the successful physician who built one of the town's more commanding homes. Every day she watched the corn in his field grow. When it at last ripened, she approached Dr. Drish and told him of her need. "No, madam," he replied. "I

Mrs. Meriwether's defiance of Dr. Drish won her the respect and generosity of other Tuscaloosans. Dr. Drish's mansion, shown here about 1907, looked much the same in 1863. (Courtesy Tuscaloosa Preservation Society)

As president of the University of Alabama, Landon Cabell Garland was also superintendent of the Corps of Cadets. Here he poses in his newly tailored uniform for Mathew Brady to take his photograph. (Courtesy The University of Alabama Libraries Special Collections)

will not allow my corn to be pulled from my field. That corn is to feed my Negroes this winter." Not to be deterred, Mrs. Meriwether followed him to his door and spoke directly: "Wait a minute. The father of my little boys is in the army. He cannot now provide food for his family. Do you not feel it is your duty to keep a soldier's children from starving?" Dr. Drish still refused. With that, she climbed over the fence, pulled several dozen ears, threw them in her carriage, and left two Confederate dollars in return. Dr. Drish afterward ordered his men to patrol his fields with shotguns. But when other Tuscaloosans heard of the incident, she regularly received vegetables for which she never paid a cent. (Dr. Drish, financially ruined by the Civil War, took to drink and gambling. He would die at his home in 1867 from a fall down the stairs during an attack of delirium tremens.)

Mrs. Meriwether heard of a newspaper contest for the best short story. Her melodramatic account of leaving Memphis, "The Refugee," won; but the $500 prize allowed her to purchase little with the inflated Confederate currency. Publication of "The Refugee" also brought a visit from another refugee: Joseph Davis, older brother of the Confederate president and one of the South's wealthiest men.

Davis and his family had reached Tuscaloosa after a protracted flight from his extensive and remarkable plantation near Vicksburg. His family found Tuscaloosans generous. Robert Jemison even invited them to live in his enormous mansion on Greensboro Street, which during the war seemed to be the center of social activities. By the spring of 1863, Davis and another family finally found a farmhouse to rent two miles out of town. Their new friends in Tuscaloosa lent them furniture. There they would stay until the war's end.

CONTRARY TO EXPECTATIONS, the war had come to Tuscaloosans. They had sent their young men off, turned their few small industries to producing war goods, converted their hotels and warehouses into prison camps, opened hospitals, and rented rooms to refugees. All of these efforts, however, were overshadowed by what went on at the University of Alabama.

A good place to begin might be in June 1858, when one University of Alabama student shot and killed another following a quarrel. This was but the worst of many violent acts that had been part of student life since opening day. The *Independent Monitor*'s subsequent editorial, which detailed the students' poor behavior and the university's worsening problem attracting students, was widely republished throughout the state. That fall, less than half as many students would be on campus as its all-time high.

President Garland began to lobby the legislature for permission to create a military department that would correct the problems of lax morals and discipline that he blamed for declining enrollments. He conveniently ignored the fact that the dropping number of students had probably more to do with the difficulties in getting to the Tuscaloosa campus. Garland's proposal to militarize the school went nowhere until John Brown's raid in October 1859. As a result, a few months later the legislature passed a massive military bill. Among its provisions were an elite volunteer corps of eight thousand men, a state flag and new militia uniform, and the transformation of the University of Alabama into the state's military academy—just as President Garland had been proposing. The cadets who arrived in the fall of 1860 were soon wearing uniforms, as was President Garland, and adhering to strict military discipline. The violence and hijinks disappeared. Enrollment soared.

Another factor helped to increase enrollment at the start of the next academic year. By the fall of 1861, parents wanted to shield their sons from being sent to the front lines, for members of the Alabama Corps of Cadets were exempt from conscription. The corps was nonetheless an organized military body in state service and could be called out at any time by the governor. In March 1862, the governor placed the cadets in charge of drilling twelve thousand of the state's volunteer troops. In July 1864, fifty-four cadets were part of a group of three hundred young Confederate soldiers headed to east Alabama to oppose Union General Lovell Rousseau's cavalry raid into central Alabama. That fall, the entire corps was ordered to north Alabama in a vain attempt to engage Union soldiers.

No one doubted that the University of Alabama was a military target. The Corps of Cadets was, after all, a military unit

University of Alabama cadet George M. Labuzan, age seventeen, in 1863 (Courtesy The University of Alabama Libraries Special Collections)

Brigadier General John T. Croxton, whose cavalry invaded Tuscaloosa and burned the University of Alabama (Courtesy Library of Congress)

and had devoted much time to drilling recruits. Besides, Union soldiers had been systematically destroying Southern military academies. They had gone out of their way in April 1863 to raze the state-supported LaGrange Military Academy in north Alabama. President Garland wrote Governor John Gill Shorter the following month of his concerns. If Tuscaloosa were ever attacked, he noted, "they would not leave one brick of the University standing on another." The following year, Union troops burned the Virginia Military Institute.

The war was essentially over by the spring of 1865. With John Bell Hood's Army of Tennessee posing no resistance after its destruction in the Battle of Nashville, the path lay wide open for Union forces to attack Alabama's heretofore untouched industrial corridor. High on their list were the iron furnaces in Jefferson County, but even more important was the massive Selma Ordnance and Naval Foundry, which continued to churn out weaponry. Alabama's military academy in Tuscaloosa was not far out of the way.

Union Major General James H. Wilson started south with more than thirteen thousand cavalrymen from Gravelly Springs in Lauderdale County, Alabama, on March 25. Only Nathan Bedford Forrest's five thousand cavalrymen could stop him. Forrest, however, remained in Mississippi after relying on false information. Repeated rumors of bluecoats and spies put Alabamians on edge as the force made its way through the mountains. The newspapers finally reported on March 30 that "Yankees, in heavy force" were in Jasper and on their way to Tuscaloosa. When the local post commander called for volunteers to add to his few troops, "some six hundred men, including the Cadets, were under arms, stationed for fight, with three pieces of artillery," boasted the newspapers, defying "the raiders to attempt to cross the Warrior!" But those Union cavalrymen headed instead for Elyton in Jefferson County. The danger had passed—or so they believed.

Meeting little resistance, Wilson decided to divide his force. He ordered Brigadier General John T. Croxton and his fifteen hundred cavalrymen to "proceed rapidly by the most direct route to Tuscaloosa, to destroy the bridge, factories, mills, university (military school), and whatever else may be of benefit to the rebel cause."

Repulsed by a Confederate brigade at Vance, Croxton and his men crossed the river and approached Tuscaloosa from the north. The bluecoats reached the bridge into Tuscaloosa at about eleven on the evening of April 3. Although he had planned to delay his invasion until the next morning, the sight of some fourteen men taking up floor planks from the bridge caused Croxton to send a company straight at them. "Who's there?" asked one of the home guards. "Friends!" was the reply. Perhaps the Michigan accent gave him away. At any rate, the guard fired, sending the ball through the crown of the cavalryman's hat. With that, the troops returned the fire, mortally wounding the guard who had challenged them, severely wounding a youth, and capturing the rest. The floor planks were quickly replaced, and the Yankees entered the City of Oaks.

Tuscaloosans had been assured that they had no reason to worry because the cavalrymen were no nearer than thirty miles. Thus the town was dark, quiet, and calm—with a single exception. Voices were heard and lights flickered at the Jemison Mansion down Greensboro Street beyond the business district. There, a wedding between Captain James Slaughter Carpenter and Miss Emily Alston Leach had just ended and the guests were dancing. The music suddenly ceased. Cavalrymen in blue uniforms burst in and went straight for the wedding cake. Captain Carpenter was allowed to say his goodbyes before being taken prisoner and hauled over the bridge to Croxton's headquarters. Carpenter would later be paroled to return to his bride, but not before performing a task for Croxton, who had known him before the war.

President Garland did not learn of the invasion until after midnight. Then he ran from the President's Mansion to the cadets' quarters shouting to the drummer boy, "Beat the long roll! The Yanks are in town." The cadets hastily donned their uniforms, grabbed their ammunition and muskets, and assembled on the campus lawn. Captain John H. Murfee, whose brother was the commandant, marched Company C, deployed as skirmishers, in open formation through a misty rain. Upon reaching the center of town, he ordered the boys—half under sixteen years of age—to "right wheel—forward march!"

"What regiment do you belong to?" came a challenge out of the darkness.

"The Alabama Corps of Cadets," came the defiant reply. And the firing commenced. The captain and a couple of cadets were wounded slightly in the exchange.

The commandant and the rest of the cadets had just reached the Dearing House, on the city's eastern edge, when they heard the gunfire. The commandant ordered the corps to double quick until they joined Company C. After some brief skirmishing, President Garland and the commandant conferred with Captain Carpenter, the same whose wedding had been interrupted, whom Croxton sent forward to explain to those three hundred boys with muzzleloaders what exactly they faced: fifteen hundred battle-seasoned cavalrymen armed with Spencer carbines—one of the most advanced weapons of the Civil War, which could fire up to twenty rounds a minute—along with the cadets' own Leach & Avery six-pounders, which Croxton's men had found and appropriated with the help of spies. President Garland wisely ordered the corps back to campus. They gathered their clothes, filled their haver-

morning to surrender the town to Croxton. But that would hardly end the matter.

About nine o'clock, Colonel Thomas W. Johnston of the Second Michigan Cavalry rode out the Huntsville Road with some of his men. Turning left at the campus gate, they proceeded up the formal cedar-lined walkway to the Rotunda directly ahead. There André DeLoffre, librarian and professor of modern languages, asked their commanding officer to spare the library, one of the finest in the South. Colonel Johnston was sympathetic and sent back a courier to General Croxton for an exemption, noting that the library had no military significance. But Croxton responded that his orders left him no discretion (perhaps an exaggeration). "It is a great pity," responded the colonel, "but my orders are imperative." Legend has it that he saved one volume, a copy of the Koran, as a memento. Explosives were then fired onto the roof, the doors opened to speed combustion, and the Rotunda was quickly reduced to ashes. The cavalrymen wasted no time in setting fire to most of the other campus buildings, leaving untouched the only military building, the Guard House.

The Yankees then applied a long powder train to destroy the brick magazine where the cadets' gunpowder was stored. The resulting explosion was reckoned the loudest sound ever heard in Tuscaloosa. They followed up by leveling the saltpeter factory. During the afternoon and the next morning, the cavalrymen continued methodically burning the cotton factory, tannery, Leach & Avery Foundry, and cotton warehouse. Local lore has it that some clever Tuscaloosans devised a ruse: they galloped into town shouting for joy that Confederate General William Hicks

The University of Alabama's librarian and professor of modern languages, André DeLoffre (above right), tried in vain to prevent Colonel Thomas W. Johnston (below right) from burning the Rotunda whose top floor held the university's library. (Above: Courtesy The University of Alabama Libraries Special Collections); Below: From Marshall P. Thatcher, *A Hundred Battles in the West* [Detroit: self-pub., 1884])

sacks with hardtack from the commissary, and marched east out the Huntsville Road. The corps would eventually turn south to Marion, disband, and each boy would head home.

Croxton's men, meanwhile, were carrying out their orders by setting fire to the Northport factory that supplied hats to the Confederacy. Mayor Obediah Berry and Father William F. McDonough of St. John's Church ventured out the next

The University of Alabama's once elegant Rotunda in ruins, as sketched by Eugene Allen Smith, former cadet and instructor of tactics (Courtesy The University of Alabama Libraries Special Collections)

Jackson's forces were on their way to deliver the town. Croxton hastily ordered his forces out—but not before rolling the cadets' six-pounders to the center of the bridge and setting the whole ablaze. In the words of one witness, "thus the town, after having been completely ruined, was rid of the enemy."

The war was over for Tuscaloosans when Croxton's raiders left that April 5. Four days later General Lee surrendered his Army of Northern Virginia. And five days after that, John Wilkes Booth ended President Lincoln's life.

Tuscaloosa had been quiet until President Garland's command to beat the long roll. The ensuing rifle volleys were followed the next morning by the roar of fire consuming the University of Alabama. That roar snuffed out more than buildings; it snuffed out decades of hopes and plans. Then came the ear-splitting explosion of the gunpowder. But the quiet sounds were more enduring and in a sense louder: the wives and mothers, sisters and brothers, friends and fellow Tuscaloosans crying for those who would never return from the battlefields. Perhaps it was the silence of the vacant chair that shouted out the loudest.

OCCUPYING UNION TROOPS were soon back in the City of Oaks. They took up residence in Washington Hall, where imprisoned Union troops had stayed a few years before. That did not last long. On November 1, 1865, one of them unintentionally set it ablaze. The original 1823

This guard house was the only military structure to survive the destruction of the University of Alabama campus by Union troops. (Courtesy Library of Congress)

two-story brick building had been expanded over the years. On the second floor were federal courtrooms, which doubled as a venue for political debates and orations. Tuscaloosa's social life played out in the hotel's rooms or in the streets below. John Gorman Barr used Washington Hall as the backdrop to one of his finest tales, "The New York Drummer's Ride to Greensboro." After having Washington's portrait defaced, after being turned into a prison, after having invading cavalrymen open fire outside its windows—after all this, it seemed somehow in character to have a Union soldier burn Washington Hall to the ground, even if it was by accident.

When considered with the remains of the university, Tuscaloosa presented more "mouldering ruins, the mournful vestiges of her former grandeur" than any other place in Alabama, according to a Chattanooga correspondent (who was unwittingly quoting from *Clotel*, the first published novel written by a black American). All this, he continued, is "the devastation of relentless war." Tuscaloosa's outspoken newspaper editor agreed, urging that the ruins be left untouched as a testament to the enemy's barbarity.

While all Tuscaloosans abhorred the losses, they were hardly of one mind about what it all meant. Defeat had only made the believers even more convinced of their cause. But the former Unionists blamed the secessionists for precipitating a needless war that had left perhaps three-quarters of a million people dead. And the former slaves found deliverance. Now that the pitched battles had stopped, the clashes would generally be less violent but a good deal more complicated. Union troops patrolled the streets, but for how long? New political alliances and even new political structures needed to be created, but what would that entail? The freed people would be assuming the responsibilities of citizenship, but how would they prepare? Tuscaloosans needed to get the University of Alabama back in operation, but who would be in charge? After first secession and then war, this seemingly unending conflict was entering a third and even more confusing phase. The battles this time would not be waged with bugles blaring on bloodied fields. This time the battles would be fought in the newspapers, by men in disguise, and at the ballot box.

BLACK TUSCALOOSANS soon began assuming responsibility for their own affairs. By mid-June the Reverend Basil Manly's former plantation slaves, now proudly deeming themselves "freedmen & freedwomen," were drawing up and signing contracts "to act faithfully as laborers and employees" for a year. Manly pledged in return to provide them with food, clothing, fuel, medical attention, and a portion of the crop. While these terms might today be regarded as fateful steps on the road to sharecropping and tenancy, their explicit legal language recognizing the rights of both parties marked a completely new status for these formerly bound men and women. Household servants in town negotiated similar agreements. The freed people were rapidly marching down their own uncharted paths.

The freed people were especially determined to worship on their own terms. State law had prohibited slaves from attending church services without white supervision, fearing their use to plot rebellion. Emancipation from slavery also meant emancipation from their masters' churches, which often had many black members. In the spring of 1866 a conference of the African Methodist Episcopal Zion Church in Mobile heard from the Tuscaloosa delegation that six hundred black Methodists were meeting in the basement of one of the white churches. They needed a church of their own, and some two hundred children needed a building in which to attend Sabbath school. That conference was the occasion for the ordination of Shandy Jones. Jones was Tuscaloosa's wealthiest free black behind Solomon Perteet. After making his fortune by barbering and investing in real estate, he had emerged during the 1850s as Alabama's foremost proponent of black immigration to Liberia. Jones returned from Mobile and immediately founded what would become Hunter Chapel AME Zion, Tuscaloosa's first black church. He soon established at the church a "thriving school for freedmen," Tuscaloosa's first. More would be heard from Shandy Jones.

Later that same spring, black members of the Tuscaloosa Baptist Church met with their white minister. They had been "impatient of any connexion with the whites, wishing to withdraw & be to themselves," according to one witness. The whites were also willing for them to separate, as long as it was in an "orderly condition." The minister addressed the black members and admonished them for the "unscriptural & disorderly . . . *quasi ordination*" of their leader, Prince Morrell. When the minister left them to come to a decision—assuming that they would defer to his advice—the black members simply walked out and established the First African Baptist Church. Morrell would serve as its pastor for thirteen years.

The new status of the freed people was hard to disentangle from the many other bewildering new problems that the war had created. Tuscaloosans were also faced with the political challenges of new constitutions and voting regulations, reopening the University of Alabama, and the mounting rage of former Confederates.

For two months after the end of fighting, authority had been in the hands of President Andrew Johnson, a Southern Union Democrat who had run with Lincoln on the National Union Party ticket. As president, he established a provisional state government in June and demanded a new constitution that repealed secession and abolished slavery, which Alabama had in place by the end of September. Johnson declared Reconstruction an accomplished fact at the end of 1865. But things turned around completely after the 1866 elections, when the North sent a substantial majority of Republicans to Congress who could override any presidential veto. Their new congressional plan for Reconstruction began by placing the former Confederate states under military rule. Alabama's elected governor would

Ryland Randolph's *Independent Monitor* newspaper was closed by federal authorities for a time and an armed guard on the second floor barred entrance to his office. (Courtesy Alabama Department of Archives and History)

serve in name only. And Congress showed its determination to establish a Republican Party in the South through a series of laws granting the vote to freedmen while removing the vote from those who had precipitated secession and war. The result was a deeply divided electorate. The Democrats—former Confederates who strongly supported white supremacy—squared off against the Republicans—an uneasy coalition of freedmen, carpetbaggers (Northerners who had come south after the war), and scalawags (Southern whites, largely former Unionists).

Tuscaloosans felt these changes acutely. The citizens, who had sent Unionists to the secession convention, had also supplied their share of men to the cause. The City of Oaks had been invaded, its factories burned, and the university destroyed. By the spring of 1867, work was finally underway to rebuild the university—just a month after Congress had called for another new state constitution to be written and approved by the voters, this time including former slaves. On October 1, while Alabamians were selecting delegates to this second postwar constitutional convention, an old Tuscaloosa Whig newspaper, the *Independent Monitor*, came under new ownership.

With no experience and unknown financial resources, Ryland Randolph moved to Tuscaloosa, purchased the *Monitor*, turned it into an extreme pro-Democrat mouthpiece, and swiftly became the most notorious editor in the South. Randolph was the prideful but underachieving scion of a famous Virginia family. The end of the fighting found the once wealthy Randolph penniless, directionless, and boasting of his brave exploits rather than acknowledging his less-than-mediocre war record while wearing the grey. Randolph railed against all the changes wrought by the Republican Congress, particularly that of giving freedmen the vote. Instead of "Save the Union," the *Monitor*'s new owner and editor emblazoned a new motto across the masthead: "The White Man—Right or Wrong—Still the White Man!" Randolph had no illusions about where black Tuscaloosans stood. But he was appalled to find many—perhaps the majority—of white Tuscaloosans "wavering" in the political winds. He set out to rally those "fence straddlers" and stop the Republican juggernaut.

EIGHTEEN SIXTY-EIGHT would be a year like no other. Randolph was seated in his newspaper office on Broad Street one Saturday morning in March when he heard "a great commotion" coming from across the street. "Two burly negro men," the editor would recount later, were attacking "a diminutive white man, beating him for all they were worth. . . . Not a white arm was raised either to protect the white man or separate the unequal combatants." Racing out of his office with a pistol and knife, he fired into the air in an effort to scare them. One of the black men fled, but the other turned and raised his stick to club Randolph. "I caught his falling stick on my left arm, whilst with my right I stabbed him till he fell, unconscious," Randolph crowed, adding that a half inch of the knife's point had broken off in the man's backbone. While the stabbed man's fellow freedmen grabbed muskets and prepared to retaliate, Randolph's friends urged him to escape. He indignantly refused, "determined to settle the matter of race supremacy right there and then." Going back to get his double-barreled shotgun from his office, Randolph walked out alone to face two hundred freedmen. He raised his gun as if to fire, and they scattered—at least according to the exaggerated account that the self-satisfied Ryland Randolph gave.

The next issue of the *Monitor* contained all sorts of warnings. To the freedmen: insubordination will not be tolerated. To "every true white man": go about "thoroughly armed." Randolph was soon arrested by Federal authorities, tried in Selma, and to everyone's surprise found not guilty. He returned a hero. The ladies decorated his carriage with flowers, and a dinner was held in his honor. When Randolph continued his attacks in print, Federal authorities closed down his office for a time and posted an armed sentry to ensure that no copies of the *Monitor* were published. He emerged from all this as the

The university's newly completed barracks (later Woods Hall) stands behind the cedar-lined walk and the rubble from the burned Rotunda. The reopening of the university was the focus of some of the state's bitterest struggles following the Civil War. (Courtesy The University of Alabama Libraries Special Collections)

The Reverend Arad Lakin (right), newly elected president of the University of Alabama, and Noah B. Cloud (below right), Republican state superintendant of education, were rebuffed when they came to Tuscaloosa to assume control of the university. Four days later, they were depicted in a scurrilous political cartoon published in the Tuskaloosa *Independent Monitor* that threatened them with lynching by the Ku Klux Klan. (Above: Courtesy the North Alabama Conference of the United Methodist Church; Below: From *Harper's Weekly*, November 27, 1858)

leader of those determined to return the old order to power.

Randolph took credit, not surprisingly, for being the first leader of Tuscaloosa's Ku Klux Klan. Like the former Confederate soldiers they were, the Klansmen rode like cavalrymen and used military tactics, which Randolph would describe all too vividly. It seems hardly surprising, for they were still at war. This time, instead of Union soldiers in blue, their targets would be insolent freedmen, traitorous scalawags, and greedy carpetbaggers—as the Klansmen characterized Southern Republicans.

This noxious brew—Klansmen, the freed people, white Republicans, carpetbaggers, the opening of the university, suffrage, and resentment—boiled over one hot August day in that decisive year of 1868. Noah B. Cloud and Arad Lakin were in Tuscaloosa to assume control of the University of Alabama. Dr. Cloud was the state's newly elected Republican superintendent of education, and the Reverend Lakin was the Northern-born minister sent to Alabama after the war to reestablish the national Methodist Episcopal Church. (Methodism had split in the 1840s over the issue of slavery.) The university's elected board of regents, all Republicans, had just chosen Lakin to be the new president. As the two began walking east along Broad Street, they heard unearthly sounds—"men screaming, and groaning, and grunting"—from behind doors and windows. At the Dearing House, they veered slightly to the right as Broad Street became the Huntsville Road.

Dr. Cloud and the Reverend Lakin reached the university, opened the gate, and entered the campus. All that remained of the once cedar-lined approach and the former architectural masterpiece of the Rotunda was mounds of rubble. Before them stood the newly completed and still vacant barracks, later to be named Woods Hall. Its towers and crenellation, like a modern version of a medieval castle, seemed to defy the Yankees to invade again.

The superintendent and new president were met by William Stokes Wyman, professor of ancient languages. Lakin asked for the keys to the university. Professor Wyman calmly refused, for he would recognize neither man's authority—legal though it was.

Flummoxed by their failed attempt to assume leadership of the university, the two returned to their homes, Cloud to Montgomery by stagecoach and Lakin to Huntsville by buggy. Eight miles out of town, Lakin stopped for the night at a farmhouse. Sitting on the porch about nine that evening, he began to hear the sounds of horses. "Sit still," his host warned. Some two dozen armed and disguised Klansmen galloped past, a rope and noose clearly visible. Lakin awakened the next morning to learn that three armed black men had spent the night guarding him. He made his way home to Huntsville without incident.

Four days later, on September 1, a woodcut appeared on page two of Ryland Randolph's *Independent Monitor*. Entitled *A Prospective Scene in the "City of Oaks," 4th of March, 1869*, the cartoon predicted the fate of Lakin (the one with the carpetbag) and Cloud after the Democrats won the election in November and their presidential candidate entered the White House the following March. The very long caption explains that the two men were particularly despised as the "great pests of Southern society": Lakin because he was a carpetbagger and Cloud because he was a scalawag. The KKK on the side of the donkey identifies the Ku Klux Klan as the enforcement wing of the Democratic Party charged with carrying out the threatened lynching. The woodcut also includes a freedman. Although not depicted visually, the caption notes that the oak limb is long enough to hang any black man who supports the Republican candidate for president, Ulysses S. Grant. The editor and Klansman, Ryland Randolph, had in mind the barber Shandy Jones—the most prominent freedman in Tuscaloosa, a solid Republican, and a Grant supporter.

Republicans immediately grasped an opportunity and reprinted *A Prospective Scene* in newspapers from Bangor, Maine, to San Francisco, California, with the warning that this is what will happen if the Democrats win the election. A Cincinnati newspaper even sent out a special edition of five hundred thousand copies that was credited with swinging enough Ohio voters to send Grant to the White House. While this may be an exaggeration, there is no question that *A Prospective Scene* created an uproar across the country. It ultimately became the most famous political cartoon to emerge during the postwar years—all this from an image a mere three by four and a half inches found on the second page of a small-town newspaper.

Randolph's cartoon may have blown up in his face, but he and his fellow Klansmen did get one thing they were after: Lakin would never become president of the university. The regents soon selected another

A Prospective Scene in the "City of Oaks," 4th of March, 1869.

"Hang, curs, hang! * * * * * *Their* complexion is perfect gallows. Stand fast, good fate, to *their* hanging! * * * * * If they be not born to be hanged, our case is miserable."

A Prospective Scene became the most notorious political cartoon from the postwar era. (*Independent Monitor*, September 1, 1868)

Northerner who, after Randolph sent him a threatening issue of the *Monitor*, never even set foot in Tuscaloosa. The intimidation of subsequent presidential and faculty appointments continued. Things got to the point that the regents voted unanimously in August 1869 to remove the university from Tuscaloosa "at the earliest moment practicable." An assassination attempt on Randolph the following year left him with an amputated leg and in chronic pain for the rest of his life. He would sell the *Monitor* and move to Birmingham a few years later. When a mere ten students enrolled in

Shandy Jones (Courtesy Ophelia T. Pinkard)

SHANDY JONES *was the leading black Tuscaloosan of the mid-nineteenth century. Freed as a child, he gained considerable wealth by barbering and investing in real estate. Jones entered the ministry and became a leading voice for black migration to Liberia.*

Fears that free blacks incited slave rebellions led Tuscaloosa's aldermen to pass an ordinance requiring them to register with the mayor, post security of $100, and to stay at home after ten at night without a special pass from the mayor. Jones received his pass the next week:

The bearer, Shandy Jones, a free man of Color, has my permission to go at large after 10 o'clock at night. He has also permission to attend Divine Worship and Class Meetings where slaves assemble for the purpose, as also any of the female members of his family.

R. Blair
Mayor of Tuscaloosa
Aug 15, 1859.

Having to ask for, and then carry, such a pass could only have been demeaning.

Jones turned his attentions to helping his fellow freed people after the war by founding Tuscaloosa's first black church, now Hunter Chapel AME Zion Church, and a school there. He was also elected to the Alabama General Assembly. Jones had hoped to enroll his son, who had served in some capacity aboard Confederate ships or boats, in the University of Alabama—a century before Autherine Lucy, Vivian Malone, and James Hood. But such was not to be. Perhaps as a result of all his efforts, the Klan hounded Jones out of Tuscaloosa. He made his way to Mobile, where he became pastor of the Little Zion Methodist Church. He was buried in the city's vast Magnolia Cemetery in the plot reserved for the local chapter of the Independent Order of Good Samaritans and Daughters of Samaria, a black temperance group. On February 4, 2017—exactly 131 years to the day after his death in 1886—a memorial service was held and a marker placed on his grave. The inscription reads:

The Rev. Shandy W. Jones
1815–1886
Born a Slave, He Championed Freedom
in the Church and the AL Legislature

the spring of 1871, a bundle of threatening letters was left hanging from a dagger. In the end, the university stayed put in Tuscaloosa, of course. And under a Democratic board of regents and new faculty (the eighth since the war) more acceptable to Randolph and the former Confederates, students finally began returning to the university in the fall of 1871. But Dr. Cloud got even. As a member of the legislature, he was in a strong position to ensure that Alabama's new land-grant school (a designation that allowed federal funds to be used to support practical education primarily in agriculture and engineering) would be separate from the state university (chartered and funded by the state to train its future political, moral, and educational leaders)—a first in the South. The newly named Agricultural and Mechanical College of Alabama was in Auburn, just a few miles from Cloud's home.

The 1868 presidential election, which had led to *A Prospective Scene*, was of less immediate significance to Tuscaloosans than the state elections. In three short years, black Tuscaloosans had gone from being bound servants to negotiating contracts. They were learning to read and sending their children to schools. They were citizens and, for the first time, voting and running for office. Shandy Jones, the successful black barber whom Randolph singled out in his hateful political cartoon, successfully won election to the general assembly, where he would join twenty-six others as part of Alabama's first class of black legislators. It was their finest moment.

THE REPUBLICANS' SUCCESS in 1868 spurred the Democrats to redouble their efforts. They refined their plan to regain political power through violent intimidation of their opponents, campaigns exploiting racial divisions to woo uncertain whites, and legal maneuvers to manipulate or stop black voting.

Shandy Jones would serve proudly in the state House of Representatives but not his Republican running mate, a white man who had also won election but died before taking office. Filling the vacated position after a special election was none other than Ryland Randolph. This left Tuscaloosans in the peculiar position of having both a black Republican and a white Klansman representing them in Montgomery.

The Republican's death was not from natural causes. He had been assassinated by the Klan while crossing the Sipsey Swamp. Such assassinations were hardly unusual. A Selma schoolteacher who came down from the North wrote to the governor in 1870 that in the past two years more than thirteen hundred Republicans had been killed. Klan violence became so intense that Congress held hearings. The testimony of Arad Lakin was the longest of any Alabamian. After his unsuccessful attempt to assume leadership at the university, he continued his church work eluding the Klan; in 1876 he joined black Alabama Methodists in founding their own separate conference within the Methodist Episcopal Church. Shandy Jones did not testify, but he should have. After being hounded out of Tuscaloosa by the Klan, he ended his days working in the U.S. Customs House in Mobile and pastoring the Little Zion AME Zion Church there.

After a brief setback during the election of 1872, the Democrats held nothing back. On Election Day in 1874, members of the White League, an open and more visible successor to the secretive Klan, attacked black voters in Eufaula, killing seven,

Dr. Charles Allen Stillman purchased this building for the Tuscaloosa Theological Institute in 1881. It remained at this location until 1897, serving as a training site for Presbyterian ministers. (Courtesy of the William H. Sheppard Library, Stillman College)

THE PRESBYTERIANS MADE THE STRONGEST CONTRIBUTION *to black Tuscaloosans' religious and educational life. They had already established a Sabbath school for children during the 1840s, which they expanded shortly after the end of the war. The Reverend Charles Allen Stillman pressed the Southern Presbyterian Church to establish a facility for "the training of Negro ministers," and the general assembly responded in 1876 by establishing such a school in Tuscaloosa under Dr. Stillman's direction. The Tuscaloosa Theological Institute met in rented houses until erecting its first structure five years later. Stillman remained the institute's leader until his resignation in 1893, and two years afterward his name was given to the school. An academic department was begun in 1893; women started attending near the end of the century; and soon after that, the Cochrane House and twenty acres of land were purchased west of the city, which Stillman College made its permanent home.*

wounding seventy, and driving off at least a thousand. The League also attacked a polling place in Spring Hill, stealing the ballot box and killing the son of a Republican judge. Ballots cast by black voters were not counted in several Black Belt counties. The result was not in doubt. Democrats in the City of Oaks lit bonfires, played music, and delivered speeches. The Republicans were gone as a political force in Alabama. No black Alabamians would be elected to the general assembly after 1878, and the Democrats would not relinquish power for well over a century.

Tuscaloosans peered through their windows around midnight one Sunday a couple weeks after the 1874 election. They saw the "ghost-like appearance" of men riding white horses in single file. Some thought they were Klansmen. The horsemen were instead the last Federal occupying troops on their way out of Tuscaloosa. That cavalcade seemed a fitting end to what began with secession and ended in the "tragic era."

But the Democrats were not yet done.

Shandy Jones was not the only black man elected by Tuscaloosa voters. Jerry Barnes, a schoolteacher, represented his majority-black ward on the city's board of aldermen beginning in 1873. When Barnes won a second election in 1875, the system of six aldermen being elected from their own wards was abolished. In its place came an at-large system of voting whereby each alderman was elected by the votes of all the citizens, regardless of residency. With white voters making the majority, this simple change was explicitly intended to end the "possibility of other negroes being elected aldermen."

But eliminating voting by wards did not stop black voters from deciding close elections, which they famously did in Tuscaloosa's 1890 mayoral election. William Carlos Jemison had first taken the oath of office as mayor ten years earlier. He quickly "injected new life into a town that had languished since the war" by launching a series of ambitious projects. These started with graveling the main streets; continued with the introduction of the telephone, electricity, and a water works; and culminated in one of the largest engineering feats that Tuscaloosans had seen, fixing the Big Gully—an enormous and growing ravine that had bisected Broad Street since an unprecedented 1866 deluge. He would later turn his attention to another ravine and develop the area there into the upscale

By the mid-1870s, former Confederates were beginning to succeed in their goal of restoring everyday life to something resembling pre-war Alabama. The university, for example, brought back the Corps of Cadets. Here Colonel Thomas McCorvey and his staff stand before Woods Hall in 1874. (Courtesy The University of Alabama Libraries Special Collections)

WILLIAM HENRY SHEPPARD *graduated from the Tuscaloosa Theological Institute, was ordained in 1888, and then pastored a church in Atlanta, Georgia—all the while waiting to be sent as a missionary to Africa. The opportunity finally came in 1890 when he and University of Alabama graduate Samuel Norvell Lapsley, a white man, were sent to the Congo, then a Belgian colony. Nearly a year after first reaching the Congo River, having endured harrowing experiences and brutal illnesses, they reached their destination of Luebo. The two soon established a mission, but constant bouts of "African fever" took Lapsley's life in 1892. Now alone, Sheppard continued his church work and began reaching out to some of the most secretive of all African tribes while taking extensive notes and collecting their decorative art.*

He returned to America, in part to marry a woman he met at the Tuscaloosa Theological Institute. He also returned to begin a speaking tour where he would sell copies of this photograph to raise funds. He went back to his mission in 1896. In addition to his duties as a missionary, Sheppard also began documenting King Leopold II's exploitation of the Congolese. By playing warring tribes off against each other, Belgian officials had created a form of state terror based on slavery. Punishments included cutting off hands. Sheppard's exposé contributed significantly to the world's condemnation of Belgium.

Sheppard finally left Africa in 1910 exhausted. Along with his family, he brought a tremendous number of African ethnographic artifacts that collectively represent one of the world's most impressive collections. In 1959, Stillman College named its library in Sheppard's honor. Here he is pointing to a map of the Congo.

William Henry Sheppard, c. 1893, photograph by Arthur S. Proctor (Courtesy The University of Alabama Libraries Special Collections. Gift of Frances Osborn Robb in honor of Clark Center)

Pinehurst neighborhood. The costs of those dramatic improvements drew some opposition. Several citizens put forward as a counter candidate to Jemison a University of Alabama alumnus still in his twenties, Henry Bacon Foster. The "Young Guard," as the young men who supported Foster were known, corralled black men, cajoled and intimidated them for hours on voting day, and then marched them in squads of eight to the polls where they dropped their ballots in the box. (Every bit of this would be illegal today. Even the voting then was not by secret or official ballots, but instead by slips of paper printed in advance and distributed to the voters by a candidate's supporters.) The Jemison backers attempted to do the same but were less successful. Those black voters delivered the election to Foster.

The pivotal role that black voters played in the 1890 election would not be repeated. Foster declined to run in 1894, and Jemison returned to office. Then, in 1900, the city's Democratic executive committee adopted a primary system for whites only. This was entirely consistent with the Jim Crow South. Local governments were increasingly moving beyond custom to segregate the two races by law. Signs began to direct individuals to separate hotels and restaurants, waiting rooms and restrooms, parks and ballfields, and countless other public places. These policies were given scientific sanction by the then-popular theory of eugenics. And they were given legal sanction by the courts, especially the Supreme Court's notorious 1896 *Plessy v. Ferguson* decision upholding racially separate—if equal—railway cars. Rarely, however, were separate services and opportunities equal.

Yes, the secession of Alabama in January 1861 and the departure of the last Union cavalrymen after the 1874 election that returned the state securely into Democratic hands makes a convenient block of time. But the era that began with secession really extends through Alabama's 1901 constitutional convention. The delegates who assembled that May elected John B. Knox of Anniston to preside. He began his opening speech by declaring that they had gathered, like their forbears in January 1861, to deal with "this grave problem of the races." Their job was now "within the limits imposed by the Federal Constitution, to establish white supremacy in this State." The problem they had been delegated to solve had been created during Reconstruction when, "by force of Federal bayonets, the negro was placed in control of every branch of our government." But the time had finally arrived when white Alabamians could by legal means reject this cruel and unjust imposition: primarily by cumulative poll taxes (that is, they had to be paid from the first year of eligibility to vote) and by tests on whether a voter understood any clause in the American Constitution (to the satisfaction of the local registrar). And that is precisely what the delegates proceeded to do. Within two years, less than three thousand of the state's nearly two hundred thousand eligible black men were registered to vote. Such misdeeds—too tame a word—would be hard to unravel.

In the late 1800s, Alabama Democrats adopted as their symbol a rooster with the motto "White Supremacy for the Right." The 1901 Constitution, which virtually eliminated black voting with poll taxes and examinations of potential voters by local registrars, was an explicit repeal of policies introduced by Republicans during Reconstruction. (Courtesy Alabama Department of Archives and History)

Tuscaloosans recruit smokestack industries… doggedly

Opposite page: Central Foundry was in full operation by 1915 when this photograph was taken of its huge operation in Holt. The steamboat is pushing barges laden with coal from the Warrior Coal Field, probably to be used at the foundry. Then cast-iron pipe would be loaded and taken down the Black Warrior River for export from Mobile and New Orleans. This combination of industry and transportation was exactly what boosters sought. (Courtesy Alabama Department of Archives and History)

TUSCALOOSANS STOOD ALONG GREENSBORO STREET watching an army march through town at the end of January 1871. But this force of two thousand carried picks and shovels instead of rifles. Many were dressed in unfamiliar baggy blue outfits, spoke in a strange tongue (Chinese), and had long queues dangling from the backs of their heads. And unlike the Union soldiers still in town, these men were warmly welcomed; for they were building the long-sought 282-mile train track connecting Chattanooga to Meridian. The successful completion of the line, which ran through Tuscaloosa, represented the first step in breathing new life into the dying town. Tuscaloosans would become convinced that their salvation lay in a simple formula: open new transportation systems (railroads and a navigable Black Warrior) to allow access to the region's vast resources (coal, iron, cotton, and timber), which could then be exported as raw materials or after refining (by furnaces, factories, and mills), as finished goods for sale.

Tuscaloosans had been thrown back and forth several times already by decisions not even of their own making. Things had looked bright after their frontier village was chosen for the state's capital and university. Then their future came unglued when the government moved to Montgomery. A little over a dozen years after that, the state seceded, joined the

NUGENT

Confederacy, went to war, and lost. Even while the effects of those earlier decisions were working their way out, Tuscaloosans themselves made another decision: to enter the industrial age.

Town boosters predicted that with access to the nearby coal and iron ore, "half a hundred manufactories will *mushroom* up." The "skill and cunning" of our workers will turn Northport and Tuscaloosa into "the greatest manufacturing and commercial center, the metropolis, of Alabama." And the Black Warrior River, that "great highway, covered with steamers and barges," would deliver coal and finished products not just to the rest of the nation, but "to all parts of the world." So they set out to remake Tuscaloosa yet again.

The renowned British geologist Sir Charles Lyell visited Tuscaloosa in 1846 after word of the Warrior Coal Field started to spread. Four of his books were listed in the catalogue of the University of Alabama library in 1848. (Courtesy Library of Congress)

TUSCALOOSANS HAD BEEN TRYING to bring a railroad to town as early as 1835, only six years after the first steam locomotive rolled down American rails. Their goal then was to create an easier route between north and south Alabama that would run through Tuscaloosa. The Huntsville and Byler Roads were arduous and took days to traverse, while steamboats could only reach Tuscaloosa about half the year during the high-water winter months. The nationwide Panic of 1837 put an end to those plans for another decade. By that time the government had left, and any efforts to link north and south Alabama was more likely to go through Montgomery and not Tuscaloosa.

Improving travel was not the only reason why Tuscaloosans pressed for a railroad. In the early 1820s, while legislators were still meeting in Cahawba, reports started to circulate even up the East Coast that coal above the Falls of the Black Warrior was "superior to the Virginia coal, and fully equal to that generally imported from Liverpool." When the legislators first met in Tuscaloosa, they discovered that the fireplaces were heated with coal, not wood. With each passing year, the possibilities and promises of a major coal field spread. Word of the Warrior Coal Field even reached England, prompting the great geologist Sir Charles Lyell to travel to Tuscaloosa to see for himself. He was surprised when he reached the City of Oaks in February 1846 to see coal at the bottom of the Black Warrior's clear waters. Later that same month, a Tuscaloosa newspaper editor confidently predicted that "the day is not remote when Tuscaloosa shall become the Pittsburgh of this section of the Union." That same prediction would be repeated well into the next century.

The excitement continued when at the end of that same year, 1846, the university's trustees created a chair of geology, mineralogy, and agricultural chemistry with the express stipulation that the first recipient make a geological survey of the state. Michael Tuomey accepted the position in the spring of 1847 and by that August had already prepared his initial findings, which focused on the nearby mineral resources. "In our coal we have a source of inexhaustless wealth, if we will but use it," an unrestrained Tuscaloosa newspaper editor exclaimed after reading Tuomey's published report; "a vast demand will arise from every point accessible to our boats. Then too will our iron come into use, and all the region about us will be alive with the sound of active labor." The change in Tuscaloosa, he predicted, "would—may we say will?—seem to us miraculous." Tuomey's continuing efforts resulted in his appointment as state geologist. His first biennial report, published in 1850, devoted many pages to describing the Warrior Coal Field and projecting its economic possibilities. Perceptive Alabamians saw the chance to balance the cotton on which the state's economy increasingly depended.

The excited newspaper editor had made a key qualification in his effusive statement: The change will be miraculous when the beds are opened, "*and the means of transport provided.*" Tuomey had pressed the necessity of improving access in his 1850 report, noting that although the Black Warrior ran through the center of the coal field, the miles of shoals above Tuscaloosa meant that only rafts and flatboats could move the coal and only when the water was high enough. He urged the construction of dams that would convert

In 1847 Michael Tuomey accepted a position on the faculty of the University of Alabama and in 1848 he was appointed Alabama's first state geologist. He was a strong proponent of better transportation to exploit the Warrior Coal Field beneath Tuscaloosa. (Courtesy The University of Alabama Libraries Special Collections)

the river into a canal. "If we had cheap methods of transportation through the State," repeated Tuomey in 1853, "the immense resources of coal, iron, and marble would be worth millions."

A railroad was needed even more than a canal, and Tuomey knew the route, which he had discovered while conducting the geological survey: a continuous valley extending from near the Tennessee River to the outskirts of Tuscaloosa. A railroad beginning in Chattanooga and coming through this valley would "pass through the very centre of the mineral region of the state" before reaching Tuscaloosa and ending in New Orleans. The implications were obvious.

The groundbreaking ceremony of the North East & South West Railroad was a great event. Businesses closed that December 7 in 1854 as a procession of railroad officials, university students and faculty, Masons and Odd Fellows in full regalia, followed by "an immense crowd of citi-

Among Tuscaloosa's first smokestack industries was a paper mill located between downtown and the river. Union prisoners were housed there during the early part of the war. (Courtesy The University of Alabama Libraries Special Collections)

zens and strangers" marched to the site of the proposed railroad line on the southern edge of town. The company's president, full of excitement and passionate optimism, predicted that the road would inevitably become "the great artery of the vast interior travel and commerce" between New York and New Orleans. The long "*winter* of our discontent," predicted the *Independent Monitor*'s editor, is "about to give place to a glorious and perennial summer." But the launch of the North East & South West was premature. The company was simply unable to raise sufficient funds. Tuscaloosa would remain at the end of a long steamboat journey, which ran but half the year, and at the end of a long stagecoach ride, which ran but once a week. "No wonder she grew up a quiet, sedate, and not overly enterprising place," judged one visitor to the City of Oaks, "for she was a little world all to herself."

A too-often shallow river and unbuilt railroad were certainly holding back Tuscaloosans from developing their resources. But that was not the end of it. Those problems were also holding back the University of Alabama. Enrollment was dropping precipitously during the 1850s. While some blamed a lack of discipline, newspaper editors across the state pointed directly to the real problem: "It is the location of the College. Tuscaloosa is not the place for it. It is too inaccessible." They noted that the academic year did not begin until mid-October, when the rains raised the river enough for steamboat travel to resume. And without a railroad, students from north Alabama had to spend days in a stagecoach or on horseback to get there.

Move "the University to some point on a railroad, or on some river navigable all the year, and its numbers will increase at once." But if Tuscaloosa were ever to get a railroad, they admitted, "the same desirable result will be attained."

Tuscaloosa's isolation also handicapped its industries by making sales and distribution difficult. An impressive paper mill with a towering smokestack took three years to build at the foot of River Hill. It was finally producing paper in 1849, and on March 8 of that year the *Independent Monitor* printed its Thursday morning edition with Tuscaloosa-made paper. Other enterprises arose to serve the needs of the cotton growers. The Warrior Manufacturing Company boasted the "largest building for manufactures in the South" when the mill opened in 1847, a few months before Montgomery became the capital. Its 150-foot-long, four-story building had looms that could hold ten thousand spindles. The opening prompted an excited newspaper editor to use the refrain that would be heard over and over again: "a new era will open to our city. Other branches of manufacturing will follow of necessity." These included furnaces to supply the machinery, which in turn "will lead to an exploration of the iron beds in our vicinity. Their richness will tempt capital. Establishments will spring up for castings and wrought iron. The coal fields will be worked, and a rail road the necessary consequence." All this could mean only one thing: "Success is certain."

It hardly worked out that way. Despite being one of only two papermaking facilities in Alabama, the Tuscaloosa mill had ceased production by the eve of the Civil War, almost surely from its inability to distribute its products. The cotton factory was sold in the early 1850s, renamed the Tuscaloosa and North Port Manufacturing Company, and by the end of the decade was sold yet again. Its closing in 1860 was what led the Ladies' Benevolent Society to sponsor the lectures for the relief of those out of work.

The Leach & Avery enterprise began its foundry and machine shop in 1848 and was soliciting orders for plows and "plantation work generally" by 1852. Like all of Tuscaloosa's first industries, Leach & Avery was at the mercy of an unreliable transportation system: rafts to float coal down the Black Warrior, wagons to haul iron from the small furnaces in the mineral district, and the occasional steamboats to ship its award-winning plows to Black Belt planters. This was hardly a recipe for success.

These industries catered to local and agricultural interests. They had little choice. And whatever hopes Tuscaloosans may have had of creating an industrial or manufacturing economy were dealt a further blow by the war. The North East & South West Railroad had completed a mere 10 percent of its line between Chattanooga and Meridian when construction ceased in 1862. Then in the spring of 1865, Croxton's raiders destroyed what little progress Tuscaloosa's industries had made. Charles Foster's tannery, in business since the 1820s, produced shoes for the Confederacy; it went up in flames, but he was able to get back in business after the war. The Tuscaloosa and North Port Manufacturing Company, which had reopened to make sheets and coarse materials for the Confederacy, went up in flames as well; it would start up east of town in 1868. And after the invasion, Leach & Avery had rebuilt their foundry yet again.

The arrival of the Alabama & Chattanooga Railroad in 1871 was an extraordinary event for Tuscaloosans. At last the town was served by a dependable and regular means of transportation. Although the tracks ran a mile south of town, that hardly kept local merchant Thomas Maxwell from boasting that the train practically ran by the front door of his Bee Hive Store on Broad Street. (*Independent Monitor*, June 21, 1871)

The combination of Tuscaloosa's continued isolation, the loss of the state government in 1847, and the Yankee invasion of 1865 left quite an impression on visitors. The same Chattanooga correspondent who in 1871 had lamented Tuscaloosa's "mouldering ruins, the mournful vestiges of her former grandeur," nonetheless went out of his way to predict a bright future for the City of Oaks. Its location above the world's finest cotton belt and at the door of a mineral district "teeming with coal and iron of the finest quality . . . will compel her to become the seat of manufacturing enterprise . . . unsurpassed by any other place on the Continent." Nothing like optimism.

TUSCALOOSANS HAD THUS BEEN WAITING a long time to see that army of railroad workers finally march down their streets that winter of 1871. The first train to roll in could only be weeks away now. And on March 6, that first train finally arrived. Tuscaloosans grasped for words. "To day the '*Iron Horse*' snorting like Behemoth, and whistling with a tremendous scream," began Tuscaloosa businessman Thomas Maxwell, "entered our station for the first time, and for miles around the '*city of oaks*' sent a thrill of joy through every heart." That "tremendous scream" may have frightened squirrels deep into the woods, but "it was a joyful sound to those who had remained here, and labored and hoped for years for its advent." It was what they heard, more even than what they saw, that was so memorable. "Waiting so many long years for the railroad," wrote a schoolgirl, "we could hear the shriek of the engines, and rumbling of the trains, as they came rapidly on. . . . Soon the locomotive came in sight, puffing and blowing, like some great war-horse, exhausted by his work . . . but the multitude—as if awed by the imposing sight—were hushed and silent."

The celebrations erupted again when the officials drove the solid silver(!) last spike of the Alabama & Chattanooga Railroad—formerly the North East & South West—two months later on May 15. And once again, the noise was striking: the roar of a mighty cannon, speeches, and "the deafening shouts . . . of delighted sight-seers, composed of men from the four continents of the globe—Europe, Asia, Africa, and America"—who had labored for so long. Someone in the crowd hoisted a placard in the shape of a shield that read in letters of gold: *A & C R. Road completed. We done it.* Another predicted that years later he would "walk again the streets of a *metropolis*" and announce proudly to the citizens, "*I helped build the first railroad to Tuskaloosa!*"

Tuscaloosa, however, was not to be that metropolis. Alabama's metropolis would instead be located some fifty miles to the northeast. The same A&C Railroad that ran through Tuscaloosa on its way between Chattanooga and Meridian also ran straight through Jones Valley, where iron ore, coal, and limestone—the necessary components for making iron—lay close at hand. Near the quiet village of Elyton, the A&C would cross another railroad running between Nashville and Montgomery. Only two days after that line's silver spike was hammered home, lots were being advertised in the Tuscaloosa newspaper for a city that already bore the name of Birmingham. The speed with which furnaces and foundries sprouted up in former fields and forests suggested its nickname, the Magic City.

The furnaces and foundries, new homes and businesses, crowds and jobs that came to Birmingham seemed always to pass by the City of Oaks, despite all the hopeful predictions. Tuscaloosa's population did jump from 1,800 in 1871, when the railroad arrived, to 2,400 in 1880—but that was still considerably less than the nearly 4,000 souls living in Tuscaloosa on the eve of the Civil War. With too little to show for five years of access to the railroad, in 1876 the Tuskaloosa Board of Industries published a nineteen-page pamphlet entitled *Reliable Information . . . for Capitalists, Manufacturers, Miners, Agriculturists* (and anyone else who would invest). The "barriers which have heretofore prevented this era of progress have been broken down," the Board of Industries announced proudly. "We present to the world a magnificent field for industrial enterprise, and cordially invite the participation of all enterprising men." The board then listed Tuscaloosa's assets, emphasizing the university and other institutions. But when it came to listing the town's commercial establishments, only the reopened cotton factory stood out.

If bringing the railroad had failed to launch Tuscaloosa's industrial and manufacturing economy, then certainly improving the Black Warrior would. By removing snags downriver and building locks and dams upriver, barges could steam directly into the mineral district and take the coal and iron to markets at far cheaper rates than by rail. Tuscaloosa's prospects would then soar at the expense of the Magic City,

Tuscaloosa's first bridge, burned by Croxton's raiders, was rebuilt by master bridgebuilder Horace King in 1872. Born a slave, King was purchased by John Godwin, from whom he learned bridgebuilding. They moved to Alabama in the early 1830s to build bridges for towns on the rivers. He was freed in 1846 with help from Robert Jemison Jr., with whom he shared business ventures. (Courtesy Collection of the Columbus Museum, Columbus, Georgia)

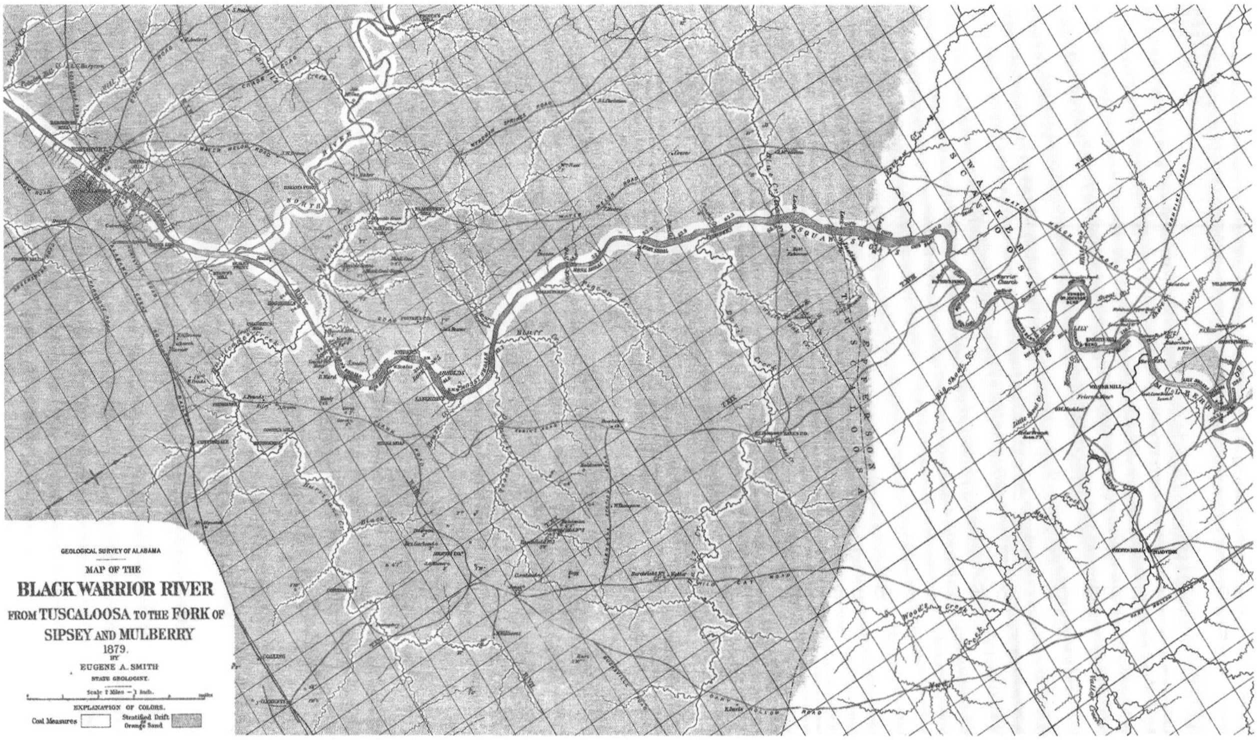

Eugene Allen Smith's 1879 map of the Black Warrior River identified the shoals that impeded navigation above Tuscaloosa. The locks and dams would be built where he marked. (Courtesy Cartographic Research Laboratory, University of Alabama)

which had no river access. So the board was careful to reprint in *Reliable Information* its appeal for a $151,000 appropriation to remove obstructions between Tuscaloosa and Demopolis. The board did not petition Congress to submerge the falls because a private firm, the Black Warrior Slack-Water Navigation Company, had shortly before sent out contracts to build a canal and to harness some of the water as power for industry. But the Slack-Water Navigation project failed. Private enterprise simply lacked the resources to build locks and canals.

Submerging the Black Warrior's shoals enough for steamboats to travel upriver could only be accomplished by the federal government, as some Tuscaloosa citizens had been insisting for years. And it just so happened that the U.S. Navy, with its fleets of coal-fed ships, was looking for an alternative to the coal that it was getting from Pennsylvania and West Virginia, which was annually held up by frozen rivers. With that in mind, the Army Corps of Engineers commissioned State Geologist Eugene Allen Smith to survey the shoals upriver from Tuscaloosa. He completed his survey and map in 1879, but it would take another six years to draft and receive approval for a plan consisting of five locks to create an eight-foot deep channel where the river could often be "easily crossed without wetting one's feet."

Construction on Lock No. 1, just upriver from the bridge rebuilt by Horace King in 1872, began in May 1887 with an immense cofferdam to hold back the water during construction. The crew removed rock from the riverbed before opening a quarry along the south bank. A steam locomotive on a narrow-gauge track was used to move the immense quarry stones to the locks. The final lock would be 322 feet long and 52 feet wide.

Construction then started on Lock No. 2, a quarter mile upriver, and on No. 3, another mile beyond it. With the work proceeding at a glacial pace, the editor of the *Times* decided that Tuscaloosans needed to remember just why the locks were needed. New mines and the opening of the river to barge traffic will bring "many and diversified industries, and will be the beginning of that era all have prayed for so long and so fervently." He gleefully passed along one visitor's conviction that Tuscaloosa was "standing on the threshold of a great business awakening." As the editor put it, "we are in sight of the promised land." Surely he was using binoculars. The gates were not even hung on Lock No. 1 until the summer of 1894. Not until early the next year would the first lock even be tested. Construction finally ended in 1896, nine years after it began.

"AT LAST!" blared the headlines. "After years of waiting, After years of wishing, After years of hoping, . . . Tuscaloosa stands on the verge of an era of industrial and material progress as full of hope and promise as her most ardent and optimistic friend could wish." This time the occasion was the first loaded coal barge to make its way through the Tuscaloosa locks on its way to Mobile. The *Baltimore* had already made quite an impression when it passed upriver through the three completed locks on January 12, especially when the skipper had courteously given rides that Sunday morning to a large party of admiring citizens dressed in their best church-going suits and dresses. A couple of weeks later, on January 27,

Cutting the channel through the shoals for Lock No. 1, looking north from the Tuscaloosa side of the river (U.S. Army Corps of Engineers)

Installing the gates to Lock No. 1, looking downriver (U.S. Army Corps of Engineers)

the *Baltimore* returned with its barge loaded full of coal from the Tidewater Coal Company's mines. Tuscaloosans ushered in the day by ringing bells and blowing whistles. Nearly every business floated streamers, hung out brightly hued bunting, and closed that Monday. Citizens formed a parade near the Baptist church. Tuscaloosa's brass band led the way, perhaps setting the pace with a stirring early Sousa march or two. They were followed by the Warrior Guards and the Alabama Corps of Cadets, carriages carrying the mayors and aldermen of Tuscaloosa and Northport, students (schools had been closed for the day), and finally whoever else wanted to join in. Arriving at Lock No. 1 where the *Baltimore* was anchored, the speeches began to what looked like thousands of people. The "Ladies of Tuskaloosa" presented a "magnificent silken banner" to the *Baltimore*'s captain. With volleys of booming cannon shattering the air, yet another "most important occasion this city and section have ever witnessed" ended.

After the railroad reached Alabama, it took five years to publish *Reliable Information . . . for Capitalists, Manufacturers, Miners, Agriculturists*. This time it took only a few months after the locks opened for the *Times* to print a Special Souvenir and Industrial Edition. The premise was the same in both cases: Tuscaloosa's new transportation links enhanced its indus-

Tuscaloosans again celebrated when the *Baltimore* took the first load of coal through the locks. The vast Warrior Coal Field could finally be reached by water. (U.S. Army Corps of Engineers)

trial, manufacturing, and commercial advantages. By 1896, the Special Souvenir and Industrial Edition listed a whopping sixty-two advantages created by the railroads and locks in its "Tuscaloosa Has" section. The list began with the town's proximity to huge coal and timber reserves; continued to include the University of Alabama, four dentists, a Chinese laundry; and ended with "a hearty welcome for all." Three years later, in 1899, the *Times* would publish an Anniversary and Trade Edition, yet again trying to attract industries and covering much of the same ground in even greater detail. By that time another railroad, this one coming between Montgomery and Columbus, Mississippi, had reached Tuscaloosa and been dedicated with the usual silver spike, speeches, and celebrations. The "Tuscaloosa Has" section in the 1899 Anniversary and Trade Edition added seven more advantages to those listed in the 1896 Industrial Edition, including a string orchestra, six secret societies, and, most importantly, "Pretty women."

Such publications must have been needed to attract industry and commerce, for the transportation systems that Tuscaloosans had so long sought were not bringing the expected bonanza of benefits. The price of coal in Tuscaloosa had immediately dropped in half after the barges reached the upriver coal mines, and yet Tuscaloosans had little else to

The construction of Lock No. 17 dwarfed anything else on the Black Warrior. (Courtesy Alabama Department of Archives and History)

show for all their efforts. So they looked again at their transportation system. The three locks, they concluded, were simply inadequate. To solve the lingering problem of navigating the Black Warrior when it was obstructed by debris, nine additional locks were constructed downriver between 1902 and 1908. The three original locks at Tuscaloosa were then renumbered—10, 11, and 12—and four more locks were added over the shoals upriver. That opened the Black Warrior only another two dozen

miles to Squaw Shoals, where a new lock and dam would allow steamboats to travel an additional fifty-odd miles. But building there would require a formidable structure rising 103 feet and spanning 1,200 feet; the lock would need to lift boats 63 feet (and the highest in the South at that time lifted but 40).

U.S. Senator John Hollis Bankhead, patriarch of the Bankhead political dynasty, spoke at the opening ceremony for Lock No. 17, recounting the long struggle to complete the project. Bankhead Lake and the Bankhead Lock and Dam on the Black Warrior River are named for him. (Courtesy Library of Congress)

Five hundred men worked continuously for four years to complete Lock No. 17 and its dam. Unlike the previous projects, however, this time they used enormous power equipment. The Hardaway Company, which constructed the dam, built a seventeen-mile railroad. On it workmen brought in a 2,000-horsepower steam plant, twenty locomotives, and twenty steel derricks each of twenty-ton capacity. The railroad was also used to transport a rock crusher capable of destroying a forty-two-inch stone (only two others in the world matched it). And then they started to work.

The official opening of the lock and dam at Squaw Shoals finally arrived on May 13, 1915—a year after the completion of the Panama Canal and a week after the sinking of the *Lusitania* by a German U-boat. The walls of the locks and the hillsides were thronged with people, and the university's band furnished the music. Tuscaloosa probate judge and future governor "Plain Bill" Brandon began the ceremony

Lock No. 17 destroyed the extensive Squaw Shoals, the Cahaba Lily's last home on the Black Warrior. (Courtesy The University of Alabama Libraries Special Collections)

by declaring that "John Hollis Bankhead has erected on this dam a monument that will last until time shall cease." (Until time shall cease?) Senator Bankhead responded by modestly recounting how he struggled for twenty-five years to get the lock and dam built. He noted that this waterway, now stretching from the heart of the Alabama coal and iron district to the Gulf of Mexico, opened unimaginable possibilities. After Governor Charles Henderson had his say, the handsome Madeliene Blair broke a bottle of water drawn from a well at Senator Bankhead's old home against the lock wall. Blair then declared Lock No. 17 open for river traffic.

The celebrations at Squaw Shoals echoed those that had accompanied the arrival of the A&C Railroad train in 1871 and the passage of the *Baltimore* through the Tuscaloosa locks in 1896. But no one seemed to notice. The waterway at last gives an "Outlet to Sea for Alabama Coal and Iron," the headlines loudly proclaimed. In just a short time, the paper continued using the same tired phrases: the banks of the Black Warrior will be lined with coal mines, iron furnaces, and industrial plants. Everyone knew that the costs of opening the waterway—an estimated $11 million—were worth every penny.

Well, not quite everyone. Roland M. Harper, the Alabama Geological Survey botanist, had visited Squaw Shoals two years before. The shoals, which Harper described in his article published in a national journal, were about three miles long and a thousand feet wide. Steep hills rising two or three hundred feet above the river began at the water's edge. Those hills were covered with a forest of virgin longleaf pine. In the shallow water of the shoals grew extensive stands of a spectacularly beautiful white spider lily, known locally today as the Cahaba Lily. The effect was breathtaking. "It is one of the ironies of fate," wrote Harper, "that the shoals, rapids and falls, which are in many ways the most interesting spots on our rivers, are the very places that are doomed to obliteration." He ended his short article by lamenting that "the effacement of any one of them is an irreparable loss," and "it is impossible to measure such a loss in money."

SURELY ALL THE WORKERS in the projected new mines and smokestack industries along the new rail and waterway systems would live in factory towns. And, in fact, a few did spring up.

The first was Kennedale. Its origins were in the mill burned by Croxton's raiders, then purchased by Baugh, Kennedy and Company. With machinery imported from England, it reopened in 1868 seven miles east of town along the future route of the A&C Railroad. Even two miles from the factory, a visitor reported that "a steam whistle, or gong, was heard, which fairly shook the earth." The plan, he soon learned, was to increase "this unearthly sound" until it could be heard from twenty miles. Once there, the visitor recognized what looked very much like an English factory: a single story with a great 150-foot smokestack piercing the air, the whole presenting "a most beautiful appearance." The windows were arranged so that the workrooms were kept light and breezy. The mill went into operation April 14, a year after the first brick had been laid, with 5,000 spindles and 120 looms—twice what had been destroyed—operated by a 100-horsepower Woodruff and Beecher steam engine.

Kennedale was named after the principle owner. The streets were named for other company members: Baugh, Seed, Leftwich, and Hays. The company would build a boarding house for girls and young women, who always made up a large portion of workers in the cotton mills throughout the country. Rows of white cottages and a large company store completed the village of Cottondale, as it would be renamed in the 1890s. The mill was never a great financial success. Three hundred workers were let go when it closed in 1876. The mill was then acquired by a consortium of

The cotton mill at Kennedale, now Cottondale, was the successor to the cotton mill in Tuscaloosa burned by Croxton's cavalrymen. The brick mill building and surrounding village reminded many of an English factory town. (From *The City of Tuskaloosa, Its Many Advantages*... [Cincinnati: Keating, 1887])

prominent Tuscaloosans and then resold several more times. Cotton production increased to where boosters were calling Tuscaloosa "the world's greatest inland center for cotton concentration." But the price for cotton kept declining. The mill would burn several times before finally closing in the 1940s.

As part of its campaign to attract investors, the Tuskaloosa Coal, Iron & Land Company published a perspective map, not only showing the City of Oaks in 1887 but the company's grandiose plans to create an industrial and manufacturing center. Vignettes in the corners of the map feature (clockwise from top left: Hill's Female College; Alabama Central Female College, occupying the old state capitol building with a dormitory wing added to the rear; Alabama State Hospital for the Insane; the University of Alabama, misidentified as Alabama State University; and the north side of Broad Street. Copies of the map were distributed like streamers at a Tide football game. (*Perspective Map of Tuskaloosa, Ala.* [Milwaukee: Henry Wellge & Co., 1887])

Two company towns—developments might be a better word—were announced in 1887, the same year that Congress approved the project to construct five locks.

In January, some twenty-five leading Tuscaloosans pooled their holdings, amounting to forty-six hundred acres, into the Tuskaloosa Coal, Iron & Land Company. Each investor was then issued stock corresponding to the acreage he had assigned to the company. With great hoopla, TCI&L published maps of the city showing its planned industries and suburban development, along with another promotional publication entitled *The City of Tuskaloosa, Its Many Advantages* . . . (the title seemed to go on forever). The booklet included a history of the city accompanied by the usual list of enticements for investors: such natural resources as materials for manufacturing iron and coke, cotton goods, brick, farm tools, and furniture; a strong agricultural base; and a prime location for commerce generally. In order to "stimulate the development of all these advantages," TCI&L included its prospectus, assets, and elaborate plans "to use every means at its command to build up a great manufacturing city." Those elaborate plans—dreams really—started with a new railroad from Tuscaloosa into the company's coal and timber lands. Those raw materials would then supply "furnaces, mills, foundries, presses, compresses, wharves, elevators, factories, workshops, and machine shops in said city of Tuskaloosa and vicinity." TCI&L would ship the products aboard its own steamboats down the improved Black Warrior River. The company expected to build houses on its subdivided property around the original Tuscaloosa townsite for the expected "large manufacturing population" employed at its one-hundred-ton coke furnace to be erected nearby. Such a plant, when complete with 125 ovens, a rolling mill, foundry, and machine shop, was easily and immediately destined to "enhance the price of every piece of real estate, in and about the City, at least 50%."

The Tuscaloosa and Castle Hill Real Estate and Manufacturing Company also filed its incorporation in 1887, in fact the month after TCI&L. Rather than pooled assets, this development project was the creation of a single family headed by James H. Fitts. Castle Hill's plans were a bit more modest: organize a yarn mill, extract coal from the Pratt seam directly east of the city, and in other ways exploit the family's disconnected 815 acres of land. The workers, like TCI&L proposed, would live on lots developed by Castle Hill, in this case east of the insane hospital.

The editor of the *Times* insisted that the two firms' plans did not overlap but rather "can only assist in the development of the other." It hardly mattered. Neither company could either build or attract any industries. Both did manage, however, to create Tuscaloosa's first public transportation system and suburbs. TCI&L, with its huge landholdings, had by far the greater impact on Tuscaloosa's growth. The days those lots went on sale were supposed to be "the liveliest and most exciting Tuscaloosa has seen since Croxton's raiders surprised the city." But none of the folks who built homes there would be working at any furnace or mine built by either TCI&L or Castle Hill.

Standard Coal built a true company town a few years later eighteen miles to the east. Brookwood "is blazing the way for developments in Tuscaloosa" beamed the *Times* editor. By the summer of 1891 the company had already constructed a

Tuscaloosans would celebrate every step toward creating an industrial economy, from the coming of the first train in 1871 through the completion of the lock and dam system in 1915. In this case, the Central Iron and Coal Company lights its furnace in Holt for the first time in August 1903. (Courtesy The University of Alabama Libraries Special Collections)

As a community unto itself, Holt had its own churches, library, schools, commissary, and baseball teams, such as the 1929 white Central Foundry team shown here. In segregated Alabama, black workers had their own team, which played several of the great Negro League teams upon occasion. Willie Mays was said to have played in Holt when he was a centerfielder for the Birmingham Black Barons. (Courtesy Judi Williams)

church, library rooms with 600 volumes on the shelves, and 150 "neat dwelling houses" along both sides of the streets. The workers were mining about six hundred tons of coal daily from its twenty-eight thousand acres. Standard Coal's combination of industry and company town presented the Tuscaloosa promoters with exactly what they had been seeking. But because it was a fair distance away, Brookwood would have a negligible effect on the City of Oaks.

Holt was a different matter. That company town's origins went back to 1900, when Frank Holt came to Tuscaloosa looking to buy land. Although he told no one, the twelve hundred acres he purchased, including two miles along the Black Warrior just upriver from the original three locks, were for the Central Iron and Coal Company. They planned to build an industrial complex to manufacture cast-iron pipes and fittings for the many municipalities then putting in their first water and sewer systems. Central Iron and Coal went on to acquire extensive property with coal, iron, and limestone deposits—the materials for making steel—between Tuscaloosa and Birmingham. Their Kellerman Coal Mines, named after the company's first engineer, would be isolated until the Mobile & Ohio Railroad agreed to build a branch line to deliver the coal to Holt.

Tuscaloosans and prominent officials once again gathered for a ceremony, this one marking the lighting of the furnace on August 3, 1903. The blast furnace began by pouring 150 tons of iron a day, but that had increased to 350 tons by 1912. Construction on the first of three foundries began in 1911. Other subsidiary plants would follow. The electricity to run it all came from a powerhouse that diverted the river water for its turbines and steam

The vigorous work of these men belies the Central Foundry's economic instability. The market for its cast-iron pipes and fittings, used in municipal water and sewer systems, was highly competitive and subject to ups and downs. Central Foundry would close during the Great Depression and reopen to supply needed products during the Second World War. Here, workers break cast-iron pipes out of their molds. (Courtesy Judi Williams)

boilers. Their finished products, the pipes and fittings, were shipped out by barge or loaded on rail cars. Central Foundry, as it was familiarly known, was always sensitive to the slightest changes in the market. When the Depression of 1920–21 slowed demand for pipe, the furnace and first foundry were shut down for months. The blast furnace would close again in 1929, on the eve of the Great Depression, and the coke ovens in 1931. Both remained idle until 1938.

Folks in Holt lived a world apart from folks in the City of Oaks. The roar from the blast furnace was "like walking up to a hurricane," according to one worker for another firm. Then came the hammering, the pounding, and all the sounds associated with turning iron ore into cast-iron pipes. It was loud, dangerous, and dirty. Smoke and grit poured out its soaring twin smokestacks. But once the shift was over, everyday life returned to familiar patterns. Even before the furnace was first fired, the company had laid out streets and begun to build houses for a workforce of fifteen hundred. The company would later add two hotels and churches, doctors' offices, a commissary (which traded in its own metal currency), drugstore, service station, and school. Central Foundry even sponsored baseball teams. Holt came to be what TCI&L and Castle Hill had promised but could never realize—a company town allied with Tuscaloosa.

Tuscaloosa's industries, such as they were, had at hand a third transportation option beginning in the 1920s that would

Above: Cleaning sand off the pipes after the casting. **Left:** Stacking the finished pipe before it was shipped out. (Both courtesy Judi Williams)

supplement the railroads and river. The new highway system allowed finished products to be delivered to specific destinations on each company's own schedule, not the trains' or steamboats'—a fact quickly learned, especially after Mack delivery trucks became available about the same time.

Tuscaloosans were just starting to use these first highways when another smokestack industry came to town. In 1927, the city government was successful in recruiting the EZ Opener Bag Company, later known as Gulf States Paper Corporation, by selling it 125 acres along the river; the city then promptly excluded the land from its taxes by reducing the city limits. The chamber of commerce added an industrial fund of $115,000 as a further enticement. Papermaking had returned to Tuscaloosa. The Gulf States mill churned out kraft paper using pulp they made from the company's vast reserves of yellow pine and then folded the paper into bags using a machine that its founder had patented. The mill's enormous sky-high smokestack was still not tall enough to prevent the distinctive sulfurous smell of papermaking from spreading across the city.

Town boosters had churned out all sorts of publicity aimed at attracting investors and entrepreneurs to the banks of the Black Warrior. As one predicted, soon Tuscaloosa "will become a manufacturing city second to none in this State" given its inestimable advantages. The year was 1884, but it could have been 1874 or 1894 or even 1924. Such was not to be—at least in their lifetimes. The industrial city was fifty miles to the northeast. The population of Birmingham in 1920—five years after the completion of Lock No. 17 had opened the Black Warrior and assured

Tuscaloosa's success—was fifteen times that of Tuscaloosa and would remain so. The completion of the Black Warrior locks and dams did in fact open new markets, and large mining companies did begin operating in the Warrior Coal Field. But the heavily laden barges just kept traveling down the river, for they had no reason to dock. Tuscaloosans did not seem discouraged for all their efforts, but they could easily have been; for by the 1930s, town boosters could brag of only two major smokestack industries: Central Foundry and Gulf States Paper. But Central Foundry closed during the Great Depression, leaving many to hope that Gulf States Paper stayed open. It would take an entirely different combination of factors to make the sort of decisive changes that the boosters wanted. Industry would indeed prove to be part of Tuscaloosa's

Holt: the booster's dream realized (Courtesy Alabama Department of Archives and History)

story—a major and immensely successful part—but that lay far in the future.

NO ONE COULD AVOID the black clouds pouring out of the Gulf States Paper smokestacks. And the smells could hardly be ignored either. Roland Harper bemoaned the destruction of the river's clear waters and spider lilies wrought by the locks and dams. That was not all. The smokestack industries introduced to Tuscaloosans the "tremendous scream" of the iron horse, the cotton mill's "unearthly sound," and the hurricane roar of the blast furnace.

At the same time that they were learning to live with new sounds, Tuscaloosans were learning to live without old and familiar ones. The Falls of the Black Warrior, cascading from the shelf that stretched across the river, had produced a constant and quiet roar long before the first Indians had ever heard it. That dull sound, which found its way to every corner of the City of Oaks, prompted some to poetry. One L. W. Reeves Jr. penned "The Waterfalls at Tuscaloosa." Two of its stanzas read:

They are rolling, ever rolling,
Their wild waters in a heap;
Ever splashing, roaring, clashing,
In their mad rush to the deep.

They are roaring, ever roaring,
No dike nor dam can hold them;
Ye men and gods behold them!
As they leap and surge and roar.

The dikes and dams did, in fact, hold them. Even as Mr. Reeves was writing in 1891, Lock No. 3 was under construction. Its completion forever silenced the Falls of the Black Warrior.

Tuscaloosans transform their everyday lives... by building a modern city

Opposite page: When the Alston Building was constructed in 1909, a seven-story building could still be considered a skyscraper. Featuring safety elevators and a roof-top garden, the building promoted the city with a "Try Tuscaloosa" sign on its roof. (Courtesy Robin McDonald)

BY 1869, ITS FIFTIETH YEAR, Tuscaloosa was considered an old town. Pigs meandered about the dirt streets of Alabama's once bustling state capital. Water came from wells, many of them located in the center of streets. The green canopy of oaks grew more majestic with each passing year, but fewer folk sought their shade during the hot summer months. Visitors to "Old Tus" found it without vitality, and Tuscaloosans agreed. "For nearly half a century this naturally beautiful place has been at a stand-still," complained one newspaper editor. Worse, noted another, the City of Oaks has "actually retrograded, in both wealth and population!"

Recognizing their plight, Tuscaloosans would set about to build a modern city out of their old town. Their decision came even as they clashed over the repercussions of secession, war, and the end of slavery; but unlike those divisive struggles, building a modern city had nearly everyone's support. Their decision was made even as they tried to attract smokestack industries; but unlike the great celebrations that accompanied the arrival of the first train or the first barge of coal, building a modern city was accomplished by a series of small and usually unheralded steps.

And this time Tuscaloosans would succeed. Once their old town had become a modern city, pigs would no longer compete for space on the streets. Their lovely but old-fashioned courthouse and town hall would

be replaced by a skyscraper and an exotic theatre. Innovative new sources of heat, light, power, communication, and clean water would change forever the idea of what a home should be. The horse would be abandoned as a series of new transportation devices—the trolley, the bicycle, and of course the automobile—took its place.

This represented more than simply modernizing a city. The collective result of these small changes was a revolution. We often think of revolutions as violent overthrows of governments. But this revolution was more comprehensive, upending the way people went about their ordinary affairs. Some revolutions can be stopped or reversed, but not this one. Revolutions frequently tend to be quick, but this revolution took a lifetime to complete; however, given its all-inclusive nature, that was a remarkably short time. From 1869 to 1939—threescore and ten years, the Psalmist's estimate of a man's lifespan—Tuscaloosans' lives were utterly transformed.

Henry Adams—that great historian and man of letters who lived through this same revolution—was said to have concluded that the simpler America of his youth had been closer to the year 1 than to the age of electricity, telephones, and automobiles of his maturity. Tuscaloosans would agree.

TIME SEEMED TO HAVE SLOWED. Tuscaloosans in 1869 conducted their legal business in a courthouse and city hall that seemed to belong in colonial Virginia. The great statehouse, then a girl's college, served as a monument to an age gone by. "Old fashioned houses" were plentiful, which was hardly surprising after the drop in population had left so many empty.

Tuscaloosa in 1869 looked just as it had twenty years before when Margaret Cammer Furman painted Cotton (now Sixth) Street looking west across Greensboro Street. From left to right: the Tuscaloosa County Courthouse, city hall, and Christ Episcopal Church. (Courtesy The University of Alabama Libraries Special Collections)

ROBERT JEMISON JR. *spared no expense to incorporate conveniences that we now take for granted when building his stunning Italianate mansion.*

He installed a modern bathroom inside the house, complete with a zinc-lined copper bathtub and a primitive flush toilet. Waste water from the toilet, tub, and kitchen drained through pipes to a brick-lined cesspool (somehow skirting town ordinances). Jemison called for a modern furnace that would heat the entire house, but the war intervened before it could be installed. The cooking range he wanted never arrived either. But at the back of his mansion, he kept his perishable food and milk in a large and very deep dry well that was said to stay forty degrees cooler in the summer. He planned to develop a small pine rosin gas-generating plant that would serve his immediate neighbors and himself, and then a larger one for the entire town. Although the war once again intervened, Jemison did succeed in lighting his own house with piped gas. And thus it was the brightly lit Jemison Mansion, in an otherwise dark town, that attracted Croxton's raiders to the wedding party that fateful April 1865 night.

The Jemison Mansion was designed by prominent Philadelphia architect Samuel Sloan, who also designed the Alabama Insane Hospital. Construction on what was then Tuscaloosa's most modern house began in 1859 and was completed in 1862. (From *The City of Tuskaloosa, Its Many Advantages…* [Cincinnati: Keating, 1887])

But whether old fashioned or not, whether a lowly cottage or an imposing mansion, all Tuscaloosa houses were basically the same: They were cold in the winter, for their stoves and fireplaces heated only one room at a time (and required about fifty pounds of coal a day). They were hot in the summer, at the mercy of handheld fans, large porches, and open windows. They were dark at night, lit either with candles (made and sold locally well into the 1880s) or with

Mrs. J. C. Perkins feeds her chickens in the backyard of her home. Nearly all Tuscaloosa families kept chickens for eggs and meat. Wealthier families had their own wells, seen here under the roof behind Mrs. Perkins. This photograph, and several others in this chapter and at the beginning of the book, are from the Perkins Family Collection, an exceptional visual chronicle of life in late nineteenth-century Tuscaloosa. (Courtesy The University of Alabama Libraries Special Collections)

oil lamps. They were sooty (because of the oil, fireplaces, and candles), full of insects (because they lacked screens), and dusty (because the streets were unpaved, the windows open, and vacuum cleaners not yet invented). True, most American houses were the same way. But streetlights, piped water, and trolleys—as well as a host of other developments that Americans were starting to take for granted—were not available in the Tuscaloosa of 1869.

Tuscaloosans lived in their homes as people had for centuries. They ate exceptionally plain fare, usually fresh. It had to be, because preservation was at best difficult. They had been able to import ice seasonally by steamboat from New England at least since the 1830s. Tuscaloosans were able to purchase locally made ice in 1869; but the machine introduced the previous year managed to produce a measly hundred pounds a day, and only hotels and the wealthy could afford its steep price of five cents a pound. Meat had to be prepared immediately upon butchering, unless preserved with salt or by dehydration. Tuscaloosans ate plenty of fish from the Black Warrior, and eggs and chickens from their henhouses. They grew their own fruits and vegetables in their backyard gardens.

Tuscaloosans' most difficult problem was certainly water, whether for drinking, cooking, bathing, washing, or refreshing "the thirsty ox or the travel-worn and mud-bespattered horse." Better homes each had their own wells, which were some sixty feet or more in depth. But without pipes, the water had to be hauled by hand—a grueling daily task. (As late as 1886, a typical housewife in North Carolina was calculated to lug in one year an extraordinary total of 36 tons of water as much as 148 miles.) That meant that clothes were only washed when necessary, and then by hand. Not only was no fresh water piped in, but spent water was not piped out. The wells were easily contaminated without sewers, so Tuscaloosa's elected officials outlawed cesspools. Waste matter was left to be dried out on the surface before the frequent heavy storms washed it away.

Tuscaloosans avidly read their newspapers sitting around the table or relaxing in a chair. But the newspapers were published only once a week; and the news they received in 1869 could be days or even weeks old, for the telegraph had yet to reach the City of Oaks. Although photographs were becoming common, none were yet printed in the newspaper. A few of the wealthier townspeople had managed to get pianos in their homes, but more often Tuscaloosans had to go to church or to bandstands in the park if they wanted to hear music. Motion pictures and recorded music, of course, were only the stuff of dreams.

Stepping out of their front doors, Tuscaloosans saw folks bustling about on their daily affairs. And they also saw a lot of horses—an estimated one horse for every five people. Horses, mules, buggies, and wagons accounted for nearly all the transportation in town besides walking. Horses also presented Tuscaloosans with untold heaps of manure and puddles of urine that mixed with the clouds of dust that blew up with every breeze. Cleaning the streets was neither a small, pleasant, nor healthful job. The smell of the flowering trees and shrubs could certainly be delightful in the spring, but the smell of horses was year-round.

Unlike the smells, the sounds that greeted Tuscaloosans when they stepped out their front doors were most agreeable, starting with singing birds and rustling oak branches and leaves. As they neared the center of town Tuscaloosans would hear "the busy hum of life on our streets" above the clopping horse hooves. That busy hum often included "a perfect jargon of voices," as boys called out the names of competing hacks, the latest theatrical production, or the best hotel. Things were quieter at night. Then the continuous muffled roar of the falls became almost loud. Its "not unmusical sound" steadied Tuscaloosans and drew them "very far back in the unchronicled centuries of the past, when these Falls first lifted their voice of waters upon the air."

In this photo titled "The butter won't come," Mrs. Perkins is pouring a liquid, possibly buttermilk, into the churner to help the milk solidify into butter. The purpose of the large homemade contraption next to her is unknown, possibly a water pump, or perhaps a machine to aid in the churning of the butter. (Courtesy The University of Alabama Libraries Special Collections)

"ALL NEEDED BY US NOW, to render ours a *real* city," pleaded Ryland Randolph in 1868, "are gas-works, railroads and telegraph wires." When not hounding carpetbaggers, scalawags, and freedmen, the volatile editor used many inches in his *Independent Monitor* columns to encourage Tuscaloosans to move their town forward. He was onto something. The City of Oaks lagged far behind when it came to providing the services found in any *real* city. Gas streetlights had first lit American city streets in 1817. Railroads had been crisscrossing the country since the 1830s. But no tracks had reached Tuscaloosa by 1869—the year that the transcontinental railroad was completed, and the total amount of track in the United States was approaching fifty thousand miles. And probably at least as many miles of telegraph lines had been strung.

This marks "the beginning of a new era for Tuskaloosa," crowed Randolph when the telegraph finally reached town in October 1869. "She has now taken the initiatory step towards casting off forever her small village-like swaddling-clothes, and will soon don the large habiliments of a full-grown city." The first messages received over the wire included market reports on the price of cotton and gold from New York. But such mundane matters would soon be making room for the more critical matches between the Tuscaloosa and Montgomery chess clubs—all conducted by Morse code.

The *Monitor*'s editor made similar comments after the first train reached Tuscaloosa in 1871. Having to rely on undependable steamboats and uncomfortable stagecoaches had left Tuscaloosa "to all intents and purposes . . . like a city in the desert." But the train's arrival "begins a new era."

Announcements of a pending gas works, the third of Randolph's require-

Oak trees down the middle of dusty streets and horse-drawn carts distinguished downtown Tuscaloosa as an old town. (From *The City of Tuskaloosa, Its Many Advantages*... [Cincinnati: Keating, 1887])

ments for a *real* city, were being floated in Tuscaloosa even before the train arrived. But nothing seems to have come of it until 1875, when the subject dominated conversations. An agent of the Needles Gas Company came to town promising to set up a plant, lay pipes, and have lights burning within six months—if enough citizens would subscribe. The light was said to be pure and soft, making it so attractive that an influx of strangers would increase the population 100 percent (the editor would soon up that prediction to 300 percent) and swell the value of real estate. The mayor and aldermen then organized the Tuscaloosa Gas-Light Company. Another year would pass, however, before construction started on the gas works near the river and workers were digging ditches and burying the tarred wooden pipes to supply the new streetlights. The not particularly successful project would be abandoned within fifteen years.

The telegraph and railroad were of significance in connecting Tuscaloosans with the "outer world," as Randolph termed it. But the gas pipes were equally important in an entirely different way. A dependable supply of gas was the first step in turning a home from a passive structure where people ate and slept into an active workshop for improving daily life. After gas lines, homes would be connected to networks of telephone, electrical, water, and sewer systems that served each household equally. Henceforth, no home—from modest to pretentious—could stand quite apart. No one could imagine what the laying of those gas pipes had started.

A gas works, railroad connection, and telegraph—Randolph's recipe for a *real* city—were in place by 1876; and yet those three services did not seem to change as much as he predicted, or at least not as quickly as he predicted. No reason for despair, the editor reassured citizens. Things

Town boosters pushed hard for railroads and improved waterways that would break Tuscaloosa's isolation and help to turn it into a modern city. The first to reach was the Alabama & Chattanooga in 1871. Here the "2:20 Express" crosses over the Mobile & Ohio's 3,600-foot trestle, constructed in 1898, on its way between Columbus and Montgomery. (Courtesy The University of Alabama Libraries Special Collections)

Well-dressed boys sporting straw boaters, old men with crumpled jackets over their white shirts and waistcoats, young women in elegant white dresses and elaborate hats, horsemen, farmers, and businessmen—all sorts of Tuscaloosans mingle under the oak trees at a dusty downtown street fair. (Courtesy The University of Alabama Libraries Special Collections)

were on the right path, and "very soon we shall have water-works, and other improvements too numerous to mention." Randolph could not possibly have known that the "other improvements" soon to be announced to a bedazzled public would include some of the world's greatest inventions. In 1876, just as Tuscaloosa's homes were finally being lit with piped gas, Alexander Graham Bell in Boston uttered his simple words into the first telephone, "Mr. Watson—Come here—I want to see you." Just two years later, on the last day of 1878, Karl Benz started the first reliable internal combustion engine. And exactly one year later, on the last day of 1879, Thomas Edison revealed to the public the first practical electric light bulb. Not merely improvements, the telephone, internal combustion engine, and light bulb were breakthrough inventions that would drive the modern age. The world would never be the same. Tuscaloosa would never be the same.

It took only six years after Bell talked to Mr. Watson for the telephone to reach the City of Oaks. The announcement was brief: the Tuscaloosa Manufacturing Company will have a telephone in operation at their cotton mills at Kennedale. "Thus the world progresses," was the understated comment of the *Times* editor. One year later, in 1883, the editor was proudly boasting of Tuscaloosa's telephone exchange, which a few businessmen had established "in a very quiet manner" to ease commercial transactions. Its twenty stations included fifteen businesses and the University of Alabama; however, noted the editor innocently, in some instances the telephone might also facilitate "social convenience." The Tuscaloosa Telephone Company had reversed those priorities before the century ended. The "phone" had become "a household necessity" for most of its nearly five hundred subscribers, but a mere "time saver" for businessmen.

Tuscaloosans waited longer for electric lights than the six years they had waited to talk on their telephones. Among the extravagant plans listed in the 1887 prospectus of the Tuskaloosa Coal, Iron & Land Company was an electric light and power plant. Nothing happened for two years, despite pleas for conquering the "plutonian darkness." Then, in late 1889, proposals for an electric plant were offered to the city council, bids for poles received the following month, and current from the steam-powered plant finally flowed to the first ten lights in February 1890. "Electricity is Life," was the title of a humorous piece depicting a naïve country fellow's trip to Tuscaloosa to see the newfangled streetlights.

The first electrical supply was not continuous. Each day for several hours, the steam engine would be powered down and the juice turned off. But the general manager of the Tuscaloosa Electric Light & Ice Company heard from citizens and by the spring of 1899 was contemplating keeping the current running "so that customers may enjoy the luxury of electric fans" both day and night. Introduced in 1882, the electric fan represented the first real breakthrough in addressing the South's perpetual problem of oppressive heat. The electric fan was itself made possible by the invention of small electric motors. Before long these would be powering all sorts of other previously unimagined appliances in the home, from vacuum cleaners and washing machines to refrigerators and mixers.

That still left the waterworks. The first Tuscaloosans cited the abundance of "crystal springs" as one of their reasons for settling at the falls. One of those springs supplied drinking water, but its location below the capitol required the water to be loaded into barrels and hauled up the hill by wagon. More convenient public wells were later dug in the center of several principal streets—with severe penalties for any damage. But the water had to be pulled out of those very deep wells with oaken buckets. Many citizens had their own brick-lined wells and used hand pumps to suck out the water—still, a laborious task. The University of Alabama had Marr's Spring and at least one brick-lined well. The insane hospital used a Worthington steam pump to fill its water tanks located in the dome. Tuscaloosans were still working out their own individual arrangements for getting water in 1869.

But the next year, when Ryland Randolph predicted that Tuscaloosa would very soon have its own waterworks, it

Selling vegetables in the middle of the street (the intersection of Greensboro and Cotton) provides a sharp contrast to the newly erected poles overhead loaded with electrical and telephone lines. (Courtesy The University of Alabama Libraries Special Collections)

was with good reason—or so he thought. A location near the old statehouse had already been selected for an immense reservoir so that "in a few weeks, at farthest," the town would be supplied with excellent water conveniently supplied through pipes that were to run all the way to the insane hospital. As with too many other projects, nothing came of it. A similar announcement was made a year later from the Slack-Water Navigation Company. Once again, nothing came of it. A sixteen-thousand-gallon cistern was in place by 1876, but this seems to have been intended more for fighting fires than for supplying drinking water. And that was where things stood until 1887, an important year for Tuscaloosa in many ways, when a private group proposed to build a waterworks. They had it up and running two years later. The water plant's powerhouse, located on high ground about three miles to the east, obtained its supply directly from the Black Warrior. Worthington steam pumps filled the 168,000-gallon reservoir atop a 136-foot tower. The water plant would remain in private hands until 1907, when its by then antiquated machinery was sold to the city. A new waterworks commission quickly doubled the equipment, extended lines and hydrants, "and gave satisfactory service for the first time in several years."

A plume of water rises from an artesian well. After the well was capped, the water would be channeled into the pipes laying on the ground and probably used to water a field. City water was available in Tuscaloosa starting in 1889 but not in the adjacent rural areas. (Courtesy The University of Alabama Libraries Special Collections)

Tuscaloosans were immediately impressed by the water system's fire-fighting potential. They went about installing fifty-three fire hydrants in the 1890s to replace their inadequate cisterns after a demonstration showed a stream from a one-inch fire nozzle rising eighty vertical feet. Although the beneficial effects of clean water on good health had long been established, Tuscaloosans took a bit longer to appreciate them fully. Americans had known that the 1849 London cholera epidemic resulted from contaminated water drawn from a single pump. Civil War surgeons had reported more men permanently disabled from diarrhea and dysentery—both due to drinking unsanitary water—than from gunshot wounds. One Tuscaloosa newspaper devoted three columns to the great yellow fever epidemic of 1878, reporting that 25,000 residents had fled Memphis and, of those remaining, a startling 5,150 had died. On the eve of getting its waterworks, Tuscaloosa newspapers were urging citizens—correctly—to use soap and clean water to prevent typhoid fever, and local physicians would be able to report a few years later that the water system had been responsible for reducing that and other maladies.

Tuscaloosa's water plant originally used steam-driven pumps, shown here, to fill a reservoir atop a 137-foot tower with water drawn from the Black Warrior River. (Courtesy The University of Alabama Libraries Special Collections)

The awareness of the role of water purity in improving health prompted the city to introduce chlorination in 1913. And with the Black Warrior's increasing pollution from industry and mining, the city dammed the spring-fed Yellow Creek, north of the Black Warrior, to create Lake Harris. From that reservoir, which opened in 1929, the water ran through a two-foot pipe for six and a half miles to the Riverview Water Treatment Plant, where it was filtered and chlorinated. The introduction of municipal waterworks and sewage systems across the nation would eventually become the single greatest cause of improved health and longevity. Clean water was estimated to have reduced infant mortality by three-quarters between 1900 and 1936.

While these improvements in health and safety were of great significance, they could never be as vivid or immediate as when children for the first time filled their basins with water by twisting a faucet knob. The memory of the daily backbreaking chore of toting water would gradually fade. And the problem with the disposal of waste also receded when, soon after the waterworks began operation, the city government began laying sewer lines—perhaps in response to the pointed criticism of the rotten-egg smell wafting from ditches. Bathrooms moved indoors, and by 1920 when mass production lowered their costs, enameled bathtubs and flush toilets had become common. Tuscaloosans were not initially billed by gallons of water used (besides, the system lacked individual meters), but by each piece of plumbing: $12 annually for the first spigot and $3 for each additional spigot, $6 per bathtub, and $8 per toilet.

Tuscaloosans' living rooms, dining rooms, and bedrooms still looked pretty much the same. But not their kitchens. No longer was food prepared in a separate building out back where, if it caught on fire, the house would at least be saved. Gas-fired ranges replaced coal-fed stoves. Enameled sinks with hot and cold water replaced metal-lined wooden boxes. Preserving food had always been a problem. The "clear as crystal" ice made by the machine owned by Joseph Voyle was expensive; but "no one should grudge the price," warned the *Monitor*'s editor in the oppressively hot month of August 1870, "for the only genuine luxury which this parched city affords." When the railroad reached town the next year, lake ice from the north became more easily available. The local Tuskaloosa Ice Company did a roaring business beginning in the 1880s. But all that changed when electric refrigerators finally replaced iceboxes in the 1920s. Modern kitchens had enormous advantages, including proximity to the dining table, efficient cooking and baking, and just plain convenience. But the smells of soup on the range top, pies baking, and bacon sizzling—all in the next room—had to rank high.

Each home had stood apart in 1869. Communication had been by voice or letter, light by candle or oil lamps, and water had to be hauled in by hand. Now those networked homes allowed Tuscaloosans to communicate by telephone at great distances; to turn on lights and run appliances with the flick of a switch; and to drink, cook, and bathe all under the same roof. The networked home was staggeringly more convenient and healthful. And, by serving everyone equally, networked homes expanded the democratic experiment.

THE ONLY CHOICES FOR GETTING into town were walking and riding when the first train reached Tuscaloosa in March 1871. But within a week, a few leading citizens pooled their resources to build a streetcar track to run from the depot, north up

The newspaper depicted the proposed steam locomotive as a pair of snorting bulls pulling passengers from the train depot into the center of town on the streetcar's first run in 1871. But like so many other dreams, years would pass before the line was finished. *(Independent Monitor, April 19, 1871)*

Greensboro Street, to the center of town. So confident was Ryland Randolph of its success that only a month later he printed another one of his woodcut cartoons, this time depicting the prospective steam locomotive as twin bulls pulling the passengers on the streetcar's first run into town.

After a year with no progress, Randolph urged the Street Car Company to substitute horse power for steam power. But the 1880s opened without a rail on the ground. Those disembarking at the train depot were forced to get to town over—or perhaps through—a deeply rutted road where carriages would sink to their axles and horses balked. "Tuscaloosa *may be* a beautiful place, celebrated for its beautiful oaks, lovely women, ugly men, [and] seats of learning," remarked one gentleman after his ordeal getting from the depot to downtown took half an hour, "but it has the blank-firedest, blank sort of a blank road to get there on, I have ever traveled, this side of blank! blank! blank!" Within six months of this gentleman's complaint, another enterprise, this one named the Tuscaloosa Street Railway Company, began soliciting investments. At long last in the summer of 1882, over ten years after the first train pulled into the depot, people could ride mule-drawn trolleys into town. It was a measure of how far Tuscaloosa lagged behind the rest of the country that only four years later, Montgomery would introduce an electric streetcar system—this before Tuscaloosans even had access to electricity. An Ohioan observed in 1884 that Tuscaloosa's chief attraction lay in "the cultivation and hospitality of its inhabitants." Yet this so-called "City of Tuscaloosa" remains "a town, nevertheless" for, quoting the prophet Nehemiah, "the people were few therein, and the houses were not builded."

Moves were afoot in 1887 to change all that—from installing a comprehensive

The Atlanta Store at the town center was built atop the ruins of Washington Hall. A streetcar on the right approaches from Broad Street preparing to make the big curve south along Greensboro. The famous block on the corner, where the city clock is today, is the pedestal that supported the hotel's George Washington sign, which was painted black during the war. (From *The City of Tuskaloosa, Its Many Advantages…* [Cincinnati: Keating, 1887])

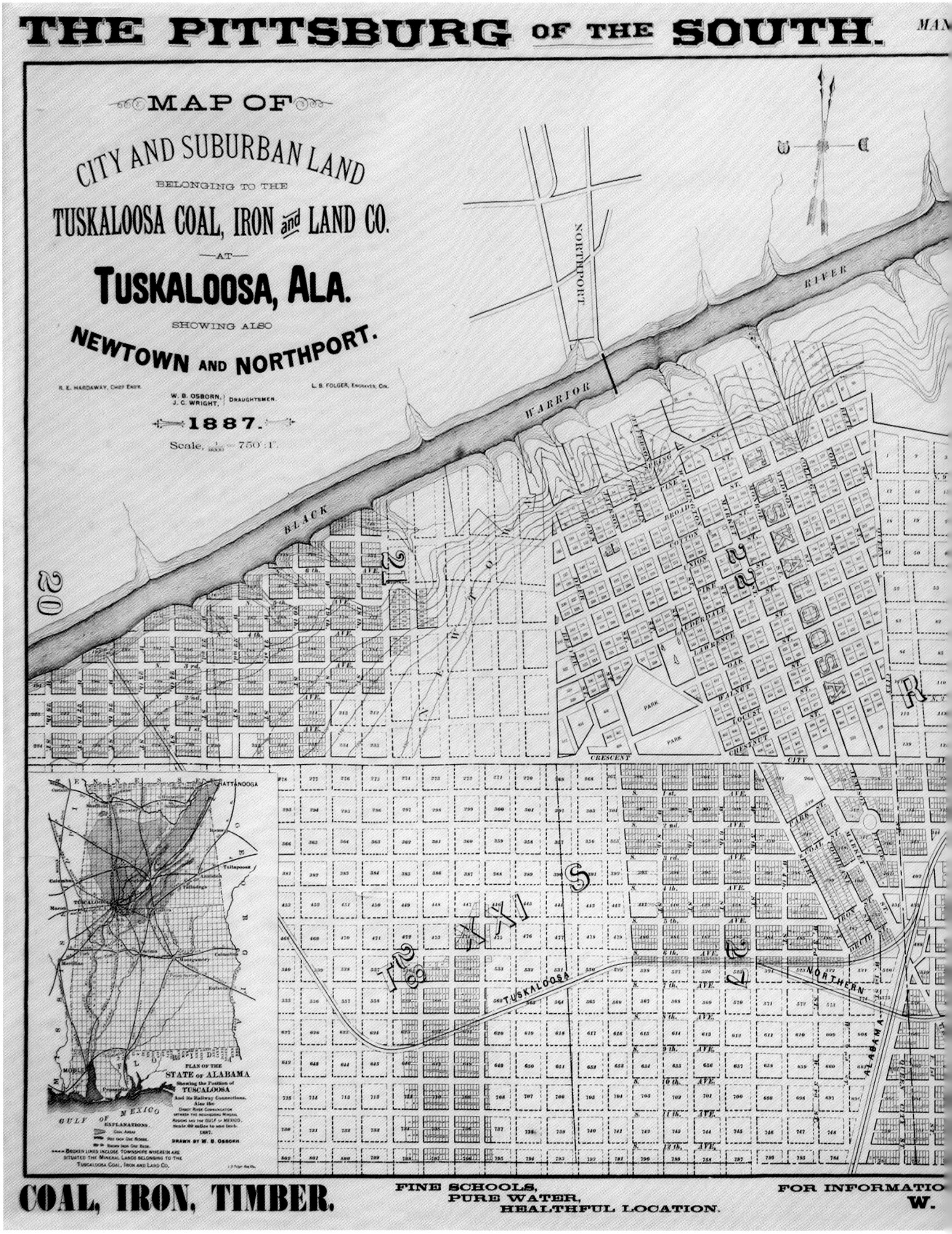
THE PITTSBURG OF THE SOUTH.
MAP OF
CITY AND SUBURBAN LAND
BELONGING TO THE
TUSKALOOSA COAL, IRON and LAND CO.
AT
TUSKALOOSA, ALA.
SHOWING ALSO
NEWTOWN AND NORTHPORT.
R. E. HARDAWAY, CHIEF ENGR.
W. B. OSBORN, J. C. WRIGHT, DRAUGHTSMEN.
L. B. FOLGER, ENGRAVER, CIN.
1887.
BLACK WARRIOR RIVER
NORTHPORT
TUSKALOOSA
PARK
CRESCENT
CITY
NORTHERN
ALABAMA
PLAN OF THE STATE OF ALABAMA
GULF OF MEXICO
DRAWN BY W. B. OSBORN
COAL, IRON, TIMBER.
FINE SCHOOLS,
PURE WATER,
HEALTHFUL LOCATION.
FOR INFORMATIO

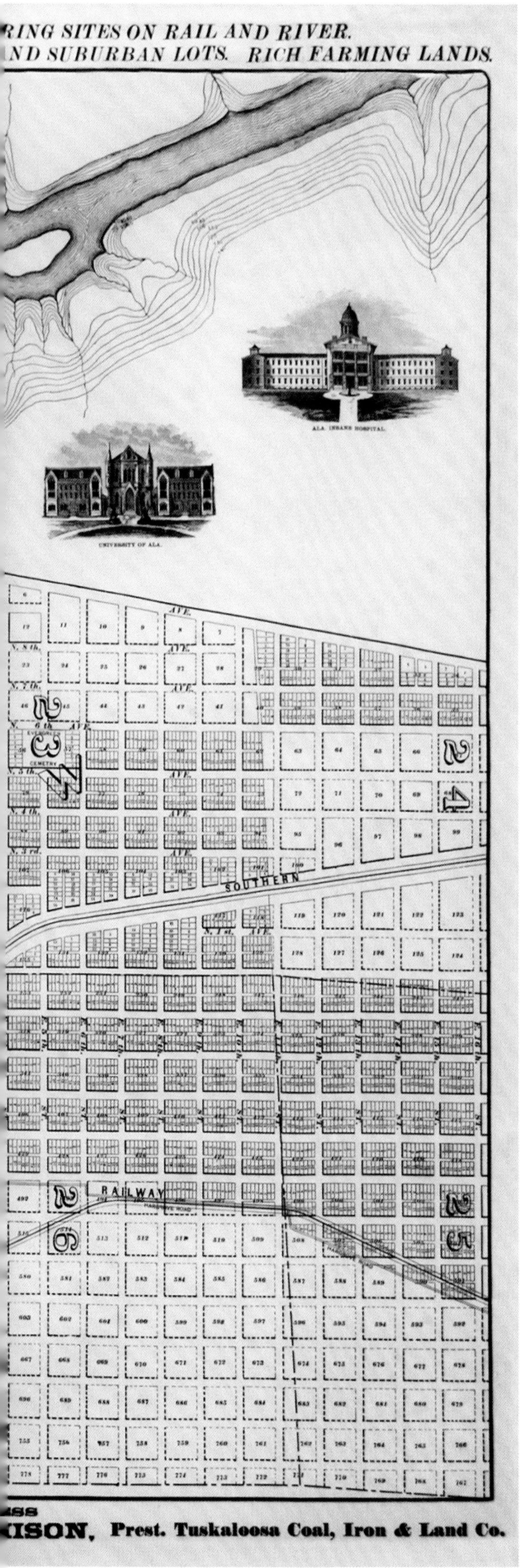

Tuskaloosa Coal, Iron and Land's 1887 grid map, a companion to its perspective map of the same year, was intended to attract new residents and investors by showing the land available for sale and its accessibility by rail. (Courtesy The University of Alabama Libraries Special Collections)

public transportation system to expanding the city's limits. In that important year, both the Tuskaloosa Coal, Iron & Land and the Tuscaloosa and Castle Hill Real Estate and Manufacturing Companies were incorporated. Their great plans to create industrial complexes were never realized, but the two enterprises did cause a great many houses to be "builded."

TCI&L subdivided its land and offered hundreds of lots up for sale. Its vast holdings abutted the original townsite with the most important lots lying east of East Margin Street, which was starting to be known as Queen City. TCI&L—significantly—announced its intention to supply those new homes with gas, light, and water.

Castle Hill located its much smaller suburb even farther out, northeast of the insane hospital. Castle Hill surveyed and sold off its property as individual lots. But because the development was beyond the TCI&L holdings, its owners decided to build Tuscaloosa's first amusement center as an enticement. Construction of Castle Hill Park began only a few months after its 1887 incorporation with sixty men using picks, shovels, and wheelbarrows to dam a small creek east of the waterworks at Riverview. The dollar-a-day wages for such back-breaking work prompted strikes, but the management prevailed. After the thirty-foot dam burst and was repaired, Lake Lorraine was stocked with fish and opened to the public. A pavilion along the shore lured Tuscaloosans with a dance floor, piano, phonograph, skating rink, bowling alley, shooting gallery, and refreshment stand. On the grounds were croquet courts, a fountain, a small zoo, and a slide beginning forty feet in the air and stretching 140 feet. A rustic bridge spanned a part of the lake's half dozen acres, designed

Lake Lorraine, northeast of town at the end of the trolley line, was a welcome retreat for Tuscaloosans. (Courtesy The University of Alabama Libraries Special Collections)

"as if on purpose to furnish quiet retreats for 'spoony' couples," reported the newspaper. Young ladies in "natty bathing costumes" tested the waters, while young men were kept out of temptation's way by the "sedate matrons" who chaperoned. Lake Lorraine proved quite popular in the '90s until the dam broke a second time and was not repaired.

These first suburbs were too far from downtown for people to walk or ride back and forth by horse or buggy. Both companies thus included plans for trolleys in their incorporation documents and promotional literature. Castle Hill acted first by purchasing the five-year-old assets of the Tuscaloosa Street Railway Company, which had operated north from the train depot to the center of downtown. New tracks were then quickly laid east along Broad Street, past the university, where it turned northeasterly until ending at Lake Lorraine, some three miles from downtown. Thirty-eight Texas mules were needed to keep it going. And they did. The Tuscaloosa Street Railway Company reported in 1889, just two years after its opening, nearly 190,000 passengers—an extraordinary number for a town of about 5,000 residents.

Only a month after Castle Hill had purchased the Tuscaloosa Street Railway, TCI&L ordered a small locomotive for its own proposed Belt Railway. Such a name represented yet another instance of overambition, for it would take many years before the tracks did more than stretch from the train depot to downtown, turn east along Broad Street, and continue past the university to the insane hospital before returning along the same route.

Both railways ran parallel in a big L for five years, making no profit until the two merged. Castle Hill's mules were retired, and the entire system was drawn by TCI&L's locomotive. Because small steam locomotives in those days were known as dummies, the Belt Railway was usually known as the Dummy Line. Tuscaloosans would finally be able to ride in a continuous loop through the Druid City after the turn of the century when the track was laid in stair-step fashion from the train depot to the eastern edge of the university campus, where it connected to the old line. Extensions from the loop reached to Riverview, and in 1904 the earlier track to Castle Hill and Lake Lorraine was extended to the newly established Holt.

No sooner could Tuscaloosans ride around the city—quite literally—on the Dummy Line, than plans were floated to electrify it. The dummy did have its drawbacks. For starters, it was loud: its noisy pistons and screeching wheels could be heard from downtown all the way to the train depot. The dummy constantly belched soot. The dummy was also notoriously unsafe: not only did enflaming sparks

The Perkins family picnicking at Lake Lorraine (Courtesy The University of Alabama Libraries Special Collections)

The Dummy Line was named for the small steam-engine locomotive that pulled Tuscaloosans around town for nearly thirty years. (Courtesy The University of Alabama Libraries Special Collections)

shoot into the air, but at least seven people were killed in only five years—between 1897 and 1902—and usually in ghastly ways. So after addressing numerous delays, petitions, failures, and equipment conversions, the Belt Railway began to run on electricity in 1915. Its three trolleys, one clockwise around the city and two others to Holt, eliminated the soot and reduced the problems of noise and lack of safety.

ALL TROLLEYS WERE LIMITED in one important way: whether powered by mule, steam, or electricity, their route never varied. Feet, horses, and buggies were not bound to a single path. But feet only were good for short distances and not for moving goods. Horses needed constant attention, and the effort required to saddle and ride them required strength and skills that many simply did not have. The time was ripe for something else.

Back in 1869, when Ryland Randolph was pleading for a *real* city, Tuscaloosans read of a phenomenon that was sweeping the country: velocipedes. These pedal-powered vehicles came in all sorts of curious configurations, according to a long article in the *Independent Monitor*. One three-wheeler was arranged with a gentleman in the back pedaling while a young lady in the front steered. Another, with eight-foot wheels, required the use of both arms and legs for power. The velocipede "designed especially for women" was propelled by the rider moving back and forth in her rocking chair seat, the oscillation transferred to the wheels presumably by means of a connecting-rod linkage. Tuscaloosans read of the role velocipedes played in promoting good health and "taking young men away from the drinking saloons." But the velocipede's real advantage, they learned, was that it "is by far more manageable than a horse, and

never runs away . . . is always saddled and in harness; it needs no veterinary surgeon or a groom."

Only in passing did the newspaper article include something called a "two-wheeled velocipede." "We want them here," wrote Randolph in 1869. But Tuscaloosans would not join the bicycle craze until 1880, when Dr. Goree brought to the City of Oaks his Standard Columbia, built by the country's first bicycle maker, the Pope Manufacturing Company. Goree's bicycle would come to be known as an ordinary or penny-farthing (so called for the great difference in size between the two wheels). When C. B. Turner and John Baskin purchased Tuscaloosa's next two Pope ordinaries, they "astonished the natives with their new steeds." Other natives were soon "riding their tall but graceful 'ordinaries' down Main street, sometimes followed by Prof. E. J. Kennedy with his old three-wheeler."

The introduction of the safety bicycle around 1890 was what shifted "wheeling," as it was known, into a practical mode of transportation. Whereas ordinaries had the pedals attached directly to the immense front wheel with a small wheel trailing behind, safety bicycles had the pedals attached to a chain which drove the rear of the two same-sized wheels. Whereas ordinaries required skill and athletic ability, safeties could be easily mastered. Safeties, in other words, were essentially modern bicycles, and they rendered ordinaries and three-wheeled velocipedes obsolete almost overnight. They were called safety bicycles for good reason: ordinaries, which lacked brakes, were prone to "headers," whereby the rider pedaling high in the air would hit something and be thrown forward over the handlebars. This happened to W. C. Cochrane, launching him into Mr. Hausman's grocery store, "having come through the show window (instead of the door) bringing the glass with him." This was all to the amazement of the Tuscaloosans who witnessed the feat, but not to the amusement to Mr. Cochrane. It would not have happened with a safety, which had brakes and a lower center of gravity that allowed the rider's feet to reach the ground. With this one technological innovation, Tuscaloosans began to ride all over town. Bicycling was no longer limited to daring young men. Girls and boys, men and women could all participate.

Some started to venture far into the country. Luther and Will Maxwell were wheeling along at a pretty brisk speed on the old Byler Road one day when Luther overran a snake sunning itself. Will did the same thing a short time later. This second snake, however, was a good-sized rattler that struck at him. The rattler missed, only to become entangled in the spokes before freeing himself and slithering away.

The first bicycle to appear in Tuscaloosa was a Pope Standard Columbia. (1881 illustration from the Pope Manufacturing Company catalog)

Another morning at half past four, the two brothers "mounted their fiery, untamed bicycles," and started for Uniontown by way of Demopolis—an eighty-mile trek. Luther would later travel to the 1893 Columbian Exposition in Chicago, where he was one of the five thousand wheelmen and wheelwomen to ride in a long lantern parade. "What would the people at home say if they could see this sight tonight?" he kept asking himself as he pedaled.

As president of Tuscaloosa's bicycle club, Luther Maxwell was asked in 1896 to pen an appreciation that he entitled "Wheels and Wheelmen in Tuscaloosa." By that time, the bone-shaking iron rims were being replaced by vastly superior pneumatic tires, probably the single most important innovation to the safety bicycle. As a result, Luther reckoned that within a year the number of Tuscaloosa's bicyclists had risen to between 300 and 350. They would ride out together to the woods around Old Wooley's Pond for an annual Fourth of July picnic.

Luther devoted most of his essay to recounting the benefits brought by the wheel. He began by repeating the oft-observed comment that bicycling, with its "peculiar fascination" of the fresh air of open spaces swiftly flowing in the face, was replacing the lure of gambling houses and beer gardens. And he stressed the bicyclists' role in improving roads. Bicycles could not be ridden on the rutted track that travelers had once trod between the train depot and downtown. He argued strongly for improved county roads, noting that the League of American Wheelmen had successfully pushed to have thousands of miles macadamized, a process that created a hard and smooth surface by compacting small rough rocks and binding them with crushed stone.

"The wheel was first looked upon as a plaything," noted Luther Maxwell, "but it has now almost displaced the saddle horse from our streets." Each day riders throughout Tuscaloosa attend to their business "on their silent steeds." He then quoted the poet Robert Burns:

> *Amidst this mighty fuss just let me*
> *mention,*
> *The rights of women merit some*
> *attention.*

Luther welcomed the "modest young misses and beautiful young ladies gliding down our oak-lined streets every afternoon," wishing Tuscaloosa had even more wheelwomen. The bicycle was, in fact, a more significant tool of social change than he realized. No longer did girls and young women have to saddle or harness a horse. Nor were they confined to the route of the trolley tracks. The bicycle allowed girls and young women to come and go pretty much as they pleased. They wrote at length in their diaries expressing the thrill of receiving a new bicycle and then using it to visit friends, go to the store, or just to go riding—on their own without chaperones. Many would pose proudly for photographs with their bicycles.

Maxwell concluded his account with a simple statement: "The bicycle is one of the greatest inventions of modern times." He had no way of knowing, of course, that in a mere four years Tuscaloosans would be introduced to an even greater invention of modern times, perhaps even the greatest.

THE FIRST AUTOMOBILE to negotiate Tuscaloosa's streets appeared in 1900. The Locomobile that D. L. Rosenau brought to town was unreliable and cantankerous. The two-seater, which lacked fenders and a windshield, took an hour to build up enough steam just to get it moving. But seeing it in the Druid City in the first year of the century could not have been more appropriate. When a few years later W. S. Persinger bought a steamer in Birmingham and drove it to Northport, his trip was certainly memorable. The poor roads "wore all the rubber off the tires," the clatter from the new invention frightened the horses, and their owners wanted to fight. But he was able to make the journey in a single day with "continuous tinkering" and frequent stops to fill the water reservoir.

Tuscaloosans did not rush out to buy automobiles after they saw Rosenau's or Persinger's steamers for the simple reason that most were unreliable or too expensive,

This Tuscaloosan was so proud of her new safety bicycle that she brought it with her for the professional photographer to include in her portrait. (Courtesy G. Ward Hubbs)

and would remain so for years. These early automobiles usually had their motors mounted under the seat and were as likely to be powered by electricity or gasoline as by steam. (One of the cofounders of Allen and Jemison Hardware drove an electrical automobile as late as 1919.) Steering was by tiller instead of a steering wheel, and few had tops of any kind. Horseless carriages they certainly were. But enough automobiles were puttering about on the streets by 1910 that Tuscaloosa began issuing licenses; Persinger would purchase the first one for a whopping twenty-five cents.

That was about when Dr. Harvey B. Searcy purchased his first automobile. Physicians liked that the automobile improved their ability to make house calls, especially when that involved going out into the country. Dr. Searcy decided on a single-cylinder Brush that used a pair of chains, instead of a differential with gears, to power the rear wheels. Turning a corner at more than five miles per hour would result in one of the chains falling off its sprocket. Nor did the single-cylinder engine render any more than vague amounts of power. "I could get about half-way up the hill, then the carburetor would run dry and I would coast back down and had to turn around and back up." After having to hitch his mechanical steed behind a living breathing steed one too many times, he sold it.

Dr. Searcy simply purchased the wrong car. He needed a Model T. Henry Ford's first sight of an automobile was probably at the Columbian Exposition. While Luther Maxwell had his eye on the thousands of bicycles, Ford was looking at the one gasoline-powered vehicle there: the four-wheeled Victoria, built by the Daimler company (which would later merge with the Benz company to produce the Mercedes-Benz). Within three years, Ford's neighbors were complaining as he drove up and down Detroit's Bagley Avenue in his own gasoline-powered four-wheeler he called the Quadricycle. Only five years after that, in 1908, Ford sold his first Model T. The "Tin Lizzie," as it was affectionately known, combined simplicity, exceptional reliability (the only survivor of a 1909 New York to Seattle race), and ease of repair—all at a low price that kept dropping. A new Model T could be purchased in the last year of production, 1927, for a third of its original 1908 price, even with loads of what had once been accessories now included as standard equipment. A network of nearly seven thousand Ford dealerships was in place by 1913. Within ten years, half the automobiles sold in the United States were Model T Fords.

By performing so many tasks, the automobile quickly took over. Horses or bicycles could only be used for short distances, and trains and steamboats were for long distances. Automobiles could be used

Early automobiles were expensive and inefficient, but the Model T Ford was a car that ordinary families could afford. (Courtesy Library of Congress)

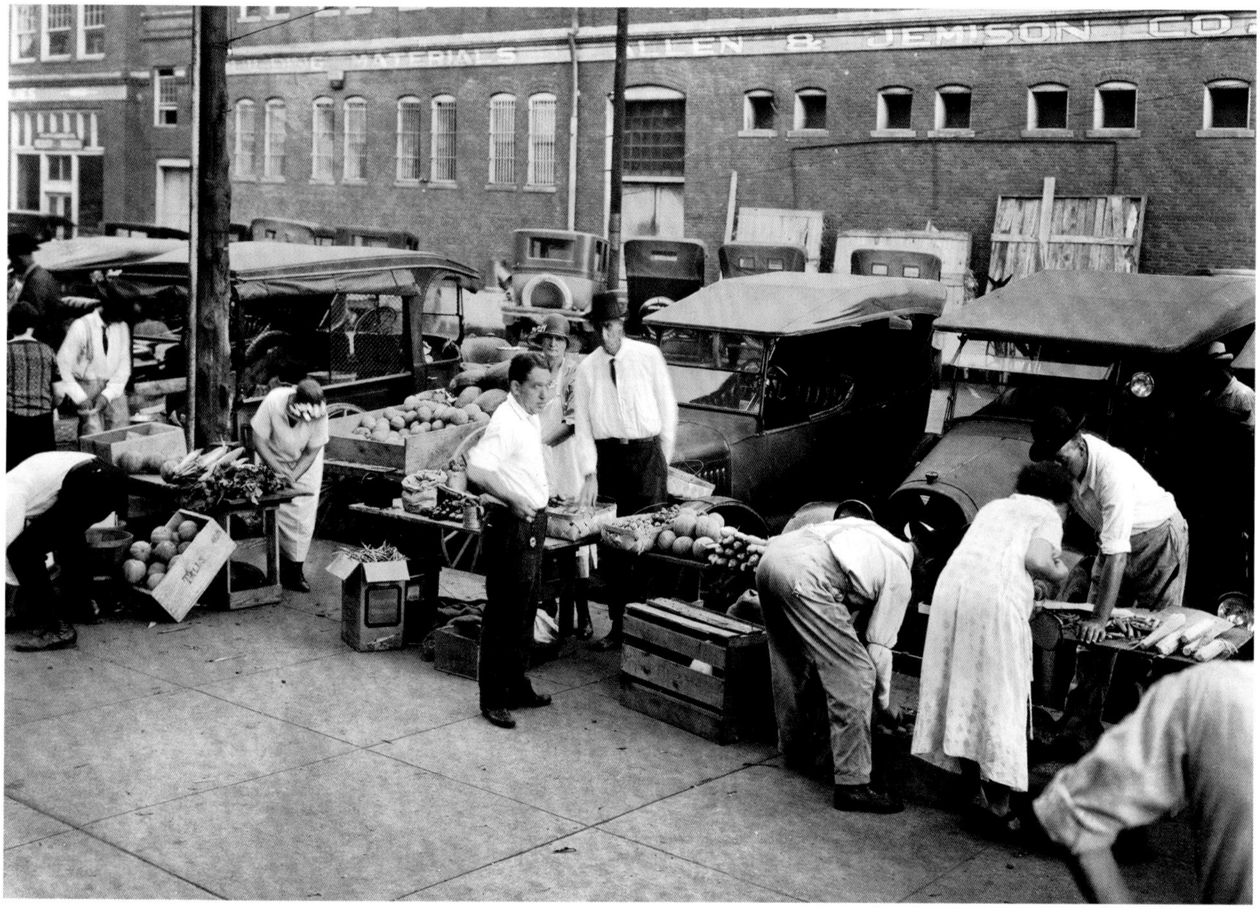

for both. Horses and bicycles were for single passengers, but automobiles could carry a family and their luggage. True, they needed more maintenance than bicycles, but not as much as horses, which not only had to be fed and boarded but their unpleasant and unhealthful waste could not be ignored. And after Henry Ford's breakthrough, workaday people could purchase their own dependable, adaptable, and easy-to-fix Model T.

And the automobile had a less tangible, but no less real, effect on the American character. While passengers aboard trains and steamboats went along the rails and rivers, automobile drivers determined where they wanted to go and when they wanted to go, limited only by the quality of the roads and availability of gasoline. Other inventions that were changing everyday life—telephones, in particular—created overlapping networks among people. But first bicycles, and then automobiles, expanded individual autonomy. The affordable Model T Ford became the great tool of democracy, at once individually liberating and socially equalizing.

Tuscaloosa County's farmers and their families took to the Model T even more than town folk. When Henry Ford introduced a truck version of the Model T in the mid-1920s, the mule-drawn wagon became obsolete. Farmers certainly appreciated how the Model T reduced their back-breaking labor, but they gloried in the opportunities it gave them just to get away. One farmer reported that he had once been "perfectly content to have my horizon bounded by the ten- or twelve-mile circle that my horses could go in a day and

The Model T Ford allowed farmers to drive to town, where they could sell their produce directly to the public. Tuscaloosans formally organized a curb market organization in 1924. Here fruits and vegetables are sold quite literally on the curb opposite Allen and Jemison Hardware on Seventh Street. (Courtesy Alabama Department of Archives and History)

The automobile revolutionized transportation—for women as well as men. Broad Street in 1869 looked nothing like it did fifty or sixty years later. (Courtesy Jason D. Townsend)

get back in good shape." The Model T had changed all that, allowing him to "make exploring trips of five times the distance. I can call on friends who have been asking me to come for twenty years." Families could hop in their Tin Lizzies and soon be in Tuscaloosa cruising down Broad Street. They could stop into the Ritz Theater to watch Al Jolson in *The Jazz Singer*. They could go shopping. Young men could find new opportunities for employment.

Automobile drivers were soon clamoring for better roads even more vigorously than did the bicyclists. Roads out in the country were certainly poor, but Tuscaloosa's streets also needed improving. When the wagons' and buggies' steel-rimmed wheels created a racket on concrete, asphalt was used to pave Greensboro Avenue and Broad Street in 1912. But it would become concrete in 1920, when the automobile's rubber tires had made the steel rims obsolete. Over the next decade, the city would pave eighteen miles in concrete.

Tuscaloosans had needed trolleys to get to and from those first suburbs built by TCI&L and Castle Hill. The new suburbs would be built for Model T Fords and paved roads. W. E. Bowers subdivided thinly occupied land to the east of Castle Hill in 1915. Few lots sold when even seventy-foot-deep wells were not hitting water. But after a water line was run in 1924 and the roads paved, the separately incorporated Alberta City mushroomed into Tuscaloosa's largest suburb. The trolley never reached that far. Over the next five years, forty-one subdivisions would be platted—all with the assumption that the residents would be driving automobiles. Retailers saw an opportunity and started opening stores near these suburbs. Before too long, they were setting up what would eventually turn into shopping centers accessible almost solely by automobile.

The 1924 water line was followed the next year with an even more important event, not only for those living in Alberta

City, but for all Tuscaloosans as well: the beginning of the federal highway system. The good roads movement had started with the bicycle craze of the 1890s; but like so many issues, it was the automobile that would make the difference. Tuscaloosa County could claim 160 miles of "improved roadway" by 1913, when the road from Tuscaloosa to Birmingham (the same that had taken Persinger a day to drive) was advertised as "one of the most delightful automobile drives in the state." "Improved roadway," in fact, meant very little. The U.S. Army Motor Transport Corps, which included Lieutenant Colonel Dwight Eisenhower, set out to drive across the country in 1919. Leaving Washington, D.C., in early July, the convoy of eighty-one trucks and other vehicles would endure countless breakdowns before finally reaching Oakland, California, in September—eight weeks later! America's roads were simply inadequate. After several initiatives finally got the federal government involved, the U.S. Numbered Highway System was inaugurated in 1925. This first federal highway system did not involve any actual construction; it instead imposed a common set of numbers to link already existing roads into a network. Federal funds were also made available to the states for improving roads.

The highway system's effects were dramatic. It now became quite easy for Tuscaloosans to hop in their cars to see the state, or the nation for that matter. And vice versa. Motorists traveling between Chattanooga and Meridian began to pour through Tuscaloosa along Route 11 on what had once been the old Huntsville Road through Brookwood. The roar of automobile engines was joined to the distinctive *kuh-thump* of the tires passing over the expansion joints spaced every fifty feet.

As motorists entered Alberta City along Route 11 (now University Boulevard East) they began to see auto camps or motor courts: clusters of tiny single-room cottages like the one famously shared by Clark Gable and Claudette Colbert in *It Happened One Night*. Motorists could in later years stay at a motor hotel, which someone coined a *motel* in 1925, the same year that the highway system began. Only motorists could get to the auto camps, motor courts, and motels—unlike the hotels, which a train passenger could reach by trolley or taxi. Much of Alberta City's growth was directly attributed to the motorists whose first encounter with Tuscaloosa was down Route 11.

The Moon Winx, easily Tuscaloosa's most famous motor court, opened with twenty cottages in the late 1920s. The Moon Winx was just one of many facilities catering to the rising number of motorists along the new highway system. (Collection of the author)

Motorists had to eat, of course. Some motor courts had restaurants; Alberta City's Moon Winx, for example, had the Barn and later, the Lamplighter. But grills and diners were more common because motorists did not want to spend the time it took to eat in a restaurant. These first grills and diners were small and locally owned, but the highway system lent itself to franchising. Tuscaloosa would one day get its own Howard Johnson's, the first national restaurant franchise—along Route 11, of course.

The number of people driving in and out of the Druid City was nothing short of extraordinary. Every day in 1937, during the middle of the Great Depression, an estimated 2,500 to 4,000 vehicles—probably well over a million vehicles per year—would travel along Route 11; and those numbers did not include cars driving U.S. Routes 43 and 82. Along with the motor courts and diners, motorists approaching Tuscaloosa from the east along Route 11 came upon a series of large public institutions.

The Veterans Hospital, only a few hundred yards south of Route 11, had just opened in 1932. Beginning with a substantial 273 beds, it would eventually grow into a massive complex of over twenty-five major buildings. Motorists continuing west through Alberta City would drive by the Partlow State School, the creation of Bryce Hospital Superintendent W. D. Partlow. He had recognized that the intellectually disabled needed different treatment from the mentally ill and opened the Alabama Home for Mental Defectives in 1923. The name was changed four years later to honor its founder, and by 1930 over four hundred patients were enrolled.

Farther west on the right was the long approach to Bryce Hospital, which had grown substantially since its opening at the beginning of the Civil War. The Alabama Insane Hospital's first superintendent, Peter Bryce, had put into effect the ideas of Dorothea Dix, who urged treating the mentally ill by improving their environment and structuring their day. Patients were accordingly set on a program of work, often cultivating plants and crops, to divert their attention and focus their minds. This had the added bonus of producing food and generating income for the hospital. Eight years after Dr. Bryce's death in 1892, the hospital was renamed in his honor. His successors continued the program of patients' growing crops and selling their own products. The unfortunate result was to encourage the legislature to reduce funding, even as the number of patients increased.

Not too far beyond the approach to Bryce Hospital, motorists passed by the newly finished fifty-five bed Druid City Hospital (DCH). The architect, D. O. Whilldin, fronted the brick three-story building with six white columns to have it blend with the University of Alabama, whose land the city leased for the hospital at no charge. Inside were the latest medical facilities, including laboratories, operating rooms, and X-ray machines. Voters in 1920 approved a $50,000 bond to build the hospital, the other half of the money needed to build the hospital was raised through contributions by local Tuscaloosans. One individual, James T. Horne, gave $20,000 to build a separate nurses' home in the back.

Just a block later, motorists reached the University of Alabama. Things were much quieter than back in 1869, when the university was still embroiled in its divisive partisan struggles. The university began accepting women in 1893, and by 1905 they were earning master's degrees. The university during the 1930s was realizing an architectural plan initiated in 1907: distinctive red brick academic buildings with white columns surrounding a quadrangle with an imposing library where the Rotunda once stood.

These many new buildings were needed to handle the university's many students, a four-fold increase from 1910 to 1920 alone. They were studying in a vastly wider array of fields than in 1869. The School of Law began in 1872, the School of Education and School of Engineering

in 1909, and the School of Commerce and Business Administration in 1919. The following year the Medical College of Alabama was transferred from Mobile to Tuscaloosa, and in 1924 the Graduate School was established to be followed by the School of Chemistry in 1929 and the School of Home Economics two years later. Nearly five thousand students would be studying at the university as the 1930s drew to a close. A fifth of those students were enrolled in engineering.

A goodly number of those thousand engineering students were enrolled in aeronautical engineering. Tuscaloosans had seen their first airplane in late 1911, only eight years after the Wright Brothers' first flight. The pilot of what was probably a Curtiss Model D took off, rose gracefully forty feet over the fairgrounds fence, swooped to one side, and promptly crashed into the ground in a "crumpled mass." He survived. That inauspicious beginning deterred few if any. Aviators could fly to Tuscaloosa after Maynor Airport, later renamed Hargrove Van de Graaff Airport, was established west of Northport in 1928. The next year the university offered its first courses in aeronautical engineering, and by 1937 its program had grown to become one of the first ten in the country to be fully accredited. Few if any could envision the role aviation would soon play in the lives of Tuscaloosans.

Passing the old Dearing House, motorists entered the original Tuscaloosa. Here

Aeronautical engineering students Winfred F. McCartney (in cockpit) and G. LaMar Hubbs (on wing) work on a biplane in the late 1930s. The university began offering courses in aeronautical engineering in 1929, and by 1937 its Department of Aeronautical Engineering was among the country's first fully accredited programs. (Courtesy The University of Alabama Libraries Special Collections) the automobile now reigned supreme. Taxis had started to replace hacks back in 1909. Motorists sometimes had to search hard for a parking spot where hitching posts and water troughs once stood. When the city commission prohibited jaywalking in 1930, they were in a way confirming the automobile's priority.

Motorists coming to Tuscaloosa for the first time certainly had an easier time finding addresses than visitors arriving in 1869. Complaining that the system of common names for streets was "like a Chinese puzzle," the editor of the *Gazette* had urged the mayor and aldermen in 1901, the year after Tuscaloosa's first automobile, to give numbers to the houses and streets as a convenience. It did not take long before Locust, College, Franklin, Cotton, Union, and so many others became numbered avenues and streets—convenient but certainly bland. (There were exceptions: Greensboro and Queen City just switched from streets to avenues, and Broad Street would finally become University Boulevard in the 1970s after occasionally being called Fifth Street or University Avenue.)

The location of the Alston Building near the Tuscaloosa County Courthouse made it a popular place for lawyer's offices. This photograph was taken for the Historic American Buildings Survey in 1993. (Courtesy Library of Congress)

Along those numbered streets and avenues stood buildings that were beyond the imagination back in 1869. Three in particular stood out from all the other buildings in the Druid City. Each did more than fulfill its function. Each made its own statement.

When the seven-story Alston Building was constructed in 1909, it utilized two late-nineteenth-century technological innovations: steel-frame construction and the safety elevator. Its location, facing Greensboro Avenue near to the courthouse, made it a popular site for lawyers' offices. Cooling was still a problem, so awnings provided shade, especially over the west-

This scene, which Margaret Cammer Furman painted c. 1850 from another angle, had by 1915 changed considerably. Greensboro Street and Cotton Street were now Greensboro Avenue and 6th Street. The Tuscaloosa County Courthouse had been replaced by Tuscaloosa's first skyscraper, the Alston Building (on the right). The well at the intersection had become a drinking fountain with a sign that read "This side for coloreds." (Courtesy Tuscaloosa Preservation Society)

facing windows. The Alston Building was considered quite the showplace for its time, and Tuscaloosans held many a dance party on its rooftop garden. Skyscrapers became popular during the twentieth century, and not just to save space. After all, it was a big country, and real estate in Tuscaloosa was hardly so dear that seven stories were needed to save money. Small cities in particular realized the benefit of the publicity that came with a tall building. At the same time that town boosters urged Tuscaloosans just to "talk growth," for example, they put up a large electric sign on the roof of the Alston Building beaming "Try Tuscaloosa." Those words may have expressed their determination, but it could hardly express their achievements; for as of 1909, Greensboro Avenue was still unpaved.

A decade later the streets were paved and automobiles were commonplace. Tuscaloosans, according to newspaper editor Ben Green, "sensed themselves on the thresh-hold of cityhood." His predecessors had been saying the same thing since Ryland Randolph announced that the town needed a gasworks, railroad, and telegraph to become a *real* city. This time Green had it right. During the 1920s, the population nearly doubled from 12,000 to 20,700, easily the largest percentage increase since the village was named the state capital. Green went on to list a number of small events that together showed "the departure of the Town of Tuscaloosa and the coming of the City."

If the Alston Building expressed determination, the towering Merchants' Bank & Trust Building announced that Tuscaloosa had at last arrived. Appropriately constructed in the middle of the 1920s on the same corner where Washington Hall

The Merchants' Bank & Trust Building, seen here in an early rendering, still dominates the Tuscaloosa skyline. Merchants' Bank & Trust failed during the Depression, and for many decades after that, the building housed the First National Bank. (From the 1926 Tuscaloosa High School *Black Warrior* yearbook)

once stood, this second skyscraper seemed to absorb elements from the columned homes of Tuscaloosa's early days. D. O. Whilldin, Alabama's leading architect, who had also designed the Druid City Hospital, used the three components of a classical column—the base, shaft, and capital—to break up the building's great height. For the base, he called for Indiana Limestone with a continuous band of Greek motifs. The shaft, floors three through eight, was of simple brick punctuated by windows. And Whilldin embellished the capital, the top two floors, with the same acanthus leaves found in a Corinthian capital.

While Tuscaloosans found the exterior of the 1925 Merchants' Bank & Trust familiar and reassuring, stepping into the lobby presented something that seemed to come from the mind of a Bauhaus architect in Germany—it was crisp and daring, with hard edges and glimmering smooth surfaces. The reporter for the *Tuscaloosa News* was enthralled. "Corridors and washrooms are tile and marble throughout. . . . Two high speed elevators with bronze doors [are accessed] from a marbled-paved lobby with ornamental plastered ceiling. The banking quarters . . . are finished in pink Tennessee marble and genuine mahogany and the architectural arrangement is such as to carry throughout the banking room the effect of the arched windows, which dignify the building's exterior. . . . The lobby itself, which is sixteen feet by sixty, is paved with marble and pink marble covers all columns." The contrast between the traditional exterior and modern interior seemed somehow appropriate for a city where the past lives with today.

The third building would set an entirely different tone. By 1936, Tuscaloosa had outgrown its city hall across the street from the Alston Building. With referendum-approved bonds supplemented by Public Works Administration funds, D. O. Whilldin drew up plans for its replacement. Nothing about the new city hall/Bama Theatre would be familiar. Architectural historian Thomas Mark Shelby describes its exterior style as PWA Moderne, incorporating "elements of Art Deco, Streamline Moderne, and Stripped Classicism with its underlying Beaux-Arts principles." No matter what you call it, "the new City Hall complex, a composition of almost abstract simplicity, was modernistic above all else and hailed as a sign of progress for the city of Tuscaloosa."

On the night that the Bama Theatre first opened, Tuscaloosans bought their tickets at the box office for *Bringing Up Baby*, the classic 1938 screwball comedy starring Cary Grant and Katherine Hepburn. They entered the lobby below a projecting marquee with stainless steel bands and twinkling lights. Above the marquee was a

The interior of the Merchants' Bank & Trust Building, with its clean and dramatic modern lines, was a stunning departure from its Classical Revival exterior. Note that the photographer had a sense of humor: in vivid contrast to the lobby's hard edges he placed a spittoon in the middle of the floor. (Courtesy Robert O. Mellown)

The old town of 1869 had become a *real* city by 1939. On the east side of Greensboro Avenue are Tuscaloosa's two skyscrapers: the Merchants' Bank & Trust in the distance, and the Alston Building on the right. Across Greensboro from the Alston Building stands the exotic and air-conditioned Bama Theatre/City Hall. (Courtesy Tuscaloosa Preservation Society)

semicircular wall of fluted limestone. The zigzag art deco patterns that started on the sidewalk continued into the front lobby and hallways. Tuscaloosans' heads must have snapped when they stepped into the back lobby, with its carpets, tapestries, paintings, and furniture that recalled the Davanzati Palace of the Florentine Renaissance—four centuries earlier. Turning left into the 1,200-seat theatre had to have been breathtaking that opening night. The romantic atmosphere began with the ceiling: randomly spaced and timed blinking lights, to give the sense of stars, recessed into a dark blue sky. But that was not all. Motor-driven projectors panned images of clouds across the ceiling. An artist known for his "unusual imagination and artistic skill" painted on the side walls vaguely Spanish or Italian scenes of gardens and stuccoed buildings with arched doorways. And all this in air-conditioned comfort—a first for the Druid City. "Toto, I've a feeling we're not in Alabama anymore."

IT HAD BEEN SEVEN DECADES since Tuscaloosans began turning their old town into a "*real* city." They drove their buggies past the ashes of Washington Hall in 1869; they drove their Ford V-8s past the commanding Merchants' Bank & Trust in 1939. Horses neighed, wagons creaked, and the falls murmured in 1869. Horns beeped and engines roared in 1939. A red brick courthouse, in

elegantly restrained Federal style, had been replaced by the yellow brick Alston Building. Across the street where the clapboard city hall once stood, Tuscaloosans now watched movies in a strange and exotic theatre. The rutted dirt roads named for presidents and trees had been replaced by smoothly paved streets and avenues identified by a string of monotonous numbers. And in place of the green parasol of oaks, a forest of creosoted poles carried miles of electrical and telephone wires. Tuscaloosans in 1869 toted water every day and lit their homes with candles and oil lamps. But long before 1939 they had only to turn a faucet or flip a switch. Motors powered everything from washing machines to refrigerators. Tuscaloosans depended on stagecoaches and steamboats in 1869 and could not even board a train. But in 1939 they motored down highways, and some even flew in the air. They could talk across town, or across the country if they had to, just by picking up the telephone.

By turning their old town into a modern city, Tuscaloosans had at the same time reinvented the way they went about their everyday lives. They, like other Americans, had gone through more basic changes in the span of a single lifetime—threescore and ten years—than during any other lifetime in human history. If theirs was an unacknowledged revolution, it was still an extraordinary one.

Tuscaloosans see the world...and vice versa

Opposite page: Tuscaloosans watch members of the University of Alabama ROTC march down Broad Street in 1943. Some 7,500 from Tuscaloosa County, plus 6,000 University of Alabama students and alumni, would serve in the Second World War, most of them overseas. (Courtesy The University of Alabama Libraries Special Collections)

"YESTERDAY, DECEMBER 7, 1941—a date which will live in infamy," began President Franklin D. Roosevelt in reporting the Japanese attack on Pearl Harbor. Tuscaloosans were listening and not for the first time; they had tuned in their radios to hear FDR deliver many a fireside chat. America's entry into the Second World War would send many Tuscaloosans overseas. At the same time, thousands of Americans from across the country, hundreds of British and French citizens, and even a few Germans would make their way to the Druid City. The war's aftermath continued this exchange of ideas, experiences, and perspectives by way of television. Tuscaloosans were giving more attention to a larger world, while the world was giving more attention to Tuscaloosans. Like the coming and going of state government, secession and its consequences, the turn toward industry, and the creation of a modern city—this exchange would force the people living along the banks of the Black Warrior to make some hard decisions yet again.

THE TELEGRAPH AND TELEPHONE both tied listeners to the ends of a wire. That set the stage for what Guglielmo Marconi called "wireless telegraphy." His success in sending a signal across the Atlantic in 1902 was a true breakthrough. The first instance of broadcasting live news to the American public occurred ten years later when distress signals from a sinking *Titanic* happened to be caught and then rebroadcast by the Marconi Wireless Telegraph Company. A few years later, the same man who took credit for

ALABAMA BOOK STORE
KRESS

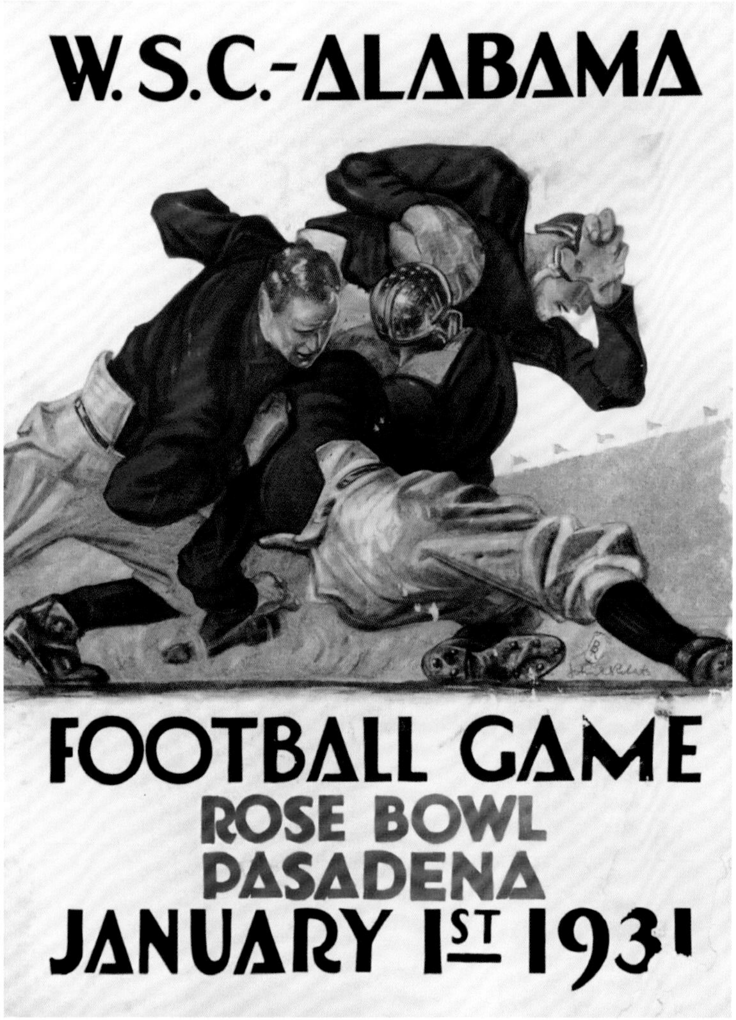

Poster for the 1927 Rose Bowl between Alabama and Stanford (Courtesy Paul W. Bryant Museum, University of Alabama)

catching the *Titanic* distress signals convinced Radio Corporation of America to market radios as an inexpensive "household utility." Radio's success was guaranteed—and so was RCA's.

Radio did not take long to reach Alabama. Birmingham's first station, WBRC, could easily be heard in Tuscaloosa when it began broadcasting in 1925. Tuscaloosans would get their own station, WJRD, in 1936. Opal Lewis recalled its impact. Because her family was among the first to own a radio in their neighborhood, friends would come over on Saturday night just to listen. Much of the programming on the Birmingham and Tuscaloosa stations was local talent, which sometimes included herself. "What a joy it was to gather with friends around the radio," she recalled.

Opal Lewis especially remembered listening to the Crimson Tide, the University of Alabama's football team, on the radio and being able to "visualize each play that the announcer described." The first broadcasts were sent by wire over Morse Code. Tuscaloosans held "watch parties" as someone read out the tickertape of the play-by-play during the University of Alabama's first Rose Bowl, the thrilling 1926 match in which the underrated Tide edged the powerful University of Washington Huskies 20–19. Tuscaloosans could later watch the highlights on newsreel clips shown at local movie theatres. The 1926 Rose Bowl has gone down as "the game that changed the South" by marking the beginning of Southern football's ascendancy.

But the often overlooked 1927 Rose Bowl may have been the more important game. Behind by a touchdown late in the fourth quarter, Alabama blocked a Stanford kick. A few grinding plays later—in what would become Bama's signature style—Hoyt "Wu" Winslett drove through the opposition's defense into the end zone. With the extra point, the final score stood at a 7–7 tie. The 1927 Rose Bowl went down in history, not for the come-from-behind tie, but as the first coast-to-coast live radio broadcast of a football game. Tuscaloosans listened intently as the NBC announcers called every play. And a thirteen-year-old boy in Moro Bottom, Arkansas, was listening just as intently. "I never imagined anything could be that exciting," he would later recall. "I still didn't have much of an idea what football was, but after listening to the game, I had it in my mind that I wanted to go to Alabama and play in the Rose Bowl." And on the first day of January 1935, the Rose Bowl would again be broadcast coast-to-coast by radio, the Tide would win its fourth national championship, and the right end would be that boy from Moro Bottom, Arkansas—Paul "Bear" Bryant.

A YEAR BEFORE THE ATTACK on Pearl Harbor, Tuscaloosans had listened on their radios as President Roosevelt promised to help Britain in its fight against Nazi Germany by providing military supplies, by turning America into what he called the Arsenal of Democracy. Tuscaloosans would soon be at work supplying the arsenal and continue doing so throughout the war.

The Great Depression hit Central Foundry hard. As the economy worsened and orders dwindled, the company had trouble paying workers and eventually closed the plant altogether. Unused equipment was eventually sold to the Japanese—before, of course, they declared war on the United States. As the blast furnace was being dismantled with parts sitting on the riverbank ready to be loaded onto barges, the federal government stepped in, stopped the sale, and ordered the furnace reassembled and the foundry back in operation.

The Central Foundry workers supplied pipes and fittings for the many posts and bases the military was building. But when that slowed, the workforce dropped nearly in half as workers entered the military or left for higher paying jobs. The company then turned to a metallurgical engineering professor at the university. Acting on his advice, it received a series of contracts for making ordnance, which included artillery shells, hand grenades, and land mines. Central Foundry also acquired contracts for casting heavy metal weights for balancing ships and for other weights to keep antisubmarine nets taut. The company's ability to deliver on schedule brought them even more contracts. Women were hired to meet the demand, and the workforce doubled from six hundred to twelve hundred. The women opened the eyes of many a seasoned employee, working "right down where the hard work was, where the high temperature metal was," Paul Singleton recalled; "it turned out they could do any job a man could do. . . . It was amazing." When Central Foundry won the Army-Navy "E" Award, for excellence, presented to the employees of firms that delivered quality goods on time, the women wore their pins on their coat lapels as proudly as the men. "Don't ever let anybody tell you that women can't do some things a man can do," Singleton cautioned. "Those women during the war did things we never thought they were capable of doing or were willing to do."

Other smokestack industries had similar stories. Near Central Foundry, Reichhold Chemical built a $3 million plant to produce phenol. National Southern Products opened its own chemical plant that used papermill waste material to manufacture soap and other products. The federal government sponsored construction of an $18 million rubber plant, but its assets were sold to B. F. Goodrich when the war ended with construction still not completed.

Tuscaloosans labored in the industries, and they sacrificed at home. Goods that they had formerly taken for granted—especially gasoline, tires, and sugar—were rationed. Housing became a problem as young men came in from the country to work in the war industries. And frequent salvage drives collected needed materials. The university's "Slap the Jap with Scrap" dance, ruled by the "King of Junk," collected more than twenty tons of metal.

Above: Starting in 1940, well before the United States entered the war, cadets started flight training at Tuscaloosa's Hargrove Van De Graaf Field. (Courtesy Tuscaloosa Regional Airport) **Opposite page:** Cover of the August 1941 *Fins and Flippers* (Courtesy The University of Alabama Libraries Special Collections)

HARGROVE VAN DE GRAAFF FIELD *became a major training center after its lease by the Alabama Institute of Aeronautics (AIA). At the instigation of the University of Alabama, the AIA signed a contract with the U.S. Army Air Corps to become one of the first to take part in the Civilian Pilot Training Program, a thinly disguised way of providing pilots for the military while America remained officially neutral. The school opened in April 1940, a few months before France fell to the Germans and the Royal Air Force was left nearly alone to prevent Britain's collapse. With the initiation of the Lend-Lease program in March 1941, Britain began sending its aviation cadets to six flying schools, including the AIA. The British cadets exasperated their American instructors with their devil-may-care attitude, sometimes flying under bridges or buzzing farmhouses. Thirteen classes of British cadets went through the ten-week course before the last finished in early 1943.*

A few months later in July, Free French cadets began training in Tuscaloosa. All personnel at the AIA—civilian and military—went through twice-daily classes to learn French six weeks before the first cadet even arrived. Eight interpreters, most of them women, would translate as the instructors slowly gave out directions. Textbooks were eventually issued in French. Except for a brief interlude, the French were the only students from October 1943 until June 1944.

In all, the Alabama Institute of Aeronautics trained some 2,305 American, 1,273 British, and 938 Free French air cadets.

THE BRITISH AND A FEW COMMONWEALTH CADETS *at the Alabama Institute of Aeronautics published their own magazine,* Fins and Flippers. *Much of it was devoted to their discovering an entirely new world. "Tuscaloosans opened their homes to us," an anonymous Canadian cadet wrote in his essay entitled "Southern Hospitality." They arranged entertainments and dances for the cadets, invited them to church, and afterward to Sunday dinner (he called it "an institution") where most of them first experienced "that most delectable of all dishes—Fried Chicken." The Canadian noted that when combined with corn on the cob and hot biscuits, the memories "will live in our minds when the sordid aspects of this war have vanished." He ended with thanks for the graciousness extended by the warmhearted Tuscaloosans.*

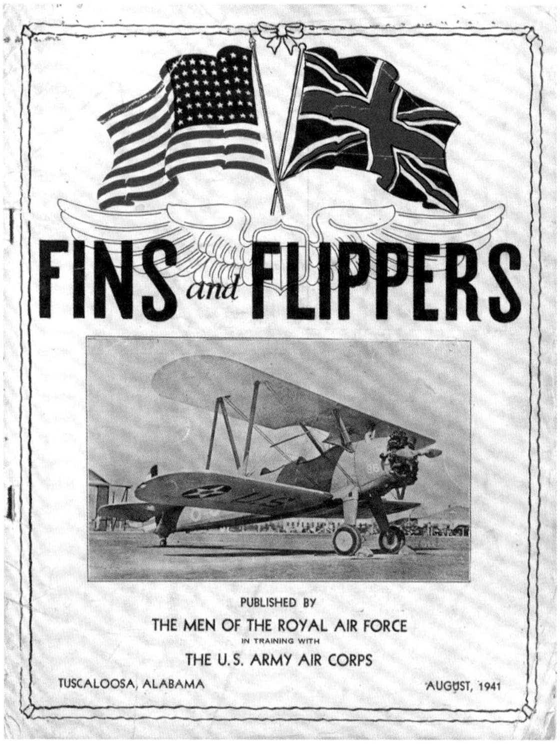

Much of Fins and Flippers *was humorous. One multiple-choice quiz, for example, asked the chief purpose for coming to Tuscaloosa. Possible answers included "The new girls," "To discover the real meaning of scrambled eggs," and perhaps as an afterthought, "Learn to fly." But the humor was a distraction from the deadly serious reason for their time in Tuscaloosa. In the back of each issue of* Fins and Flippers *were photographs of every cadet with, in some copies, the date he later died in combat written in beside.*

An unfortunate consequence of these drives was the loss of some historic artifacts from before the Civil War. War-loan bond drives in the Tuscaloosa district were said to have raised enough money to help purchase four heavy bombers, three medium bombers, and eighteen fighters.

Thousands of young men came to Tuscaloosa for military training. British and Free French air cadets joined Americans in learning to fly at the Alabama Institute of Aeronautics across the river at Hargrove Van de Graaff Field. The University of Alabama would host nearly thirteen thousand Americans receiving academic and physical training in a variety of programs during 1943 and 1944. The university's president noted proudly that its military programs were among the largest in the country.

That was hardly the end of it. Injured Americans were sent to the Druid City for medical care. Tuscaloosans had a long-standing commitment to healing that stretched back to the Civil War. Tuscaloosa's Veterans Hospital had already been in operation nearly a decade before Pearl Harbor. So it was entirely in keeping with this tradition when, in July 1943, the doors officially opened on Northington General Hospital. (Its namesake, Lieutenant Colonel Eugene Garland Northington, was a University of Alabama alumnus who presided over the army's largest hospital; his pioneering use of the X-ray would lead to cancer, the loss of two arms, and eventually take his life.) The rambling $4 million facility was hastily erected on a sixty-five-acre cotton patch along

Opposite page: Four University of Alabama students were among the first to apply to the Civilian Pilot Training Program when it opened soon before the United States entered the Second World War. From left: Virginia Richards, Orene Putnam, Nancy Batson, and Sue Clarkson. After graduation in 1941, Nancy Batson joined the Women's Auxiliary Ferrying Squadron in which she flew planes from factories to the armed forces. Batson piloted some of the great aircraft of the Second World War, including the twin-engine, twin-tail Lockheed P-38s and the massive Republic P-47s. (Courtesy Nancy Batson Crews' private collection, via Sarah Rickman)

Hargrove Road. A *Birmingham News* reporter joked that a full day and a road map were needed to go through the maze of interconnected buildings, which would eventually number more than a hundred. Its original 2,000 beds and staff of over 2,300 civilians and military personnel would prove inadequate. By the end of the war, some 3,900 patients were receiving care and some 12,000 had already come and gone. The press was proud that a fifth of those were Alabamians—but that meant that over 9,500 patients were not. And those were in addition to the hundreds of officers, Women's Army Corps nurses, and others at the hospital who came from out of town. One congressman called Northington General "Alabama's most important war-time establishment."

Tuscaloosans had seen outsiders come to town before, from Creek Indians to Union prisoners to Chinese workers. This war had already brought cadets from Britain and France as well as Americans from every state. And then came the German prisoners of war. They worked in Northington General's kitchens and laundries from Germany's surrender until the hospital was deactivated a year later. One Tuscaloosan remembered seeing the prisoners "sullenly staring at passersby" from behind the barbed wire fence surrounding their temporary houses on Fifteenth Street. When all were counted—the wounded, the hospital staff, the flight students, those training at the university, the German prisoners, and others—something on the order of thirty thousand people, mostly young men, saw Tuscaloosa for the first time during the war.

And many Tuscaloosans were seeing the world for the first time. The Warrior Guards had been to Mexico during the Mexican War, northern Virginia during the Civil War, and in 1916 had been sent out west to find Pancho Villa. No sooner had they returned, than the United States declared war, and they, along with perhaps eighteen hundred others from Tuscaloosa County, went into the army or navy. Forty-five oak trees were planted along University Boulevard to memorialize those who never returned from the First World War. Participation in the Second World War would dwarf those numbers. Seventy-five hundred from Tuscaloosa County—more than four times as many as during the First World War—would wear uniforms. And at the University of Alabama, about 6,000 students and alumni would serve, many leaving to join before graduating. Some 325 of those had fought on the gridiron for Bama before joining to fight overseas for their country. And nearly 100 members of the faculty enlisted. Of those 6,000 former students in uniform, 343 men and 1 woman would not return.

Everyone left behind "was worried about your family that was in the war," recalled Mary Morris, a nurse at Northington. "We didn't talk about it." After listening intently as CBS and NBC broadcast the D-Day landings on radio, many Tuscaloosans gathered at church to sing and pray. Those included Nancy Hughes of the Bethany community, a mother of three whose husband and five brothers went to war. "It was a gloomy picture, but we had to make the most of it." When the war ended in 1945, many of those Tuscaloosans who returned—and too many did not—had seen atrocities that they could never have imagined.

The postwar years were good for Tuscaloosa. Enrollment at the University of Alabama reached nearly ten thousand by 1948, almost double what it had been in

ABAMA INSTITU
ERONAUTICS
TUSCALOOSA, ALA

Above: Some 13,000 servicemen from all over the country and the free world trained at the university. (Courtesy The University of Alabama Libraries Special Collections) **Right:** Six Crimson Tide players join the Marines at halftime during Bama's last home game of the 1942 season. (Courtesy Paul W. Bryant Museum, University of Alabama)

1941. Jobs were plentiful, contrary to predictions, in the manufacturing industries that had geared up during the war. Even more jobs were to be had in constructing the houses needed by all the young people getting married. Most of these homes had to be built increasingly farther away from downtown, thus accelerating people's dependence on the automobile and the popularity of shopping centers. The city's population again jumped, from twenty-seven thousand immediately before the war to forty thousand in 1950.

THIS GENERATION had been through a lot—first a depression lasting a dozen years and then a world war lasting an interminable four. When called upon to defend both their own country and their allies', they stepped forward only to endure wretched conditions in unfamiliar places, often with unpronounceable names. They lost friends and family. They saw ghastly horrors committed in the name of twisted ideologies—Fascism, Nazism, and Japanese imperialism—that extolled the superiority of their own races while denouncing American ideals of equality and freedom. As a result, many soldiers returned uncomfortable with what some called the American Dilemma: the contradiction between, on the one hand, the shared values of individualism, civil liberties, and equality of opportunity that held Americans together and, on the other, a racially segregated society that kept Americans apart by law.

The American Dilemma had become an ever-increasing part of life in Tuscaloosa since the days of Ryland Randolph and Shandy Jones. The 1901 Alabama Constitution had been explicitly, and successfully, drafted to prevent black Alabamians from voting and entering political office. More

The Weather

The Tuscaloosa News

Born In 1818

GIRL THOUGHT MURDERED BY 'FRIEND'

INSTALLMENTS ON WAR DEBTS TOTAL ONLY 9 PER CENT

More Wages, Less Hours Aim Of Industrial Chief

VETS AGREEMENT SUSTAINED WHEN DEMOCRATS VOTE

FOUR PRISONERS ESCAPE FROM GREENSBORO JAIL

DELEGATES PICK COX AS HEAD OF MONETARY GROUP

Monetary Chairman

JAMES M. COX

DEPUTIES SEARCH COMMUNITY FOR CLUES TO MURDER

GUS RAIFORD, 46, KILLED IN FALL FROM WINDOW

GRAVES IS ONLY ONE NOMINATED TO HEAD LEGION

FIRE ENDANGERS SUMMER HOME OF PRESIDENT'S SON

POTTER DEFEATED IN $100,000 SUIT AGAINST SHERIFF

The Daily Washington Merry-Go-Round

FLAPPER FANNY SAYS

MERCURY GOES TO 53 AS COOL SPELL CONTINUES

R. O. T. C. CAMP IS CUT DOWN TO FOUR WEEKS

The murder of Vaudine Maddox and its aftermath showed the worst violence of white vigilantes during the Jim Crow era. (From the *Tuscaloosa News*)

than that, it was part of a larger plan to dampen educational, social, and economic opportunities for black citizens while emboldening white Alabamians. A second Ku Klux Klan emerged when in 1915 an Alabamian burned a cross atop Stone Mountain in Georgia. This new Klan was initially concerned with the influx of immigrants coming to America but soon turned its attention elsewhere.

Extralegal violence betrayed a stark racial bias. Of the 138 victims of lynching in Alabama from 1900 to 1921, all but five were black Alabamians. Tuscaloosa County had become a particularly violent place by the early 1930s. This would culminate in June 1933 when Vaudine Maddox was murdered in Big Sandy, a dozen miles down the Greensboro Road. Three young black men were arrested, jailed, and charged with rape and murder—despite alibis, physical disabilities, and records of faithful church attendance. A mob of some three hundred men came to Tuscaloosa to get at the accused but were turned away by the circuit judge and sheriff.

While the mob bided its time, three lawyers from the International Labor Defense (ILD) arrived in Tuscaloosa. The ILD, established as the legal advocacy branch of the American Communist Party, achieved international renown in 1921 by defending the anarchists Nicola Sacco and Bartolomeo Vanzetti in their bitterly controversial murder trial. The ILD lawyers arrived at the Tuscaloosa courthouse not long after defending the Scottsboro Boys in a sensational rape case that they would appeal all the way to the U.S. Supreme Court. Several hundred gathered outside the courtroom "to mumble to each other about those Communists from the North" who came to defend the three accused of murdering Vaudine Maddox. The governor sensed a riot in the making and ordered National Guardsmen to disperse the growing mob with tear gas. The ILD lawyers left that afternoon on the train.

Before the trial was set to open on August 22, the circuit judge sent the three prisoners to Birmingham to protect them. They would never make it. The deputies and prisoners had traveled about half the way when they came across a dozen hooded and armed individuals blocking the road. The three prisoners were forced out of the car and the deputies told to

Every new development in the Vaudine Maddox murder case and the events that followed was announced with banner headlines on the front page of the *Tuscaloosa News*. (From the *Tuscaloosa News*)

The Tuscaloosa News
VOL. CIX—NO. 144. TUSCALOOSA, ALA., FRIDAY, JUNE 16, 1933. PRICE FIVE CENTS
NEGRO JAILED AS ATTACK SUSPECT
HISTORY MAKING SPECIAL SESSION CONCLUDES TODAY
Congress' Achievements Unequalled In History
GERMANS SEEK COLONIAL EMPIRE AT WORLD MEET
THREE MEASURES OF VAST IMPORT SIGNED INTO LAW
YOUTH OF 20 WHO LIVES NEAR SITE OF CRIME, TAKEN
OUTLAWS KIDNAP SHERIFF; LEAVE IN AUTOMOBILE
PLANS APPROVED FOR 25 MILLION IN PUBLIC WORKS

EXTRA The Tus[caloosa News]
MASKED B[...]
MADDOX C[...]
Pippen, Harden, Cla[...]

The Tuscaloosa News
VOL. CIX—NO. 146. TUSCALOOSA, ALA., MONDAY, JUNE 19, 1933. PRICE FIVE CENTS
NEGRO SAYS HE SAW GIRL MURDERED
Huge Cotton Leasing Project Announced
YOUTH, 15 CLAIMS PIPPEN ATTACKED VAUDINE MADDOX
GIGANTIC SCHEME TO HELP GROWERS EMBRACES SOUTH
FRENCH HINT FOR ADJOURNMENT OF ECONOMIC PARLEY
KIDNAPED BREWER RELEASED UNHURT BIG RANSOM PAID
FIVE KILLED AS GANG BATTLES OFFICERS
DR. W. J. COOPER OPENS CAPSTONE EDUCATION MEET

keep going. Two of the three prisoners were found the next morning just across the Bibb County line, their bodies full of bullet holes. The third, Elmore Clark, was discovered the following day in Vance, recuperating from three gunshot wounds. Judge Henry Foster called in 125 National Guardsmen to protect Clark. They were soon stretching barbed wire around the Tuscaloosa courthouse, giving it "the appearance of a military fort."

Responsibility for the murder of the two prisoners, and the attempted murder of the third, immediately fell on—of all people—the ILD lawyers. "There was a threat of grave disorder in Tuscaloosa," observed Judge Foster, "and it all is the fault of the International Labor Defense." Had the ILD not gotten involved, "I am confident there would have been no lynchings."

Letters published in the *Tuscaloosa News* were even more direct, asking God's forgiveness for the carpetbaggers who had "returned lynching to our midst" because forgiving them is something that "human hearts cannot." Another accused the ILD of deliberately making the defendants into dead martyrs to advance "a mock Cause." A grand jury would conclude in early October that it lacked sufficient evidence to bring an indictment for the shootings.

But outrage over the lynchings and subsequent failure to take responsibility began to get the attention of important individuals, organizations, and newspapers. First the governor put up a reward for the lynchers' arrest and conviction. Then newspapers added their say. "Alabama is put to shame by a lynching," wrote the *Birmingham News*, and once again "it is

August headlines on the front page of the *Tuscaloosa News* report on the progress of the grand jury investigation into the the lynchings. The front page of the October 3 issue (bottom), reports the ultimate failure to bring any charges. (From the *Tuscaloosa News*)

SHALL WE ACCEPT THE CHALLENGE? *(excerpted from original article) Tuscaloosa is a proud city, her citizens are a proud people. We are very much like a well bred family which suffers long and silently rather than wash its dirty linen before the public gaze, but there comes a time when patience ceases to be a virtue and the choice between self humiliation and the continued living in filth must be made.*

Within the span of six days ending Sunday morning, three murders were committed, two in the city and one in the county.

We cannot permit present conditions to continue, for it offers a great peril both to individuals and the people as a whole. When a band of men, taking law into its own hands, escapes without penalty, will it not be more apt to repeat its performance? Will it not inspire other bands with a similar daring? Will these men, bearing a grudge, not outrage an innocent man, black or white, whose sole offense is a personal one?

Failure of the law abiding to accept the challenge of the lawless can no longer be construed as anything less than condoning the flouting of the law, and to that extent becoming parties to the crimes committed. So far as THE NEWS is concerned our conscience, and our self respect demands that we no longer accept the judgement of some of the finest and most honorable leaders in our public life that "the less said about the problems we face the easier it will be to solve them and the better it will be for all."

—*W. Bruce Shelton,*
"Shall We Accept the Challenge,"
Tuscaloosa News, *September 27, 1933*

The Tuscaloosa News
TUSCALOOSA, ALA., WEDNESDAY, AUGUST 16, 1933
GRAND JURY VISITS LYNCHING SCENE
PRESIDENT TAKES HELM ON CODES OF CHIEF INDUSTRIES
POISONING OF 4 IS ADMITTED BY AKRON ATTORNEY
PROPERTY PROBE OF MACHADO MEN BEING LAUNCHED
Clark Gives Sworn Statement, Mob Had 'Drop' On Deputies
ORDERS BULLETS TO BE TAKEN FROM BODY OF PIPPEN
JOHNSON ACCEPTS TEMPORARY CODE FOR NEWSPAPERS
PATROL LIFTED AT COURTHOUSE, HOLIDAY IS ENDED

The Tuscaloosa News
TUSCALOOSA, ALA., THURSDAY, AUGUST 17, 1933.
GRAND JURY CALLED BACK MONDAY
220,000 Jobs For Idle Sought In Alabama
JUDGE OVERRIDES 17-DAY RECESS IN LYNCHING INQUIRY
DETAILS OF BANK CRISIS BARED BY
COTTON FARMERS TO REPAY TENTH

The Tuscaloosa News
TUSCALOOSA, ALA., MONDAY, OCTOBER 2, 1933.
'MAY RUN FOR GOVERNOR', DR. DENNY
Grand Jury Reports 'No Bill' In Lynching
EVIDENCE IS NOT THOUGHT ENOUGH FOR INDICTMENT
Ministers Urge All Citizens To Enlist In Crime Crusade
20 SOLDIERS DIE AS GUNS BLAZE IN HAVANA STREETS
UNIVERSITY HEAD TO ENTER RACE IN MAY, HE BELIEVES
QUAKE INJURES 4 AT LOS ANGELES; DAMAGE IS LIGHT
NEGRO MURDERED IN NORTHPORT AS HE TRIES TO FLEE

Tuscaloosa County that is the scene of the outrage." Women's clubs and then men's organizations started to voice their disgust. The Southern Commission on the Study of Lynching published a report, *The Plight of Tuscaloosa: A Case Study of Conditions in Tuscaloosa, County, Alabama, 1933.* Finally bowing to pressure, W. Bruce Shelton, editor and publisher of the *Tuscaloosa News*, wrote a front-page editorial entitled "Shall We Accept the Challenge?" (This would not be the last time that the *News* published a front-page editorial on the consequences of racial violence.) The editorial called for a return to order—a point that would be heard again—and urged local organizations to take responsibility for purging the community of violence.

While all this was going on, Dennis Cross was accused of tearing the dress of Alice Johnson, an eighteen-year-old member of a poor white farm family. A black man who had to be dressed and undressed by his brother, the forty-nine-year-old former coal miner had not worked in the four years since a stroke left him partially paralyzed. On September 24, Cross was awakened by seven men claiming to be police officers; driven to the Black Warrior River, where the assault was alleged to have occurred; and shot dead.

"Tuscaloosa is 'on the spot' before the eyes of the world," warned the County Council Against Crime. And in a sense, the eyes of the world were never diverted. Outrage over the lynchings following the Vaudine Maddox murder—horrific as they were—did fade with time. But the lynching of the partially paralyzed Dennis Cross did not. *To Kill a Mockingbird* eerily recounts the story of Tom Robinson, a crippled black man wrongly accused of raping a nineteen-year-old from a poor white farm family. And while Atticus Finch turns the lynch mob away before the trial, Robinson would also be shot dead—by prison guards. Harper Lee, the book's author, entered the University of Alabama only a dozen years after Cross was killed nearby.

Young black men returning from the Second World War had a newfound confidence needed to confront the laws and social mores that gave rise to such outrages. Having once faced murderous armies overseas, they refused to yield when back in the States. Small things that would once have been ignored would no longer be tolerated. Tuscaloosans sensed that something new was afoot when they read of Jackie Robinson joining the Brooklyn Dodgers in 1947. President Harry S Truman mandated equal treatment in the armed services the following year. Then came the pivotal 1954 *Brown v. Board of Education* Supreme Court decision

Autherine Lucy's arrival for classes at the University of Alabama in February 1956 provoked the first successful violent resistance to the Supreme Court's decision outlawing racial segregation. (Courtesy The University of Alabama Libraries Special Collections)

reversing its "separate but equal" ruling in *Plessy v. Ferguson*. Only a year and a half later, the nation's eyes would be watching Tuscaloosans test the *Brown* decision.

Autherine Lucy finally learned that she had been accepted into the University of Alabama on January 29, 1956. (The next night, during the second month of the Montgomery Bus Boycott, the home of Martin Luther King Jr. would be bombed.) Lucy had first applied—and been accepted—to study librarianship. But that was before the university learned of her race. After her case wound through the courts for nearly three and a half years, she arrived in Tuscaloosa on February 3 to begin attending classes. Lucy spoke to the over two hundred reporters at the end of the day, admitting that one student had indignantly walked out of her first class that Friday. Some students sat alongside her during her second class and even wished her well. But the mood was changing after she left to return home to Birmingham.

After eleven that evening, fraternity boys set afire a small cross of sticks wrapped in socks. Soon a crowd marched to the President's Mansion. Mrs. O. C. Carmichael addressed them there, explaining that her husband was in New Orleans. Chanting "Keep Bama White" and singing "Dixie," some five hundred protestors then moved down University Boulevard to the flagpole at the intersection with Greensboro Avenue. There Leonard Wilson, a student and member of

Saturday evening, 1956, protestors burned desegregation literature in front of the student union building. (Courtesy The University of Alabama Libraries Special Collections)

Klansmen were conspicuous during the Autherine Lucy protests. (Courtesy The University of Alabama Libraries Special Collections)

the White Citizens' Council, rallied them against desegregation and urged them to meet again the following night after the basketball game.

Lucy attended classes Saturday morning and then headed back to Birmingham again, all without incident. But after the Alabama basketball team trounced rival Georgia Tech that evening, students headed over to the quad to watch another burning cross. Shouts of "Keep Bama White" and "To hell with Autherine" were even louder than the night before. Older men, clearly not students, swelled this crowd to an estimated two thousand. Ku Klux Klansmen were milling about. Marching again to the center of town, the angry protestors violently rocked a Greyhound bus until the frightened driver and passengers escaped. Confederate battle flags and clinched fists were prominent. Leonard Wilson once again baited the crowd from his perch on the flagpole, urging that they all assemble at Smith Hall on Monday morning as Lucy entered her first class. The crowd headed back to campus calling for President Carmichael. He addressed the estimated twelve hundred to fourteen hundred protestors from the balcony of the President's Mansion. His

Buford Boone, publisher of the *Tuscaloosa News*, won the Pulitzer Prize for his front-page editorial after the Autherine Lucy debacle. (Courtesy Calvin Hannah and Boone Newspapers, Inc.)

WHAT A PRICE FOR PEACE—AN EDITORIAL

When mobs start imposing their frenzied will on universities, we have a bad situation.

But that is what has happened at the University of Alabama. And it is a development over which the University of Alabama, the people of this state and the community of Tuscaloosa should be deeply ashamed—and more than a little afraid.

Our government's authority springs from the will of the people. But their wishes, if we are to be guided by democratic processes, must be expressed by ballot at the polls, by action in the legislative halls, and finally by interpretation from the bench. No intelligent expression ever has come from a crazed mob, and it never will.

And make no mistake. There was a mob, in the worst sense, at the University of Alabama yesterday.

Every person who witnessed the events there with comparative detachment speaks of the tragic nearness with which our great University came to being associated with a murder—yes, we say murder.

"If they could have gotten their hands on her, they would have killed her."

That was the considered judgment, often expressed, of many who watched the action without participating in it.

The target was Auth[e]rine Lucy. Her "crimes"? She was born black, and she was moving against Southern custom and tradition—but with the law, right on up to the United States Supreme Court, on her side.

What does it mean today at the University of Alabama, and here in Tuscaloosa, to have the law on your side?

The answer has to be: Nothing—that is, if a mob disagrees with you and the courts.

As matters now stand, the University administration and trustees have knuckled under to the pressures and desires of a mob. What is to keep the same mob, if uncontrolled again, from taking over in any other field where it decides to impose its wishes? Apparently, nothing.

What is the answer to a mob? We think that is clear. It lies in firm, decisive action. It lies in the use of whatever force is necessary to restrain and subdue anyone who is violating the law.

Not a single University student has been arrested on the campus and that is no indictment against the men in uniform, but against higher levels which failed to give them clea[r]-cut authority to go along with responsibility.

What has happened here is far more important than whether a Negro girl is admitted to the University. We have a breakdown of law and order, an abject surrender to what is expedient rather than a courageous stand for what is right.

Yes, there's peace on the University campus this morning. But what a price has been paid for it!

—*Buford Boone, "What a Price for Peace,"* Tuscaloosa News, *February 7, 1957* words were drowned out by shouts and the popping of camera flashbulbs.

Reading their Sunday papers over breakfast the next morning, Americans learned of the chaos. The accompanying photographs, sent by wire, made a more lasting impression than the journalists' reports. One image showed President Carmichael pleading for the protestors to stop. Another was of an inebriated fraternity boy stomping on the roof of a frightened black man's car. Back in Tuscaloosa, President Carmichael warned protesting students that they faced punishment and set up meetings with faculty and students.

The climax came on Monday, February 6. Lucy entered Smith Hall for her first class. The crowd of protestors outside quickly turned into an angry mob. Under a hail of gravel and eggs, university officials managed to get her into a car and over to her next class across campus. The mob by this time had perhaps swollen to well over a thousand. Many of these were workers from Central Foundry and the Goodrich tire plant. Protestors had also come from Birmingham and even Mississippi, Tennessee, and Georgia. Lucy remained trapped for several hours on an upper floor of the education library. When a fortuitous altercation distracted the crowd's attention, Lucy escaped into a police car that sped off in the opposite direction. A couple of hours later she was on her way to Birmingham. That evening's demonstrations followed a now familiar pattern: marching to the flagpole, speeches, marching back to the President's Mansion, Mrs. Carmichael pleading with the crowd to disperse, and the crowd drowning out her words before throwing rocks and eggs. President Carmichael was not on campus because at that moment he was meeting with the trustees in a downtown Tuscaloosa hotel. There they voted to "exclude Autherine Lucy until further notice from attending the University of Alabama."

In the wee hours of that night, *Tuscaloosa News* editor and publisher Buford Boone sat down before his typewriter. "What a Price for Peace" appeared, like "Shall We Accept the Challenge?," on the front page. Lucy's "crime," he boldly stated, was that she was born black and decided to move against Southern custom and tradition, "but with the law, right up to the United States Supreme Court, on her side." He then asked, "What does it mean today at the University of Alabama, and here in Tuscaloosa, to have the law on your side? The answer has to be: Nothing—that is, if a mob disagrees with you and the courts." Buford Boone's "What a Price for Peace" would win the *News* its first Pulitzer Prize.

Lucy lost her chances of returning when her attorneys, including future Supreme Court Justice Thurgood Marshall, disregarded advice and sued the university. They alleged that she had not been suspended in the interests of safety as the university claimed; rather, they charged the university, including its trustees, with conspiring "to assimilate the air of riot and disorder and rebellion" by using the protesting students as a ruse to refuse her an education at the University of Alabama. That was enough. When the conspiracy charge could not be proven, the university expelled her. Leonard Wilson, who had led the demonstrations at the flagpole, was also expelled. Thus ended the nation's first successful resistance to the *Brown* decision.

The *Tuscaloosa News* had covered those four days extensively, as had newspapers from across the nation. The university issued over 260 passes to members of the press. Photographs and stories of Saturday's demonstrations were wired across the nation and even across the globe. On Monday while Lucy was trapped in her second class, a reporter from the *Times* of London had tried to reach her by telephone. Radio stations stretching from East Germany through the Soviet Union to North Korea had used her four days at the University of Alabama as propaganda. Lucy went on the Voice of America, a government-funded international radio network, to broadcast her response to the world. She would spend a great deal of time over the following months holding press conferences and giving interviews, consistently maintaining that she was no communist but instead a Christian dedicated to democracy.

The nation followed Autherine Lucy's four days in Tuscaloosa by reading in the newspaper and listening on the radio, but they got little from watching television. John Cameron Swayze made reports on the fifteen-minute NBC evening news program; unfortunately, his report used a film clip from Montgomery mistakenly identified as Tuscaloosa. Dave Garraway on the *Today Show* interviewed the editor of the student newspaper, the *Crimson White*, whose editorials had urged the university to bow to the inevitable and desegregate as the law required. But America never watched any broadcasts of the insults, the marches, the rock throwing, or Lucy's escape.

Television was truly a product of the '50s. Only six stations were in operation by the end of the Second World War. But on that Saturday when Autherine Lucy attended class, about five hundred were operating across the nation. Tuscaloosans read about the programming of Birmingham's two stations in the *Tuscaloosa News* that day alongside Tuscaloosa Furniture's ad for the new Philco twenty-one-inch television with "top-touch tuning." And that evening they could watch *Gunsmoke* and *The Honeymooners*. But they could not watch the events in Tuscaloosa, because the technology was not yet able to broadcast the unfolding events in the hinterlands.

The impact of live broadcasting would become increasingly influential. Popular sporting events dominated from the start. The first Crimson Tide game to be carried live on radio was the 1927 Rose Bowl, but the first game carried live on television was not until 1951 (a loss to Tennessee). Television would build new fans beyond the bleachers—and beyond the city and state—who were able to watch events in the present tense. Television was not merely a supplement to the radio announcer; television created new experiences. By not knowing the outcome, viewers felt that they were actively participating, contributing even, to the unfolding events. Critics complained that television dulled the senses, isolated people in their homes, enthroned mediocrity, was addictive, and worse. Yet the immediacy of television could also be used as a tool for enlisting support in various causes—a fact not lost on politicians and civil rights leaders.

Television had reached nearly a third of American homes by 1952 and 90 percent of American homes by 1963. That summer on the *CBS Evening News with Walter Cronkite* and NBC's *Huntley-Brinkley Report*, Americans watched as Eugene "Bull" Connor directed fire hoses and attack dogs against children in Birmingham, as Martin Luther King Jr. delivered his "I Have a Dream" speech at the Lincoln Memorial, and as family and friends grieved following the killing of four young girls when Birmingham's Sixteenth Street Baptist Church was bombed. They also watched events playing out in Tuscaloosa, when once again an attractive and articulate young black woman came to the University of Alabama. Unlike the chaos surrounding Autherine Lucy's four days on campus, however, this incident would be carefully orchestrated.

The curtain for this drama known as the Stand in the Schoolhouse Door—and indeed, the confrontation would be theatrical—rose with George C. Wallace's repeated campaign pledge "to stand in the schoolhouse door" to prevent integration. "Segregation now, segregation tomorrow, segregation forever," he vowed at his January 1963 inauguration. Governor Wallace raised the stakes after Vivian Malone and James Hood, two exceptionally courteous young people, were accepted to enroll. He appeared June 2 on NBC's *Meet the Press* at their invitation. Wallace found the television cameras stimulating and, by easily neutralizing every question the reporters posed, came across as a masterful intellectual jouster. When a federal judge barred Wallace from standing in the way of the two students' enrolling, Wallace noted that the judge had not barred him from coming to the campus. And when the Kennedy administration reached out to the governor in hopes of defusing the situation, Wallace refused to answer their phone calls.

While the governor stoked the segregationists' fires, others prepared to avoid a repeat of February 1956. *Tuscaloosa News* editor Buford Boone, who had been writing about the inevitability of desegregating the university since his Pulitzer Prize–winning

Deputy Attorney General Nicholas Katzenbach first asked Governor George C. Wallace politely to allow Vivian Malone and James Hood entrance into Foster Auditorium to register as students. Wallace interrupted him with "we don't need your speech," and held his ground. After Katzenbach's fourth request, Wallace folded his arms, jutted out his chin, and stared straight ahead. (*Birmingham News* photograph courtesy Alabama Department of Archives and History)

After President John F. Kennedy federalized the Alabama National Guard, Governor Wallace was asked "to step aside, on order of the President of the United States." Vivian Malone and James Hood then entered to register as "a forest of TV cameras and scores of reporters" recorded the historic event. (Courtesy Library of Congress)

editorial, met with fellow editors, businessmen, industrialists, and even Coach Bryant (who had led the Crimson Tide to the first of his six national championships a year and a half before). All agreed that the end of segregation was at hand and that upholding order and the rule of law was paramount. And no one wanted Tuscaloosa, Alabama, to become another Oxford, Mississippi. There a 1962 riot protesting the first black student at Ole Miss had ended with two men shot, one of them a French journalist. In the White House, President John F. Kennedy and his brother, Attorney General Robert F. Kennedy, turned to their deputy attorney general, the lanky Nicholas Katzenbach, to deal with the situation on the Alabama campus. The three believed that Wallace did not want to provoke violence but that he did want a nonviolent confrontation of some sort.

Everyone prepared for an invasion by the news media. The administration arranged for a worldwide communications system that included direct lines to the White House. Buford Boone leased the now vacant former *Tuscaloosa News* building (strategically off campus) for the university to use in accommodating the 324 registered members of the media, two-thirds of whom came from outside Alabama. The old newsroom was quickly outfitted with telephones, telegraphs, darkrooms, and—most importantly—air conditioners. Some of America's finest journalists were coming to Tuscaloosa. The *New York Times* sent two reporters as did the *Washington Post*. But once again, the story wasn't confined to the United States. Reporters also arrived from Japan, the Netherlands, South Korea, and Britain (which sent eight). Five Tuscaloosa radio stations were on hand for live coverage. Television cameras stood ready; but in recognition of the new medium's power and the uncertainty surrounding Wallace's behavior, live broadcasts were disallowed.

At last came the main event. The day: June 11, 1963. The place: Foster Auditorium. The atmosphere: overheated, with sky-high humidity and the thermometer reading nearly one hundred degrees. The actors: a governor, deputy attorney general, and two students. A Greek chorus of reporters and film crews stood to the side.

The governor had chalk lines drawn prescribing where everyone should stand when the two students came to register. Katzenbach was annoyed "to be cast in a supporting role to Wallace," as he recounted later. Refusing the reporters' pleas to speak into the television microphones, Katzenbach approached the schoolhouse door.

Wallace, the five-foot-seven former state boxing champion, stood in the shade having just emerged from an air-conditioned room. He held his left hand up "like a traffic cop" to stop Katzenbach, the six-foot former B-25 navigator and POW. As the television cameras rolled and sweat dripped off the deputy attorney general standing in the intense sun, the governor read from a prepared speech ending with "I . . . hereby denounce and forbid this illegal and unwarranted action by the central government." Several times Katzenbach asked Wallace to reconsider but was met with stony silence. And with that, Katzenbach walked Vivian Malone to her dormitory, where she was warmly greeted by the house mother. After going through the cafeteria line at lunch, she sat alone before two young women joined her. Meanwhile James Hood got settled in his dormitory.

A smiling Vivian Malone, now a registered student at the University of Alabama, leaves Foster Auditorium as the media is held at bay. (Courtesy Alabama Department of Archives and History)

President Kennedy then ordered the Alabama National Guard into federal service and General Henry Graham to Tuscaloosa. Graham in turn ordered a hundred armed infantry to campus. At three thirty he waded through what Katzenbach described as "a forest of TV cameras and scores of reporters," saluted the governor, and spoke. "It is my sad duty to ask you to step aside, on order of the President of the United States." Wallace then uttered a parting shot at "federal interference," turned, and got into his car. Pulling away he invited the press to "come back to see us in Alabama." Vivian Malone and James Hood entered, registered, and fifteen minutes later walked out as University of Alabama students.

Americans watched their televisions that evening as Chet Huntley and David Brinkley on NBC and Walter Cronkite on

James Hood studied at the University of Alabama for only two months following his enrollment. He returned to the university three years later to attend Emphasis '66, an SGA program on the subject of students in a democratic society. The featured speaker was Robert F. Kennedy, seen here shaking hands with Hood. (Courtesy The University of Alabama Libraries Special Collections)

CBS reported on the incident over film footage. They stayed tuned to watch the president speak to the nation an hour later. Kennedy sat behind his desk in the Oval Office unsmiling. He began by recounting the university's admission that afternoon "of two clearly qualified young Alabama residents who happened to have been born Negro." He then moved on to larger issues. The university's integration, he said, should be understood as an example of the "worldwide struggle to promote and protect the rights of all who wish to be free." The basic point was that "every American ought to have the right to be treated as he would wish to be treated, as one would wish his children to be treated." After recounting the educational, financial, and health discrepancies between the races in America, the president insisted that inequality based on race is neither a sectional nor partisan issue; "is not even a legal or legislative issue alone, [for] law alone cannot make men see right. . . . We are confronted primarily with a moral issue. It is as old as the Scriptures and is as clear as the American Constitution." The "heart of the question," he insisted, "is whether all Americans are to be afforded equal rights and equal opportunities" in this, the centennial year of the Emancipation Proclamation. Kennedy's landmark speech in response to the Stand in the Schoolhouse Door marked a decisive turn. He asked Congress to enact civil rights legislation and directed the Justice Department to pursue illegal segregation in the courts.

But Kennedy lay dead that November. James Hood was gone before September but would return to earn his doctorate in 1997. Vivian Malone graduated in the spring of 1965 and shortly afterward married Stillman College alumnus and future physician Mack Jones. After serving in several capacities in government supporting civil rights, she was chosen by the George Wallace Family Foundation as the first recipient of the Lurleen B. Wallace Award of Courage. Autherine Lucy married divinity student Hugh Foster in 1956 and lived elsewhere before moving back to Alabama with her family in 1974. She earned her master's degree from the University of Alabama in 1992 and sent two of her children there. The Malone-Hood Plaza outside of Foster Auditorium and facing the schoolhouse door was dedicated in 2010. In the center of the plaza stands the forty-foot Autherine Lucy Clock Tower.

ENDING SEGREGATION at the University of Alabama did not end segregation in Tuscaloosa. Water fountains, restaurants, hotels, drug stores—even waiting rooms at Druid City Hospital—were all divided by race. "When black people went to buy shoes," recalled Louise Crawford, "they were not allowed to try the shoes on; they had to measure their foot size with a string." Only whites could swim in the Queen City Pool. "That's all I knew," was the judgment of Dr. W. N. Dansby, a local dentist, who could have spoken for both black and white Tuscaloosans.

The first steps toward ending segregation began on a city bus, as it had in Montgomery. A white bus driver one day ordered three Stillman College students and one Druid High School student to vacate their front seats for two white passengers. The four refused, noting that this was May of 1962 and that the bus driver's order violated a policy in effect since the Montgomery bus boycott ended in late 1956. The argument grew heated and did not end until the four were arrested and charged with disorderly conduct. A few black ministers and community leaders met that evening to organize the Tuscaloosa Citizens for Action Committee (TCAC). As TCAC's president met with bus line officials, Stillman College students marched and blocked buses approaching the campus. The bus officials assured TCAC and the black community that discrimination and harassment would end. And then Vivian Malone and James Hood stepped through the schoolhouse door in June 1963.

That's where things stood that fall when Tuscaloosa's First African Baptist Church was looking for a new minister. The congregation hired T. Y. Rogers, the former assistant minister at Martin Luther King's Dexter Avenue Baptist Church in Montgomery. Rogers, who had plenty of experience as a civil rights organizer, became deeply involved in TCAC, which launched a nonviolent campaign in April 1964 following the dedication of Tuscaloosa's new county courthouse. The city had assured black Tuscaloosans that the

The signs in the newly constructed Tuscaloosa County Courthouse still specifically divided the citizenry by race in 1964, despite assurances to the contrary. Protestors, mostly Stillman College students, first began marching on April 23. The culmination would come on June 9, Bloody Tuesday. (Courtesy *Tuscaloosa News*)

As pastor of the First African Baptist Church, the Reverend T. Y. Rogers Jr. (second from left) would lead many of the civil rights protests in Tuscaloosa. He led the march against the signs in the new courthouse that culminated in Bloody Tuesday. Rogers would remain pastor of First African Baptist until 1971, when he died in an automobile collision.

seven-story concrete box was not going to have signs reading White and Colored, but when Governor Wallace dedicated the building that spring, the signs were there nonetheless. Those signs quickly came to symbolize not just segregation but the city's lack of good faith. Four days after the dedication, TCAC sent a letter to the probate judge demanding an end to all such signs and discriminatory hiring practices at the courthouse. TCAC called for a boycott of downtown businesses when no changes were forthcoming. "We refuse to spend integrated dollars and receive segregated service," said Reverend Rogers.

THREE HUNDRED PROTESTORS, mostly Stillman students, gathered at the First African Baptist Church on the morning of April 23. They began walking toward downtown in pairs because the Tuscaloosa police had denied TCAC a permit for a parade. Some carried signs reading "Segregation Must Go." They gathered at the steps of the courthouse, where Rogers began reading a statement. The police quickly broke up the demonstration and arrested a few. TCAC responded by ratcheting up the boycott. The Reverend Rogers continued his campaign from the pulpit. "We're gonna march around that wall of segregation," he thundered; and like Jericho's wall, "it's gonna come tumbling down." Attendance at First African Baptist soared. Schools for voter registration were started in six churches and two homes. Ralph David Abernathy and Martin Luther King Jr. came to encourage the protestors. TCAC soon turned to larger issues than just discriminatory signs in the courthouse. When

TCAC sent local officials a letter requesting that segregation in all public buildings—schools, hospitals, hotels, and restaurants—be forever ended, the officials refused even to acknowledge receiving the letter.

Tensions steadily mounted in the early days of June. On the second, protestors attempted without success to eat at lunch counters at Woolworth's, the Kress Five & Dime, and H&W Drugs. All left without incident. The next day, an attempted parade was stopped by the police. The climax came on June 9, which came to be known as Bloody Tuesday. After some staged sit-ins and marches by teenagers, the police chief put an end to further demonstrations. Five hundred college and high school students nonetheless assembled in the First African Baptist Church. The Reverend Rogers then led them out on a march to the downtown businesses about three blocks away. The police chief stopped him after a hundred yards to ask whether he intended to march in defiance of the ban. When Rogers nodded and answered "Yes," he was arrested. The police officers then started pushing the protestors back into the church using cattle prods, nightsticks, and fists. A few of the students responded by throwing rocks and bottles. With that, the police fired teargas into the church, forcing the protestors outside where they were met with more nightsticks and fists. "All bedlam broke loose," reported the pastor's wife, Lepezia Rogers. "We almost suffocated. I saw a couple of people carrying others who had passed out. They wouldn't let us out for about 30 or 45 minutes, after that they came in with their gas masks on." Ninety-four of the demonstrators were arrested and thirty-two injured, some badly, according to a report on the front page of the *New York Times*.

Bloody Tuesday was a turning point. Black men, many of whom had heretofore stayed clear of the protests, were particularly outraged. Dozens immediately armed themselves and even drove downtown that very evening seeking revenge. "I have never in my life seen so many folks walking down the street with shotguns on their shoulders," recalled labor activist Joseph Mallisham. Fearing the worst, he persuaded a few to form a defense organization to protect their fellow black Tuscaloosans. Mallisham had returned fearless from the Korean War, and he had been among the armed defenders of Autherine Lucy. This new defense organization, whose numbers would eventually reach about a hundred, accepted only married veterans who had served in active combat. To avoid publicity, Mallisham insisted that the group never adopt a name. They first set about protecting the home of the Reverend Rogers. Armed guards requested identification and fired at cars whose drivers would not halt. Other TCAC leaders were similarly protected by about ten men each. They even protected a handful

Reverend T. Y. Rogers (second from left) learned the techniques of nonviolent protest as an assistant pastor under Martin Luther King Jr. at Montgomery's Dexter Avenue Baptist Church. In 1968 he served as one of Dr. King's pallbearers along with Andrew Young (immediately to the right of Rogers) and Jesse Jackson (right foreground). (Courtesy Alabama Department of Archives and History)

of white friends, particularly University of Alabama professors.

Subsequent events only inflamed tensions. On June 25, just a bit over two weeks after Bloody Tuesday, federal Judge Seybourn H. Lynne ordered the discriminatory signs removed from the Tuscaloosa courthouse. Two days later, Ku Klux Klansmen held a huge rally, where Imperial Wizard Robert Shelton and others spoke to nearly fifteen hundred cheering segregationists. The Civil Rights Act of

Tuscaloosans on March 13 mourned the assassination of the Reverend James Reeb during the 1965 demonstrations in Selma. Two days later, President Lyndon Johnson would invoke Reeb's name when presenting a draft of the Voting Rights Bill to a joint session of Congress. (Courtesy the *Tuscaloosa News*)

1964, which prohibited racial segregation in public facilities, emboldened black Tuscaloosans when it was enacted on July 2. Several restaurants refused them service on the morning of July 8, but the public library did issue library cards. That evening about seventeen paid for tickets and entered the Druid Theater to watch the Peter Sellers comedy, *The World of Henry Orient*. A crowd of about two hundred were waiting when they left the movie and hurled sticks, stones, and bottles. White men and youths then drove the streets looking to provoke more incidents. Buford Boone penned another front-page editorial in the next day's *Tuscaloosa News*. "The Price of Our Silence" called once again for law and order especially now that desegregation was an accomplished fact.

That evening several hundred rowdy white men returned to the Druid Theater. No black movie-goers were there, but the actor Jack Palance was there with his family (who were in town to visit relatives). According to sources at the time the mob apparently mistook Palance and his wife for a black man with a white woman. Rocks and bottles again soon filled the air, and the police resorted to teargas and water hoses from a fire truck. They handed helmets to Palance, his wife, and three children and escorted them to their rental car—now sporting slashed tires, scratched paint, and a sign that read "The Knights of the Ku Klux Klan is Watching You." Policemen patrolled downtown, and the city commissioners immediately imposed a curfew for minors. By that time Palance and his family were gone from Tuscaloosa. The next day's *Tuscaloosa News* published yet another front-page editorial by Boone.

TCAC returned to the segregated seating problem on the Tuscaloosa buses the following month. Despite the agreement of two years earlier, individual drivers were known to direct verbal, and even physical, abuse at black passengers. After no action by Druid City Transit, TCAC began a bus boycott on August 10. It took only three days before the management laid off more than twenty employees. Three months later, Druid City Transit folded. A new company, Tuscaloosa Transit, started bus services in the spring of 1965, this time with an integrated workforce and a clear policy forbidding discrimination. The need for the Tuscaloosa Citizens for Action Committee was largely over. Their last organized event was a march to protest the death of Episcopal seminarian Jonathan Daniels, who had been involved with the 1965 Selma protests.

Tuscaloosa's school system was a tougher nut to crack. When the 1954 *Brown v. Board of Education* and subsequent decisions overturned legalized segregation, school districts responded by improving black schools in hopes that the federal government would stay out. Druid High and Tuscaloosa High were both constructed about the same time with nearly identical floor plans and costing about the same. But the equality ended there, with better textbooks, furnishings, and more experienced teachers going to the white schools.

Separate-but-equal had its backers in Montgomery. Governor George Wallace successfully pushed a law through the legislature in 1966 that invalidated any local school board's attempts to comply with the Supreme Court's decision. His wife and successor, Tuscaloosa native Lurleen, pushed for laws providing tuition grants to children attending private schools.

That same year, 1967, a U.S. district court ordered all Alabama school districts not already under court order to integrate. Tuscaloosa's solution was to allow parents to pick the schools that their children would attend. Angry black parents staged a two-week sit-in, but Tuscaloosa school officials had already implemented the policy. "I didn't want to go," recalled Deloris Warrick, one of the first black students to attend a white school, "but mom made me. She wanted to make sure we really could attend. She'd been fighting for so long that she wanted me to prove it was real." The freedom-of-choice policy ended up pleasing no one, and in the end only a handful of black students moved over to the white schools—5 percent across the state.

The federal courts then listed Tuscaloosa's school district among the seventy-six in Alabama where freedom-of-choice had failed and ordered that better and faster ways to integrate be implemented. This time it would be the teachers who would move. In the fall of 1968, seventy-seven transferred to different schools. Some complained, with good reason, that the white schools received the best black teachers while the black schools were sent the youngest and least experienced white teachers.

The board of education was ordered the following year to gain a more balanced distribution, this time by moving the children to different schools. Once again, no one seemed pleased. Black parents feared that their children would face discrimination, while many white parents simply did not want the schools integrated. This conflict reached its nadir one day in 1970, when a couple hundred white parents took over a county school scheduled soon to be closed and taught their children there in protest. White enrollment doubled that year in Alabama's private white academies. "It wasn't open resistance," observed Jeanette Bell, then a teacher at Skyland Elementary, but rather "quiet decisions." A compromise of sorts was reached in 1981 when the courts allowed some Tuscaloosa elementary schools to remain all-black, thus sidestepping many of the problems that massive busing and school closings brought.

With a shrinking student population and white flight blamed on federal oversight, the Department of Justice, NAACP Legal Defense Fund, and the Tuscaloosa City Board of Education reached a compromise in 1998 that lifted the federal court supervision in place since 1970. In return for being allowed to control such matters as student and personnel assignments, transportation, physical facilities, and allocation of resources, the school board agreed to adopt plans for special needs and honors education, student discipline, and retention problems. Sixty Tuscaloosans formally objected. "I can't understand why we want to settle for this," argued Chykeitha Roshell. "They have not desegregated the schools. Is George Wallace still standing in the doorway?" But Judge Sharon Blackburn of the federal district court went ahead and verbally granted unitary status, which was formally confirmed in 2000. Three decades of direct federal intervention ended. Single-grade schools were immediately replaced with neighborhood schools, zone lines changed, and new construction projects started as the school board turned its attention to other problems.

Breaking the segregated city government was yet another problem. Black voters had helped to elect Jerry Barnes to the board of aldermen in the 1870s. But the system of at-large voting put in place as a result made that unlikely to happen again. Black representation was made nearly impossible by the whites-only primary and by the reduction of the ten aldermen to three commissioners about 1911. The system of three commissioners, including the mayor, stayed in place until the 1980s. By that time the city became open to lawsuits challenging at-large voting as unconstitutionally depriving minorities of equal opportunity. In consultation with local black leaders, the Tuscaloosa County legislative delegation introduced a bill to replace the three-member commission government, elected at large, with a government of one mayor elected at large and seven council members elected by districts. And in October 1985 Charles Steele and John England, who would later serve as an Alabama Supreme Court associate justice, became the city's first black office holders since Jerry Barnes.

John H. England Jr., a graduate of Tuskegee University, was one of the first black students admitted to the University of Alabama School of Law. In 1985 he was elected to the first of two terms on the Tuscaloosa City Council, and later served on the Alabama Supreme Court. (Courtesy the Collection of the Alabama Supreme Court and State Law Library)

THE SCRUTINY OF THE TELEVISION camera had played a large part in wrenching Tuscaloosans off their time-worn paths. Other inventions—air-conditioning, computers, and the internet—would continue to bring changes as the twentieth century unfolded.

During the transformation of everyday life that began in the 1870s, only the electric fan had made any sort of dent in the South's perennial problem of oppressive heat and humidity. And it was only a dent. The problem was most keenly felt in movie theaters. Windows needed to be kept shut to dampen the noise and light, but that turned the theater into an unbearably hot oven. It was hardly surprising then that Tuscaloosa's three movie theaters were among the first businesses to experiment with placing blocks of ice in front of their electric fans. The Bama Theatre, built in 1938, was Tuscaloosa's first air-conditioned building of any kind, and it would have been more remarkable had a rudimentary air-conditioning system not been installed in a Montgomery movie theater over twenty years before.

Southerners flocked to buy the box window units that became available after the Second World War. Over a million were sold in 1953 alone. A dozen years later, whole-house air conditioners were becoming standard in new houses. "The greatest contribution to civilization in this century may well be air-conditioning," wrote the British scholar S. F. Markham in 1947, "and America leads the way." While Markham's prediction was a bit extreme and all-encompassing, the introduction of cooled dry air would nonetheless bring far-reaching changes to the South and with it Tuscaloosa. Store owners and office managers rushed to install air conditioners after studies repeatedly demonstrated that their employees' efficiency and productivity improved during the summer months. New houses dispensed with the traditional grand front porches, or they became mostly decorative. Neighbors saw less of each other as they spent more time watching television in their dens and living rooms.

Air-conditioning would also make summers in the South bearable to those

The Bama Theatre was the first building in Tuscaloosa to offer its patrons the comfort of air-conditioning. (Courtesy Skip Baumhower)

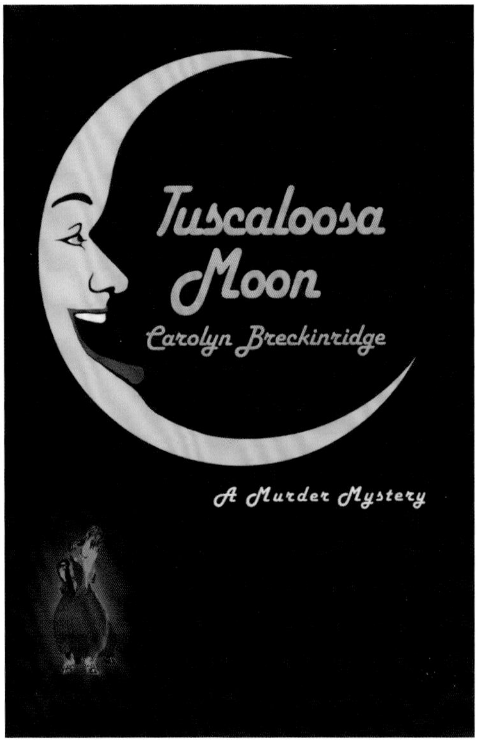

Far Left: Cover of *Tuscaloosa Sam or Life in the Wilds* by W. J. Hamilton (Published by the Arthur Westbrook Company, Cleveland, Ohio, 1909)
Left: Cover of *Tuscaloosa Moon* by Carolyn Breckinridge (Courtesy Carolyn Breckinridge)

"A DESTINATION FOR DREAMERS"

Tuscaloosa has captured the imagination of untold numbers. Perhaps it all began with the mystery surrounding the Indian chief who nearly destroyed Hernando de Soto's 1540 expedition—and then was never heard from again. That simple story just wouldn't do for Albert J. Pickett, an historian writing three centuries later. Out of his imagination came a Chief Tuscaloosa of "gigantic proportions . . . a head taller than any of his attendants." The imaginative possibilities continue today with Carolyn Breckinridge's 2013 murder mystery, Tuscaloosa Moon.

Or perhaps part of the attraction to Tuscaloosa comes from the word itself, the way if flows off the tongue. Tuscaloosa Sam *(what a name!) was the title and lead character of an 1867 dime novel set on the Mexican border of west Texas; Alabama is never mentioned. Then there are the puns. The explorer Captain Spaulding (Groucho Marx in the 1930 madcap comedy* Animal Crackers*) preferred Alabama elephants because the Tusks-are-loosa.*

But even more than the mysteries and the sound of the name, people seem to get more nostalgic for Tuscaloosa the farther and longer they are away. In a 1906 article, one fellow coined the term "Tuscaloosa Idea" to describe his determination to get back as soon as he could to the banks of the Black Warrior. The Tuscaloosa Idea subsequently found its way into songs: "Hey Gus, is that the bus to Tuscaloosa?" asked Johnny Mercer in his 1944 hit, "Tuscaloosa Bus." John Forsythe sang "Flaggin' the Train to Tuscaloosa" in Alfred Hitchcock's 1955 black comedy, The Trouble with Harry. *And the title of the 1976 off-Broadway musical,* Tuscaloosa's Calling Me, *captured the Tuscaloosa Idea perfectly—except for its subtitle:* But I'm Not Going!

unaccustomed to the heat. New people with new ideas and new economic plans would come to "Try Tuscaloosa," as the sign atop the Alston Building had once urged. JVC, the Victor Corporation of Japan, paved the way when it announced in 1985 that it would be the first foreign manufacturer to open a plant in Tuscaloosa. JVC was attracted in part by Interstate 59/20, completed in the mid-1970s. JVC was also attracted by a partnership with the University of Alabama forged by President Joab Thomas. Not only did the university's engineering and computing departments work with JVC managers, but the university's Japanese Studies Program provided opportunities for the managers' children to study in a Japanese-language school. JVC's success in Tuscaloosa would prove an important precedent.

JVC opened its plant in 1986 and began manufacturing compact discs the next year—as the world was experiencing a breathtakingly rapid explosion in personal electronics and computing. Apple's first consumer product was the Apple II home computer in 1977. IBM followed with its PC, launched in 1981 with Microsoft software. Steve Jobs then raised the ante in 1984 with the Macintosh, which introduced the mouse and shifted personal computing into a new realm of graphics. Then in 1991 the first web page was posted on the World Wide Web. The University of Alabama's campus-wide email service started the following year (although certain departments had been using their own email since the early 1980s), and the university's first official website was launched not long after. While personal

The announcement by Mercedes-Benz in 1993 that it would build a state-of-the-art production factory was the culmination of boosters' dreams stretching back into the mid-nineteenth century. (Courtesy Mercedes Benz U.S. International)

In 1997, employees at the Mercedes-Benz U.S. International plant marked the completion of 50,000 vehicles. In early 2018 they built their 3 millionth vehicle. (Courtesy Mercedes Benz U.S. International)

electronics and computing were making the headlines, mainframe computing and robotic manufacturing were also moving ahead at a dizzying pace.

All of these—air-conditioning, computers, and electronic communications—came together on the first of October 1993. This is "a new day for Alabama," beamed Governor Jim Folsom Jr., "a day when we move to the forefront of economic development." Standing by his side was Helmut Werner, president and chief executive officer of Mercedes-Benz AG. They were announcing that one of the world's finest automobiles would be built in the Druid City. "Is this as good as a national football championship?" asked Governor Folsom referring to the Crimson Tide's destruction of the heavily favored Miami Hurricanes in the last Sugar Bowl; "I think it's better." Probate Judge Hardy McCollum echoed the governor: "What this tells the world is that Tuscaloosa and the state of Alabama can be equated with the best. Obviously, we do have football, and now we can do it with the finest automobile maker in the world!"

For six months, officials from Mercedes-Benz had been weighing a host of factors—including transportation costs, the quality and productivity of the workforce, state and local incentives, distance to residential areas and suppliers—in deciding where to locate their first manufacturing plant outside Germany. They finally chose a thousand acres near Vance. The $253-million incentive package and the prime location between Interstate 59/20 and the Norfolk Southern Railroad were important considerations. So was JVC's success in working with Tuscaloosa's city government and the University of Alabama. But none of these factors were decisive. What finally tipped the scales, according to Mercedes-Benz officials, was

Tuscaloosans' warmth and commitment. They also voiced, in so many words, their sense that Tuscaloosans were ready and eager to adapt to the Germans' commitment to quality.

When the first M-Class sport utility vehicle rolled off the assembly line in February 1997, the company had projected sixty-five thousand annual sales. But demand was so great that production was immediately increased to eighty thousand. Matching demand with production so easily was only made possible because of the robotic manufacturing system. Demand continued to increase as new car lines were added, so Mercedes-Benz expanded the plant every few years. By January 2018, the Tuscaloosa County Mercedes-Benz plant celebrated the assembly of their 3 millionth vehicle.

The city of Tuscaloosa, the county, and the state all reaped benefits. Mercedes-Benz has invested over $4.5 billion in its Tuscaloosa plant. In return, some 3,600 individuals are employed (an estimated 22,000 jobs when subsidiary companies are included) with an annual economic impact estimated at over $1.5 billion. The example set by Mercedes-Benz attracted other automobile manufacturers to Alabama: Honda in Lincoln, Hyundai in Montgomery, and Toyota in Huntsville. Together they turn out about a million vehicles each year, many for overseas markets—by far Alabama's largest export at $7.9 billion in 2016.

The impact of Mercedes-Benz on Tuscaloosans has been more than economic. The company has become involved in such local projects as the YMCA, food banks, Habitat for Humanity, and Adopt-A-School; it has sponsored marathons and Oktoberfests. During their stays in Tuscaloosa, many of the German population join the Prentice Concert Chorale to perform major works of choral literature, including original compositions by Alabama composers. And Tuscaloosans are not the only ones to be influenced by this mingling of cultures. After a year or two, many Mercedes-Benz officials return to Germany with a newfound appreciation for barbecue, Crimson Tide football, and Southern hospitality.

The Mercedes-Benz U.S. International plant in Tuscaloosa County has a workforce of about 3,700, producing almost 300,000 SUVs and cars annually, which are sold in 135 countries. (Courtesy Library of Congress)

THOSE LISTENING ON THE RADIO to President Roosevelt denounce Japan's attack on Pearl Harbor could not possibly have imagined welcoming the Victor Corporation of Japan to Tuscaloosa, building Mercedes-Benz automobiles just down the road, or electing black Tuscaloosans to political office. Across those years a great deal happened to change attitudes: going off to fight totalitarian regimes, bringing tens of thousands to Tuscaloosa for training or medical treatment, watching and being watched on television, dramatic national events unfolding on the university campus, and others. This was not the same sort of revolution that turned Tuscaloosa from an old town into a modern city, not the sort of revolution that could be seen in the automobiles driving down the street or by flicking a switch to turn on a light. This was instead a revolution in values. And it came only after people decided to reject some of "the past that lives...with today," to reject Dr. Dansby's "that's all I knew." It was a revolution as profound as any other.

Tuscaloosans endure six minutes...and everyone comes to lend a hand

Opposite page: The April 27, 2011, tornado cut a diagonal swath through Tuscaloosa beginning in the southwest corner and exiting through Alberta City in the northeast. The profound and overwhelming nature of the destruction can be judged by this photograph, which was taken almost two months after the storm. (Courtesy Robin McDonald)

TORNADOES HAVE ALWAYS ROARED through the Black Warrior Valley. One destroyed most of Newtown in 1842. Northport lost thirty-seven lives (over 10 percent of the population) to a tornado in 1904 and thirty-eight to another in 1932 that destroyed over a quarter of the town's homes. Tuscaloosa County has, since 1950, led Alabama in the number of severe tornadoes.

But no one had ever seen anything like what came in April 2011.

The destruction was not for lack of preparation. Mayor Walt Maddox had led a delegation of sixty to Emmitsburg, Maryland, to attend a course held by the Federal Emergency Management Agency (FEMA). During their week there in January 2009, the FEMA personnel simulated a variety of emergency scenarios beginning with a riot after an Auburn-Alabama basketball game and culminating—wisely, it would turn out—with a massive tornado ripping through Tuscaloosa. While the team learned a great deal, few of them left FEMA's National Emergency Training Center expecting ever to need those lessons.

The National Weather Service warned on the morning of Wednesday, April 27, of the strong possibility of tornadoes later in the day. Governor Robert Bentley prudently declared a state of emergency at 11:00 A.M., thereby putting a thousand National Guardsmen on alert. Mayor

Maddox did the same with the city's incident command system. Utility companies in the Midwest started sending repair crews south before any reports of damage. Schools were closed, thankfully, as were many businesses. The owner of H&W Drugs East on Fifteenth Street had sent everyone home after storms earlier that day knocked out computer service.

Tuscaloosans joined others throughout the state and the nation in watching live radar track a fearsome front as it headed

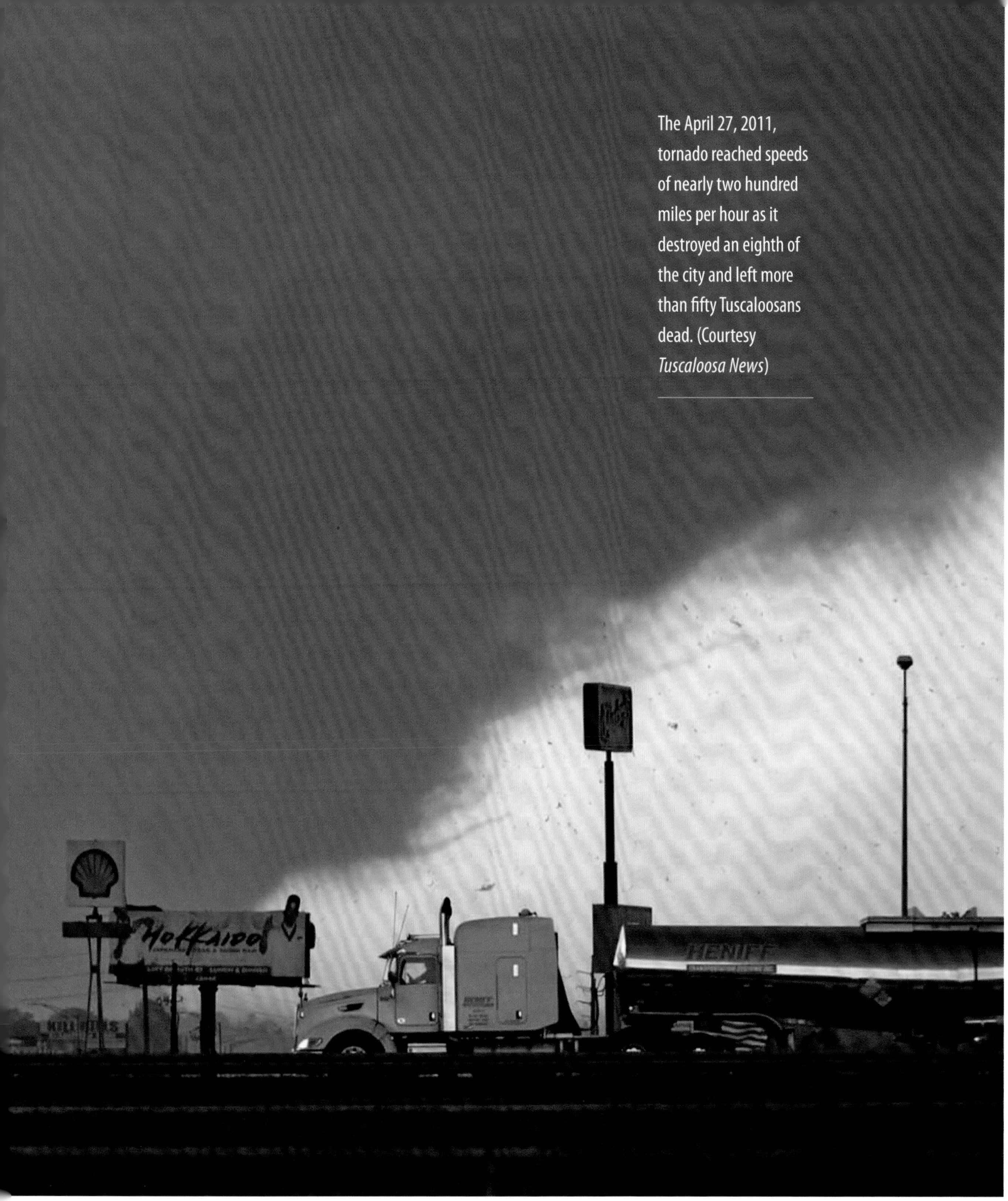

The April 27, 2011, tornado reached speeds of nearly two hundred miles per hour as it destroyed an eighth of the city and left more than fifty Tuscaloosans dead. (Courtesy *Tuscaloosa News*)

northeast from the Gulf of Mexico. With each passing hour, the worst elements seemed to be converging on the Druid City. The skies darkened. With the danger mounting during the late afternoon, weathermen began warning people to start moving into their safe places—basements, closets, bathrooms. From strategically placed cameras, such as the one on the roof of the former Merchants' Bank & Trust Building, television viewers stared in disbelief as the black whirlwind entered

The author, Pat Hubbs, and Matthew Keogh cross the viaduct into Alberta City two days after the April 27 tornado. (Courtesy G. Ward Hubbs)

Tuscaloosa's southwest corner at 5:13 P.M. "It was a larger tornado than any of us had ever seen," judged Deputy Fire Chief John Brook.

Folks desperately began piling mattresses above them. Some clung to each other to keep from being sucked away. Some prayed. Randy Lambert and his family in Alberta City put on bike helmets, crouched behind the only substantial wall in their frame house, and waited.

Six minutes later, at 5:19 P.M., the tornado exited Tuscaloosa's northeast corner and entered Holt. City leaders had assumed that this tornado, like previous ones, would bounce and touch down in multiple places. But it stayed on the ground "like a giant lawnmower," in the words of Fire Chief Alan J. Martin. A six-mile swath of destruction, up to a mile wide, ran diagonally from one end of town to the other. An eighth of Tuscaloosa lay in ruins. Croxton's 1865 raid paled in comparison.

Buildings were not what mattered, of course. People mattered. And too many were left injured or dead.

The residents of Rosedale Court, a 188-unit public housing development in southwest Tuscaloosa, were among the first to be struck. Robbie Thomas ran inside with her mother, daughter, and niece. "My nephew was in the red truck," she said through tears. "We told him to come in, but the wind blew the door shut and that was the last time we saw him. . . . We saw everything fall apart and we were buried. We unburied ourselves." It took some time to find the body of Robbie's nephew, fifteen-year-old Justin Le'Eric Thomas.

"Rosedale Court is gone," was former resident George Weatherspoon's simple assessment. "It looks like a war zone."

The tornado continued on its deadly appointments. At Twenty-Fifth Street, Crimson Tide long snapper Carson Tinker wrapped his big arms around Ashley Harrison as they crouched in a closet. "I'm scared," she said.

"It's going to be OK," he reassured her. But it wasn't OK. They were both sucked out of the closet. Carson Tinker landed sixty-five yards away in a field, badly injured. Ashley Harrison landed lifeless not too far away, her neck broken.

Some twenty employees and customers cowered in the back-corner breakroom of the Hobby Lobby in Wood Square. The air pressure plummeted as the tornado's winds, approaching two hundred miles per hour, came upon them. A manager tried to hold the door to the breakroom shut. The tornado won, ripping the door open. But the tornado failed to pull out one woman whom the manager held tightly.

THE TORNADO IN NUMBERS

ACROSS THE SOUTH, APRIL 25–28, 2011

349 tornadoes officially recorded
11 of those were rated EF4 on the Enhanced Fujita scale
4 were rated EF5 (typically one EF5 tornado is recorded annually)
Estimated $10.8 billion in damage
One of the deadliest tornado outbreaks ever
324 deaths from tornadoes, 24 from related events
Some 2,775 injured

IN ALABAMA, APRIL 27

62 tornadoes (the most in a single day)
238 confirmed deaths

IN TUSCALOOSA, APRIL 27

Path of Destruction

80 miles total length
5.9 miles in Tuscaloosa city limits
Entered Tuscaloosa at 5:13 p.m., left 5:19 p.m.

Deaths and Injuries

53 Tuscaloosans died, some immediately and others later of their injuries.
More than 1,200 people were treated at DCH Regional Medical Center on the evening of April 11

Damage

Some 12 percent of the city was destroyed

Residential structures:
5,362 affected
61 percent of rentals with residential median income less than $28,000
2,493 damaged
1,612 severely damaged
1,257 destroyed

Commercial structures:
356 affected
178 damaged
64 severely damaged
114 destroyed

City government infrastructure:
Fire and Rescue Station No. 4 destroyed
East Precinct, Tuscaloosa Police Department destroyed
Communication tower destroyed

Environmental Services vehicles:
25 destroyed, 26 damaged

"Somehow, the walls stayed up," recalled employee Alison Tucker a few hours later. "For some reason, they stayed up."

Many of the homes in Alberta City were smashed or blown away. "Everything was moving," recalled Fred Jackson, who was holed up in his bathroom when the winds hit. "The house is destroyed. We had to get out through a window." When Tuscaloosa police officer Preston Grammer crawled out of the Alberta City precinct office, he learned about a young woman trapped under the collapsed Arlington Square Apartments, along Twenty-Fifth Avenue East. He could not see her, but he could hear her screams. Reaching her took hours of digging by hand through literally tons of materials. "Please don't let me die," she said to Grammer as he touched her hand. And he didn't. Also living on Twenty-Fifth Avenue East was a grandmother with three of her grandsons. They were among the fatalities. "We covered them with sheets," recounted Grammer. "We had orders just to leave them there, there on the side of the road," said the veteran of Afghanistan, and "that was one of the hardest things I have ever had to do."

The tornado reached its peak as it passed Alberta City and entered Holt. On Crescent Lane East, David Bayode and his wife fell face down on their two boys to protect them from the approaching winds. They had no place to hide as the storm tore their home off its concrete slab and sucked the Bayodes up. David Bayode was awakened 150 yards away from his home by his son telling him, "Daddy, Daddy, Mama's gone."

Robert Reed, manager of nearby Crescent Mobile Home Estates, was a big man

Robert Reed is seen at the site of his home near Crescent Ridge Road in Tuscaloosa a month after the tornado. Reed played football in college and kept up weightlifting in the years since. It paid off on April 27, as he used what witnesses called superhuman strength to pull people out from the rubble of a trailer park where he was the property manager. (Courtesy Dusty Compton/*Tuscaloosa News*)

who could bench press 415 pounds. That would help. The storm threw Reed and his family across the street. A truck flew over, and an air-conditioning unit landed on his fiancée's head. After throwing the unit off, he knelt and prayed. "I went numb," he recalled. "I didn't notice nothing about my surroundings." But he jumped up when he heard screaming and calls for help from his neighbor John Hayes, who had managed to crawl out of his own trailer but was unable to rescue his wife and mother. Reed rushed over and threw off the double-door refrigerator that had pinned the two down. "I don't know how he done it," recounted Hayes, "but you do extraordinary things that you don't know how in times like these." Reed moved on to eighty-eight-year-old Annie Lois Sayer's home. As he lifted up the two brick walls that pinned her down, another neighbor pulled her out. Like Carson Tinker, Reed told her that it would be OK. And once again, it wasn't OK. "By the time we got to the road, she took her last breath." A sheriff's deputy took Reed's loved ones to the hospital while Reed continued to pull out some dozen people in all.

Reed was but one of the untold many ordinary Tuscaloosans who immediately turned to help their neighbors. Brandon Reid moved from house to house in his Forest Lake neighborhood calling out for people inside the wreckage. "I really don't know what I'm doing," the shaken University of Alabama student admitted; "I just know that Jesus said to love your neighbor as yourself, and I know I would want help if I were trapped inside my house."

When Robbie Wyatt emerged from his own damaged Alberta City home (which would take more than eight months to repair), his first words to his neighbor were, "We've got to see about those folks down there," referring to those living in the heavily damaged Chastain Manor retirement community. So off they went, climbing over, under, and around the immense downed oaks that blocked the way. Robbie and his neighbor were able to help a few folks escape the rubble, but for each person they helped, there seemed to be a dozen more in need.

As night began to fall over the mangled city, the Moon Winx sign still stood at its post—unlit, but reassuringly intact. Downed power lines and power poles littered University Boulevard East, and

Alberta City's landmark neon sign survived the tornado. It was designed by local artist Glenn House in 1959 who, after spending about three hours one day—at fifty cents an hour—came up with a winking crescent moon. House had but one regret: "I have kicked myself for fifty years because I didn't give that moon a bow tie." (Courtesy Robin McDonald)

beams from flashlights punctured the incoming darkness. The day may have ended, but the turmoil was far from over. Dozens of dazed and frightened families huddled on the concrete slab where AutoZone once stood. A few blocks further, the walls of Alberta Baptist Church no longer had a roof. Two miles down the road, a crowd of people were flooding into DCH hospital.

This time the cliché could not have been more appropriate: the streets in front of the hospital had turned into a parking lot. People drove in with injured survivors strapped to doors and pieces of plywood lying in the backs of their damaged pickup trucks. All Tuscaloosa physicians and medical personnel had been asked to come assist, and they were treating the injured in hallways and anywhere they could find. One nurse called it "organized chaos." When patched up and told to go back home, most responded that they no longer had a home. DCH grew ever more crowded as the night grew longer and the staff attended to some twelve hundred Tuscaloosans. One of those was a college student in the emergency room. Nurse Sharon Allen held his hand. "I needed to be with him," she recounted. "So many times, I wanted to contact his family and say, 'he wasn't alone' when he died." Nothing heroic. "We were just doing our job."

While some were digging out the injured and taking them to the hospital, others cleared the streets to allow emergency vehicles to pass—often using just their hands. Volunteers would drive up to fire and rescue personnel and shout out, "I've got a chainsaw in the back of my truck. Where do you need me?"

"Take your pick," was the answer. "Wherever you want to go." Some individuals, upon learning that they had lost someone, nevertheless continued in their efforts to help others.

As George White, Tuscaloosa fire and rescue assistant chief, put it, "People didn't just stand on their porch and say 'poor me.' They got out there and they helped their neighbors."

These gestures certainly grew out of a generous spirit, but many were spurred on by necessity. The three agencies most responsible for disaster relief—the Salvation Army, the Red Cross of West Alabama, and the Tuscaloosa County Emergency Management Agency—were all among the first to lose their buildings. Added to this were the fire and police precinct stations in Alberta City, which were also in the middle of the storm's path. "One of the firefighters," according to Fire Chief Martin, "said it took him an hour to walk just a few blocks" with all the debris making the roads impassable.

"The scene looked like something out of a big-budget Hollywood disaster movie," quipped a *Tuscaloosa News* reporter.

The mayor addressed the media at eight forty-five that evening. "Tragedy and destruction have encompassed our city," he said, "but it will not conquer us. Rather, it will inspire us to demonstrate our patience, our faith, and our confidence that a new day will certainly dawn."

The next day did dawn with the mayor and city council's list of emergencies growing. Pressure in the water system was dropping in east Tuscaloosa, which would make stopping fires impossible and could contaminate the drinking water. The city asked residents to boil and conserve their water as a precaution. The city council granted the mayor his request for emergency powers, and he in turn asked

Tuscaloosa Mayor Walt Maddox, right, speaks with President Obama as they tour damaged areas in Tuscaloosa's Alberta City area on Friday, two days after the storm. Along with President Obama and Mayor Maddox, Alabama Governor Robert Bentley, U.S. Senators Richard Shelby and Jeff Sessions, and other local and national dignitaries visited Tuscaloosa that same day. (Courtesy Dusty Compton/ *Tuscaloosa News*)

the University of Alabama police to take responsibility for the Cedar Crest neighborhood, which was all but destroyed. A couple hundred National Guardsmen had started to arrive on the scene only a half hour after the tornado hit. The city would request another five hundred the next afternoon and an additional three hundred a few hours after that. Mayor Maddox announced a curfew. He also announced thirty-seven known fatalities (of an eventual fifty-three). "The amount of damage I've seen is beyond a nightmare," he said.

Unrecognizable was the word that Tuscaloosans kept repeating. When a police officer called for assistance in rescuing some trapped babies, the dispatcher asked for his location. "I can't give you an address because there aren't any addresses anymore." Brad Lawrence drove around after the storm and reported being "lost in my own town." Mayor Maddox recalled "walking through streets you grew up with your whole life and didn't know where you were." And twelve-year-old Jonna said "It looked like a war zone outside, like a bomb just hit. It was scary." When her family later returned to their home, "We passed our street four different times, and then we almost passed the house, which was kind of weird because, I mean, you're supposed to know your own house."

President Barrack Obama's declaration of a major disaster on Wednesday night made federal funds available. He arrived in Tuscaloosa on Friday morning less than an hour after ordering the Navy SEALs to take out Osama bin Laden. "I've never seen destruction like this," was his reaction. Standing with Mayor Walt Maddox in the ruins of Alberta City, the president vowed to "do everything we can to help these communities out." And in the months and years ahead, the government would indeed reach out, in no small part because of the hard lessons learned in New Orleans after Hurricane Katrina. President Obama was just the first and most prominent of a long list of public figures to visit—from politicians (including Alabama's governor, senators, and some representatives) to pop stars (beginning with Charlie Sheen) to athletes (too numerous to list).

Volunteers from all over began to organize using cell phones, tweets, emails, and other media. Cross-state rival Auburn started a Toomer's for Tuscaloosa Facebook page the day after the tornado, mirroring the Tide for Toomer's Facebook page set up to help restore the oaks poisoned by a pathetic, and since jailed, Bama fan in 2010. "Helping with the rescue and people in need is what you do," said Warren Tidwell of Opelika, the driving force behind the campaign. "Football only goes so far. This is what you do." Tidwell proceeded to coordinate volunteers who drove to Tuscaloosa. Auburn University officially joined the relief effort with a tweet reading, "AU president Jay Gogue is leading the charge to create an avenue for Auburn alumni to help our friends in Tuscaloosa. Stay tuned." The Mobile Auburn Club sent out its own tweet soliciting goods to take to T-Town.

Members of the *Tuscaloosa News* staff celebrate and congratulate one another after the announcement that the paper had won a Pulitzer Prize for their coverage of the April 27, 2011, tornado that destroyed much of Tuscaloosa. (Courtesy Robert Sutton/ *Tuscaloosa News*)

After pitching in to help Tuscaloosans, Toomer's for Tuscaloosa would head to Joplin, Missouri, after another devastating tornado, to Brooklyn and New Jersey after Hurricane Sandy, and to north Georgia after a tornado there. "Let us not grow weary in doing good" they posted on their Facebook page. We Are T-Town organized within a week to provide all sorts of material needs for the victims of the Tuscaloosa tornado. They too would go on to expand their mission to provide relief for natural disasters elsewhere. We Are T-Town named "one of our biggest resources" to be the networking made possible through their Facebook page.

Social media and other means of electronic communication were incredibly important in raising support for Tuscaloosans. That the April 27 tornado had been watched in real time by millions on their televisions made it almost certainly the most widely seen tornado ever. It did not take long before personal videos of the tornado were loaded onto YouTube. Had the storm hit at night or before television and the internet, its enormity would not have struck home to anyone living much beyond Tuscaloosa. Television and internet video were just two of the communication systems that became important tools of recovery. Immediately after the winds had died down, Tuscaloosans picked up their cell phones to call their loved ones. This alone would have overloaded the cell phone system's capacity, but the storm had knocked out several towers to boot. City officials lost two of their three channels. Phoning in, for some reason, was easier than phoning out. Local Tuscaloosa radio stations stepped in by broadcasting the needs of individuals and organizations to a public that could then respond.

With generators supplying only enough current to run a few computers, reporters at the *Tuscaloosa News* used Twitter to give updates to Tuscaloosans in town and around the world alike. They posted photos and videos online and set up an interactive bulletin board to assist those looking for friends and loved ones. The paper edition was printed in Birmingham for two days. A year later, the *Tuscaloosa News* would receive its second Pulitzer Prize. The committee specifically cited "its enterprising coverage of a deadly tornado, using social media as well as traditional reporting to provide real-time updates, help locate missing people and produce in-depth print accounts even after power disruption forced the paper to publish at another plant 50 miles away."

Another factor in rallying support was Walt Maddox. The thirty-eight-year-old mayor was not only telegenic but articulate. He projected concern, of course, but also a sense of resolute confidence. "The people of this city will not let us down," he told President Obama after two hours of sleep—a pace that he would keep up for another three weeks. And Maddox was a quick study. He observed how the president and first lady's arrival raised spirits. At first Maddox thought that leaving his office or high-level meetings was "taking time away from my job." But he soon realized that getting out to talk with Tuscaloosans "*is* my job." Maddox would become the face of Tuscaloosa on national television. That evening, after the president was gone, the mayor would be interviewed by CNN while standing in what had once been the Cedar Crest neighborhood. A few weeks later the *New York Times* ran an article, "Mayor's World Remade in an Instant," which described him as the "efficient, earnest,

unwavering hero of the storm, praised by federal officials and tornado victims alike."

Over the following weeks and months, nameless and numberless individuals would grab hammers and nails to begin the slow process of rebuilding. These people would need food and especially beverages as the summer wore on. For those residents left without a functioning kitchen or electricity, the simple notion of feeding oneself became an immense hurdle. In response, many businesses and individuals opened their doors to the hungry. Moose Lodge on Paper Mill Road was serving barbecue, potato salad, and slaw. They asked only whether you wanted chicken or pork, a Coke or iced tea. They never asked for a dime. No one walking along University Boulevard East through Alberta City, or pretty much anywhere along the path of destruction, could go more than fifty yards without passing a stand giving out free food and beverages. Tuscaloosa Academy adjourned at lunch for the rest of the school year so that the students could spend their afternoons helping in the recovery.

Many of the volunteers came from faith communities, which clearly led

Members of the Alberta Baptist Church gather in the parking lot outside their church for Sunday services following the tornado, which had destroyed their sanctuary. (Courtesy T. G. Paschal/*Tuscaloosa News*)

much of the rebuilding efforts. Churches were packed on the Sunday following the storm—but not at Alberta Baptist Church. Their sanctuary had been destroyed, so the congregation held services in the parking lot. Nor was that the end of it. Their members were among those along University Boulevard East, standing in the hot sun with the ruins behind them, giving out free refreshments to any and all. The Salvation Army, whose office and shelter had been among the first hit, set up a distribution center at McFarland Mall. Tuscaloosa's American Red Cross headquarters near the Salvation Army had also been destroyed, so members of the undamaged Woodhaven Church of the Nazarene in Alberta City opened their doors for the Red Cross to use for six weeks. And when church groups across the country asked about coming to help with the rebuilding, Woodhaven would house many of them as well. Holy Spirit Catholic Church put much of its effort into helping Tuscaloosa's displaced Spanish speakers. "After the tornado, we organized a shelter," explained Dorothy McDade, Holy Spirit's Hispanic ministries coordinator. "We provided people with their needs, clothing, car seats, diapers. We had a little medical place here, and then we helped people with paying bills, starting up again to pay for the light bill and stuff like that." First Presbyterian Church would house a couple thousand volunteers over the next two years. Such examples were multiplied throughout the city as nearly every faith community got involved. Mayor Maddox—a confirmed Methodist—saw in these efforts more than just Tuscaloosans working together to help the needy. He saw what he called "putting faith into action," the sort of thing that Christ had been talking about.

And not just locals came to help. "City Expects Wave of Volunteers" read the headlines of the May 7 edition of the *Tuscaloosa News*. Only ten days after the tornado, an estimated ten thousand volunteers had already arrived from out of town, some having driven twelve and fourteen hours straight. Such organizations as UMCOR, the United Methodist Committee on Relief, arrived soon, as did Samaritan's Purse, an evangelical humanitarian aid organization led by Franklin Graham. Members of World Changers, an organization of Christian high school and college students, removed debris. Students at St. Joe's Catholic High School in Philadelphia came to work in early June. Within a month, the number of known volunteers had risen to over eighteen thousand. This was a low estimate because many had not bothered to register with the Volunteer Reception Center, which was trying to keep track. Some would even come from overseas.

Many volunteers worked with Habitat for Humanity. Founded in 1976 by University of Alabama School of Law alumnus Millard Fuller and his wife Linda, a Tuscaloosa native, Habitat promotes "partnership housing," where volunteers work alongside those in need to build affordable and substantial homes. One of the groups that worked on Habitat homes following the tornado was Project Children, an organization promoting peace in Northern Ireland by bringing Protestant and Catholic young people to work together on common projects in the United States. "Habitat Tuscaloosa is like family," said Denis Mulcahy, founder of Project Children. He has brought a delegation from Northern Ireland to Tuscaloosa to work on Habitat homes every year since the tornado. What really stood out for Maoiliosa Scott, a student at Queen's University Belfast, after spending a week in Tuscaloosa's "scorching" heat "was the immense gratitude shown by everyone we met . . . their appreciation of our choosing to help their community was genuinely moving." Project Children is but one of many such organizations. More than twenty-two thousand volunteers have worked on Habitat Tuscaloosa homes following the tornado. They come—and continue to come—from all fifty states and from six continents. Habitat Tuscaloosa is still waiting for an Antarctican volunteer.

The storm united Tuscaloosans of all stripes—across socioeconomic, racial, and political divisions. The storm even managed to blur geographical boundaries. All who came to help—whether from the other side of the state, the other side of the country, or the other side of the ocean—were welcomed by Tuscaloosans as fellow Tuscaloosans.

The new amphitheater had first opened only a few weeks before the tornado hit; and on May 27, just over a month after, country music singer Kenny Chesney was onstage leading the sold-out audience in singing "My Home's in Alabama." He had considered canceling, but Mayor Maddox urged him to come. Tuscaloosans needed a break. Chesney and his band not only performed; they, along with their managers and booking representatives, all donated their fees—thought to be in the hundreds of thousands of dollars—to the GiveTuscaloosa.com relief fund. "The heart of the country is with everybody's who's dealing with this tragedy," Chesney told the crowd. "The whole world knows this town is hurting." Chesney set a precedent. The rock band My Morning Jacket donated their performance fees to benefit the United Way of West Alabama. "I think that's just why we're on the planet," lead singer and guitarist Jim James explained, "to help each other." When the country band Alabama reunited at the amphitheater in September for their only full concert since officially retiring in 2004, they raised nearly $170,000 for the City of Tuscaloosa Storm Recovery Fund. All performers at the Tuscaloosa Amphitheater that first season reportedly donated their services to the relief efforts.

And the popularity of the Crimson Tide certainly brought people back to Tuscaloosa to help in the recovery. Former coach Gene Stallings, who led the Tide to its 1992 national championship, brought some 150 former players back home. They would be joined by Bama players stretching far back over the decades.

And the 2011 team would have its own role to play in the recovery. Two days after the storm, Coach Nick Saban addressed his team assembled at Bryant-Denny Stadium. The Tide "has got a community to support," he told them. "We can't just be a team for them on Saturdays. The fans are with us in the best times, and we have to be with them in the worst times." Several of the players had already pulled injured Tuscaloosans out of the debris, and the coach gave those who were emotionally and physically damaged the opportunity to go ahead and leave for home. (The university, which had just missed the tornado's path, had canceled classes and final exams.) He ended on a strong note. "Once we all get back here and really start preparing for the season, we're going to have a chance to do something very special for our community. These people are hurting, and we're going to be able to show them that we've got their backs." And with that Coach Saban left for DCH to visit long

A memorial across the street from the house where University of Alabama senior Ashley Harrison was killed while taking shelter with her boyfriend, Carson Tinker, long snapper for the Crimson Tide. (Courtesy Michelle Lepianka Carter/ *Tuscaloosa News*)

snapper Carson Tinker, whose girlfriend Ashley Harrison had been ripped from his arms. Tinker's teammates and coaches would also come to visit.

The opening game of the 2011 season was against Kent State University, Coach Saban's alma mater. That summer, Kent State had sent several players to work on a Habitat for Humanity home for Bob and Dana Dowling, whose own home in Holt had been destroyed by the tornado. The Dowling's new home was one of several sponsored by Coach Saban's Nick's Kids Foundation, named in honor of his father. The Kent State volunteers joined others from Auburn who had also come to help. "All of these people just care," noted Mrs. Dowling of those from Kent State, Auburn, and Alabama all working together. "They don't care who it is. They just want to help." While in the Druid City, the Kent State players also conducted a clinic for underprivileged kids. Tuscaloosans took notice: unlike the usual good-natured booing when the opponents take the field, this time the Kent State Golden Flashes were greeted with a standing ovation. Before the kickoff, the governor shook hands with representatives from the police, firefighters, and emergency medical technicians. All stood in silence to honor those who had died, especially the six University of Alabama students. Then it was on to football. (Kent State lost 48–7.) "That first game didn't build one house, or bring a business back or a loved one back," Mayor Maddox said after the game, "but it gave us a sense of unity."

The Tide did well during the season gathering, if possible, even more support as fans rallied behind the team from Tuscaloosa. After defeating the twelfth-ranked Florida Gators 38–10 and several other SEC opponents, the Tide moved up to no. 2 in the rankings. The game of the year came on November 5 as the unbeaten no. 1 ranked Louisiana State University (LSU) Tigers came to Tuscaloosa to battle the unbeaten no. 2 ranked Crimson Tide. A reported fifty thousand fans without tickets were outside Bryant-Denny Stadium at kickoff. A staggering forty-six of the players who ran out on the field would go on to play in the NFL. The game lived up to the hype with a classic defensive struggle producing a 6–6 tie as time ran out. The Tide got the ball first in overtime but failed to score on its possession. The Tigers, however, managed to kick a field goal. Final score: LSU 9, Bama 6.

With Alabama falling back to third in the rankings and LSU remaining no. 1, many thought the chances of winning a national championship were gone. But not Coach Saban. As the season was ending, no. 3 Bama had a tortuous path to get to the final game: the Tide would have to win out, and no. 2 Oklahoma State University, no. 4 University of Oregon, and even no. 5 University of Oklahoma would all have to lose. The Bowl Championship Series (BCS) was not about to invite Alabama and LSU—two teams not just from the same conference but from the same division of the same conference who had already played each other—to a rematch unless forced. But everything fell into place. On Friday, November 18, 2011, Iowa State University beat no. 2 Oklahoma State in double overtime, 37–31. And on the next day, no. 4 Oregon failed to make a field goal on its last play, and the University of Southern California won 38–35. Meanwhile down in Waco, Baylor University upset no. 5 Oklahoma with a 34-yard touchdown pass in the final eight seconds. In a mere twenty-four hours, three games each went down to the wire and were decided in the exact and only way that could put the Tide back in the hunt. Bedlam broke out in Tuscaloosa. But Alabama first had to take care of Auburn in the Iron Bowl, which it did with remarkable ease, 42–14.

New Orleans on January 9 was awash with LSU fans. Bedecked in garish combinations of purple and gold with the occasional green thrown in for good measure, they had practically taken over the French Quarter. They were in high spirits (in several ways), utterly convinced that if LSU had been able to squeeze out a win in Tuscaloosa, then certainly the Tigers' superior talent could only mean victory in their own backyard. The Alabama fans were outnumbered, more reserved, and far more sedately dressed. They knew that when Coach Saban had enough time to prepare his team—and he had—then Bama could be nearly unstoppable. Moreover, the Tide would be playing for more than a championship this time. The Tide would be playing for Tuscaloosans.

The Bama defense obliterated the LSU offense. In the first half, the Tigers were unable to cross midfield and gained a first down only once. During the second half, the Tigers did cross midfield, but two plays later they were pushed back into their own territory. They never saw Bama's side of the field again. So near to perfection was the Alabama defense that an offsides call in the waning minutes of the game accounted for Alabama's only penalty. And the Bama offense was formidable against a very good Tiger defense. Quarterback

The Alabama Crimson Tide celebrates winning the 2011 season national championship—its fourteenth—with a 21-0 victory over the LSU Tigers in the BCS National Championship Game played January 9, 2012, in New Orleans. (Courtesy Crimson Tide Photos)

AJ McCarron threw for 23 of 34 passes with no interceptions. Trent Richardson's coffin-nailing 34-yard touchdown run with 4:44 to go in the game made the final score 21–0. The score should have been far worse, for Alabama had run up 384 yards to LSU's 92.

But by that time—really, by midway through the third quarter—the LSU bleachers were practically empty. Bama fans stayed seated as the clock wound down to victory, not allowing a second to pass uncelebrated. Inside the Mercedes-Benz Superdome, along the Tuscaloosa streets, and in front of television sets across Alabama and the nation, Tide fans were still cheering. In Bama's locker room, Coach Saban signaled for silence. "We buried the pain tonight," he said with emphasis.

A fourteenth national championship was a good way to end a hard year.

A past that lives with today

Opposite page: Capitol Park stands on the site of the great statehouse designed and built by William Nichols. During the mid-1980s, professor and architectural historian Robert O. Mellown directed the location and reconstruction of the capitol's foundations—all that remained following the devastating 1923 fire. Tuscaloosans generously returned pieces of the structure that had been removed and placed in their gardens decades earlier. Mellown's efforts stand to remind us that the past and the present converge in Tuscaloosa. (Courtesy Robin McDonald)

TENS OF THOUSANDS EAGERLY ENLISTED to restore Tuscaloosa after the 2011 tornado. They came from across the state, the nation, and even farther afield. They came for several reasons, including their own good will and faith, a winning mayor, and loyalty to the Tide. They also came because Tuscaloosa was worth fixing. And Tuscaloosa was worth fixing because, several times over a span of two centuries, Tuscaloosans recharted their course to create a town that would intrigue Carl Carmer and so many others. Even today's wailing sirens and traffic jams on McFarland Boulevard cannot obscure how, as Carmer observed, the past lives with today in Tuscaloosa.

The decision to make the frontier trading village at the Falls of the Black Warrior into the young state's new capital led directly to the creation of the University of Alabama in 1831. What began as a small "Seminary of Learning," as they called it, is now a major research university. Over twelve thousand faculty and staff work in more than three hundred buildings on a site perhaps twice the size of the original Tuscaloosa townsite. Nearly forty thousand students are drawn in by an attractive campus and the university's serious investment in scholarships. Another great attraction, unquestionably, is the Crimson Tide's unparalleled success as college football's gold standard: seventeen national championships under coaches Wallace Wade (1925, 1926, and 1930), Frank Thomas (1934 and 1941), Paul "Bear" Bryant (1961, 1964, 1965, 1973, 1978, and 1979), Gene Stallings (1992), and Nick Saban (2009, 2011, 2012, 2015, 2017)—with more to come. Bryant-

Denny Stadium has nearly 102,000 seats where some of those screaming fans do, in fact, occasionally sit. But millions of other fans across the nation and even across the globe are rooting with their eyes glued to the TV and their ears tuned to Eli Gold.

A hundred and fifty years on, the ghosts of secession and its aftermath still haunt the streets. Croxton's destruction of the university is noted by the outline in stone of the Rotunda's foundation, half obscured by the Amelia Gayle Gorgas Library front steps. Historical markers and the annual J. C. C. Sanders Lecture Series also recall the role of the Corps of Cadets during Tuscaloosa's invasion. Proposals are occasionally heard to raise the ironclad CSS *Tuscaloosa* from its muddy grave in the Mobile River. The bitter divisions of Reconstruction seemed to be forgotten until the recent efforts to honor Tuscaloosa's leading freedman, Shandy Jones. A memorial service was held in 2017 at his recently discovered grave in Mobile, and a few months later Hunter Chapel AME Zion Church inaugurated an annual Shandy Jones commemorative dinner.

Just when those ghosts seemed to be fading, however, new ways of fighting the old battles emerged. Some argue, for example, that Civil War memorials do not honor great men so much as honor their going to war to defend an evil cause. The University of Alabama's Morgan Hall is named for a Confederate general and purportedly (the evidence is thin) a leader of the Klan. But John Tyler Morgan was also the U.S. Senator who successfully obtained federal funds essential for rebuilding the university after Croxton's raid. After a student-led campaign to replace his name, the university instead removed Morgan's framed portrait. That the past lives with today in Tuscaloosa makes dealing with these thorny issues all the more difficult. In so many ways our forebears are like us, and in so many other ways they are different.

Tuscaloosans once poured their energies into building railroads and locks that "in no great space of time" would turn the City of Oaks into "one great pulsing heart of manufacture and commerce." Town boosters believed that their dreams had been realized in Central Foundry. But the iron industry was already peaking when its furnaces were first lit in 1903, and after a series of ups and downs, Central Foundry closed for good in 1982 after plastic pipe made cast iron obsolete. Gulf States Paper employed over twelve hundred Tuscaloosans in its heyday; but the machinery was not updated, and the mill was shuttered in 1978. Other smokestack industries, including the B. F. Goodrich tire plant and the Hunt Oil refinery, continue. And then, out of the blue, the boosters' wildest hopes were more than realized. It may have taken a century, but still, the coming of Mercedes-Benz in 1993 represented industrialization of an unimaginably high quality. Yet without an infrastructure that includes the University of Alabama, transportation systems, and a ready workforce—all of which were pushed by nineteenth-century boosters—Mercedes-Benz would have gone elsewhere.

The introduction of domestic inventions between the Civil and Second World Wars is now such a part of everyday life that it is difficult to appreciate just how significant that revolution was. But imagine a Tuscaloosan of 1869 suddenly whisked to 1939. He would be completely lost confronting automobiles speeding along where horses once ambled, children lighting a room with the flick of a switch, indoor plumbing, refrigerators, movies, and even air-

Students from Williams College in Massachusetts joined tens of thousands to help rebuild Tuscaloosa after the deadly 2011 tornado. They and others have continued to come each summer to work on Habitat for Humanity homes. Tuscaloosans all. (Courtesy Habitat for Humanity Tuscaloosa)

conditioning. He could fly in an airplane! By contrast, a Tuscaloosan living in 1939 would adjust rather quickly to today's city. Homes are still connected to networks of electricity, gas, water, sewer, and (now cell) telephone—as they were then. An LED is certainly more efficient and lasts longer than Edison's incandescent—but it is still a light bulb. Members of the Druid City Bicycle Club ride about on safety bikes—just as Tuscaloosa's wheelmen and wheelwomen did in the 1890s. A 2019 Mercedes-Benz SUV loaded with safety and luxury equipment makes for a better ride than a '39 Ford Tudor Sedan Deluxe—but drivers still use a steering wheel to steer down the right-hand side of the road. The FM radio in that Mercedes-Benz has a far richer, static-free sound than the old AM units that had to be housed in furniture cabinets—but it still broadcasts the Crimson Tide games just as they did in 1939. The great inventions introduced and adopted during those seven decades are still with us. The more recent inventions, primarily electronic, have contributed in important ways to Tuscaloosans' lives. The Mercedes-Benz plant uses computer-driven robots to produce higher quality automobiles at a faster rate than in the days of mind-numbing jobs along assembly lines. And social media helped immensely in the rescue and rebuilding efforts following the 2011 tornado. But the effects of these new inventions on everyday life have not yet approached the revolutionary effects created by the inventions of a century before.

The entry of Tuscaloosa into the larger world that began with radio, the Second World War, and television also permeates everyday life—but in very different ways. Black and white members of the city council sit across the same table. And the same holds true for tables at restaurants, at civic organizations, and pretty much wherever Tuscaloosans meet. Entering the larger world has also brought people from beyond our shores to do extraordinary and once undreamt of things. This revolution lies not in new inventions that change the way we conduct our daily routines, but in the ideas and values we use to live with each other. In this respect, the Tuscaloosans of today are certainly not the Tuscaloosans of 1939.

The tornado's legacy lies not in the new or rebuilt buildings, but rather in the volunteers. They came to a storied town, two centuries in the making. It was built by Tuscaloosans: frontier settlers and itinerant politicians, artisans and educators, town boosters and factory workers, Autherine Lucy and Vivian Malone, clergy and protestors on Bloody Tuesday, Crimson Tide fans, Mercedes-Benz officials, everyday folk, and surely—surely—those volunteers who came to help. All are Tuscaloosans, even those whose zip code is far outside city limits.

Yes, the volunteers restored this town because it was special. But it was special because Tuscaloosans built it that way.

Chronology

1816
Settlers begin arriving at the Falls of the Black Warrior River

1819 December 13
Territorial legislature incorporates the village as *Tuskaloosa*

1819 December 14
Alabama enters the Union as the twenty-second state

1825 December 13
Tuscaloosa becomes Alabama's second state capital upon the general assembly's vote

1831 April 12
University of Alabama dedication ceremonies in Christ Church

1834
First bridge over the Black Warrior River constructed by Seth King

1834 December 27
Chief Yoholo-Micco addresses the legislators as the Creek nation exits the state

1842 March 4
Tornado destroys Newtown and damages the bridge, which would be replaced ten years later

1847 November 1
Upon completion of a new statehouse, Montgomery succeeds Tuscaloosa as Alabama's capital

1853 July 14
Alabama Insane Hospital cornerstone laid

1854 December 7
The North East & South West Railroad holds its ground-breaking ceremony in Tuscaloosa

1860 February 23
University of Alabama becomes the state's military academy

1861 January 11
Alabama secedes from the Union

1861 May 4
Warrior Guards depart

1865 April 3–5
Union cavalrymen enter Tuscaloosa, burn the university and factories, then burn the bridge as they retreat

1868 September 1
Ryland Randolph publishes *A Prospective Scene* in the *Independent Monitor*

1869 October 11
Telegraph reaches Tuscaloosa

1871 February 7
North Port incorporated

1871 March
First train reaches Tuscaloosa

1872
Horace King rebuilds the bridge destroyed by Croxton's raiders

1874 November 22
Last occupying Union troops leave Tuscaloosa

1876
Tuscaloosa Theological Institute, later Stillman College, established

1879
William Carlos Jemison first elected mayor

1880
First bicycle ridden in Tuscaloosa

1882
First iron-girder bridge over Black Warrior installed, replacing bridge that was destroyed in an 1880 tornado

1883
Tuscaloosa telephone exchange created

1887 January–March
Tuskaloosa Coal, Iron & Land Company and Castle Hill Real Estate and Manufacturing Company organized

1887 May 19
Project to build five locks and dams approved by Board of Engineer officers of the U.S. Army

1887 September
Production of ice and electricity begins

1887
Tuscaloosa Water Works established

1887
Tuscaloosa Belt Railway constructed, eventually encircling Tuscaloosa

1888
Five-ton cornerstone laid at Lock No. 1 (later known as Lock No. 10)

1890 February 8
The first (ten) electric street lights are turned on

1896 January 12
The *Baltimore* makes the first passage upriver through the locks system

1896 January 27
The *Baltimore* descends through the locks with first load of coal

1898 May 12
Last spike driven in the Mobile & Ohio Railroad route from West Point, Mississippi, through Tuscaloosa to Montgomery, Alabama

1900
First automobile driven in Tuscaloosa

1903 August 4
Central Foundry lights its furnace for the first time

1911 December 6
First airplane takes off from Tuscaloosa

1915 May 13
At Squaw Shoals, the last lock is declared open

1923 August 22
Capitol burns

1923 September
Partlow State School opens

1924
City water system reaches Alberta City

1925
Merchants' Bank & Trust Building completed; U.S. Numbered Highway System inaugurated

1926 January 1
The University of Alabama defeats the University of Washington in the Rose Bowl in "the game that changed the South," the first of Bama's string of national championships

1927 January 1
The Crimson Tide ties Stanford in the Rose Bowl

1932 March 21
Tornado destroys much of Northport

1932 July 6
Veterans Hospital formally dedicated

1933 August 12
A. T. Harden and Dan Pippen Jr. lynched

1933 September 24
Dennis Cross lynched

1933 September 27
"Shall We Accept the Challenge?," published on front page of *Tuscaloosa News*

1936
WJRD, Tuscaloosa's first radio station, begins broadcasting

1938 April 12
Bama Theatre opens, Tuscaloosa's first air-conditioned building

1938
Alabama Institute of Aeronautics opens

1943 July
Northington General Hospital opens

1956 February 3
Autherine Lucy first arrives at UA

1956 February 6
Lucy escapes a mob; that evening the board of trustees suspends her until further notice

1956 February 7
Buford Boone publishes Pulitzer Prize–winning "What a Price for Peace" on front page of *Tuscaloosa News*

1962 May 5
Stillman College students ordered to vacate bus seats; Tuscaloosa Citizens for Action Committee (TCAC) formed

1963 June 11
Stand in the Schoolhouse Door; John F. Kennedy addresses the nation

1964 April 12
George Wallace dedicates Tuscaloosa County Courthouse containing racially discriminating signs

1964 June 9
Bloody Tuesday

1964 June 25
Federal judge Seybourn H. Lynne orders Tuscaloosa County to remove all discriminatory signs in courthouse

1964 July 9
Jack Palance center of race riot at Druid Theater

1964 August 10
TCAC starts bus boycott

1964 November
Druid City Transit gives its franchise to the Tuscaloosa City Commission

1965 April 12
Tuscaloosa Transit resumes bus services with integrated workforce and nondiscrimination policy

1976 July 11
West Alabama General Hospital dedicated

1985 May 18
CSS *Tuscaloosa* discovered in Mobile River

1986
JVC opens its manufacturing plant

1993 October 1
Formal announcement that Mercedes Benz AG would build its first foreign manufacturing—not just assembly—plant in Vance

1997 February 14
First customer-ready Mercedes Benz M-Class rolls off the assembly line

1998
Compromise lifts federal court supervision of Tuscaloosa city schools

2011 April 27
Tornado destroys 12 percent of Tuscaloosa, eventually claiming fifty-three lives

2012 January 9
The Crimson Tide defeats the LSU Tigers 21–0 to win its fourteenth national championship

For further reading

TUSCALOOSA: TWO HUNDRED YEARS IN THE MAKING is set into the larger context of the events, choices, innovations, and social movements occurring across the state and nation. *Tuscaloosa* is also built up from seemingly endless unrelated details gleaned from newspaper articles, letters, and the like. But *Tuscaloosa* also relies on the research, writings, and arguments of fine historians, many of whom are personal friends. For those who wish to go into a little more depth on particular topics, their writings form the core of my suggestions for further reading.

TO BEGIN WITH

Those interested in the history of Alabama should start with Edwin C. Bridges, *Alabama: The Making of an American State* (Tuscaloosa: University of Alabama Press, 2016). A handsome and engaging book, *Alabama* not only introduces many of the issues that have been central to Alabama's story but also provides the larger backdrop that explains much of what happened at a local level.

The standard books on Tuscaloosa's history are collections of newspaper articles. Matthew William Clinton's *Matt Clinton's Scrapbook: One Hundred and Fifty Years in the Life of Tuscaloosa and Northport* (New Orleans: Portals Press, 1979) reprints what he wrote in the *Tuscaloosa News*. Clinton relied a great deal on his father, Thomas Clinton, whose original newspaper articles and reminiscences are more difficult to locate. Former *Tuscaloosa News* editor Ben A. Green's *A History of Tuscaloosa, Alabama, 1816–1949* (Tuscaloosa: Confederate Publishing, 1980) is largely an undigested chronicle of events drawn primarily from newspaper articles. He did seem to have consulted city government records that have since been lost. I have, however, found contradictions between some of his assertions and contemporary sources that he seems not to have consulted. I have also discovered outright errors.

In 2011, James N. Ezell privately published his complete transcription of E. A. Powell's *Fifty-Five Years in West Alabama*, which was originally serialized in the *Tuskaloosa Gazette* from 1886 to 1889. This represented an enormous improvement over the flawed and incomplete version of Powell's memoirs that had been previously published in the *Alabama Historical Quarterly*, for it included a glossary, place name gazetteer, and index. Ezell also compiled *The Ferryman's Last Trip: An Index of Persons from Articles Published in Twenty-Six Tuscaloosa County Weekly Newspapers from 1821 to 1928 Containing over Twenty Thousand Names* (self-pub, 2010). Non-circulating copies of these two works are available at the W. S. Hoole Special Collections Library, University of Alabama, and at the Tuscaloosa Public Library; and searchable electronic versions of these two works are freely available from him. Ezell has also compiled an immense collection of unusual facts about Tuscaloosa from which he writes columns for the monthly magazine *Druid City Living*.

CHAPTER 1. TUSCALOOSANS SECURE THE STATE CAPITAL . . . ONLY TO LOSE IT

The best overview of Alabama before the Civil War is found in Herbert James Lewis, *Clearing the Thickets: A History of Antebellum Alabama* (New Orleans: Quid Pro, 2013). Chronicling Tuscaloosa before the war was the aim of Matthew William Clinton in his *Tuscaloosa, Alabama: Its Early Days, 1816–1865* (Tuscaloosa: Zonta Club, 1958).

A study of Tuscaloosa's frontier years can be found in Thomas Chase Hagood's "Alabama Fever Rages: Migrations to the Frontier of Early Alabama," *Alabama Heritage* 125 (Summer 2017): 48–59, which is taken from "Rewriting the Frontier: Making History in Tuscaloosa, Alabama," his 2004 dissertation from the University of Georgia. William Ely's description of Tuscaloosa was reprinted in W. Stanley Hoole, ed., "Elyton, Alabama, and the Connecticut Asylum: The Letters of William H. Ely, 1820–1821," *Alabama Review* 3, no. 1 (January 1950): 36–69. Archibald Bruce McEachin's *A History of Tuscaloosa, 1816–1880* (Tuscaloosa: Confederate Publishing, 1977) consists largely of biographical sketches.

How fortunate that architectural historian Robert O. Mellown chose to devote his energies to Tuscaloosa's antebellum buildings. On the statehouse: "Alabama's Fourth Capital: The Construction of the State House in Tuscaloosa," *Alabama Review* 40, no. 4 (October 1987): 259–283; and "Variations on a Capitol Plan," *Alabama Heritage* #77 (Summer 2005): 8–17. On the University of Alabama: "The President's Mansion at the University of Alabama," *Alabama Review* 35, no. 3 (July 1982): 200–229; "The Alabama Rotunda," *Alabama Heritage* 44 (Spring 1997): 32–37; and *The University of Alabama: A Guide to the Campus and Its Architecture* (Tuscaloosa: University of Alabama Press, 2013). On the Alabama Insane Hospital: "Construction of the Alabama Insane Hospital, 1852–1861," *Alabama Review* 38 (April 1985): 83–104; and "Mental Health and Moral Architecture," *Alabama Heritage* 32 (Spring 1994): 5–17. On domestic architecture: the Hardin Perkins House and Garden, "Where Katie Was Born: Adventures in Provenance," *Alabama Heritage* 96 (Spring 2010): 53–56; and "The Jemison Mansion and Longwood," *Alabama Heritage* 26 (October 1992): 24–34.

F. A. P. Barnard, including his achievements in photography and astronomy, is addressed by Robert O. Mellown and Gene G. Byrd in "The Extraordinary Frederick Augustus Porter Barnard," *Alabama Heritage* 56 (Spring 2000): 6–25. John Gorman Barr's southwestern humor is collected in *Rowdy Tales from Early Alabama: The Humor of John Gorman Barr*, ed. by G. Ward Hubbs (Tuscaloosa: University of Alabama Press, 1981).

John W. Quist's extraordinary study, *Restless Visionaries: The Social Roots of Antebellum Reform in Alabama and Michigan* (Baton Rouge: Louisiana State University Press, 1998), contrasts the reform impulse in Tuscaloosa with Ann Arbor and Ypsilanti, Michigan. *Restless Visionaries*, make no mistake, is a formidable read, but he published a much more digestible version focusing strictly on Tuscaloosa: "Slaveholding Operatives of the Benevolent Empire: Bible, Tract, and Sunday School Societies in Antebellum Tuscaloosa County, Alabama," *Journal of Southern History* 62, no. 3 (August 1996): 481–526.

CHAPTER 2. TUSCALOOSANS BECOME CITIZENS OF THE CONFEDERACY...AND REAP THE WHIRLWIND

Tuscaloosa companies during the Civil War are listed in Beasey S. Hendrix Jr., *Tuskaloosa's Own: A Short History and Muster Roll of Confederate Units from Tuskaloosa County, Alabama* (Tuscaloosa: Colonial Press, 1988). Much of the material on the Tuscaloosa prisons can be found in Robert Pickenpaugh, *Captives in Blue: The Civil War Prisons of the Confederacy* (Tuscaloosa: University of Alabama Press, 2013).

Croxton's raid and the University of Alabama are the subjects of Helen Eckinger, "The Militarization of the University of Alabama," *Alabama Review* 66, no. 3 (July 2013): 165–168; Rex Miller, *Croxton's Raid* (Fort Collins, CO: Old Army Press, 1979); James Pickett Jones, *Yankee Blitzkrieg: Wilson's Raid Through Alabama and Georgia* (Lexington: University Press of Kentucky, 1976); and Clark E. Center Jr., "The Burning of the University of Alabama," *Alabama Heritage* 16 (Spring 1990): 30–45.

Christopher Lyle McIlwain Sr. puts the invasion of Tuscaloosa and burning of the university in the larger context of the end of fighting and beginning of Reconstruction in *1865 Alabama: From Civil War to Uncivil Peace* (Tuscaloosa: University of Alabama Press, 2017).

My own *Searching for Freedom after the Civil War: Klansman, Carpetbagger, Scalawag, and Freedman* (Tuscaloosa: University of Alabama Press, 2015) uses Ryland Randolph's threatening political cartoon, *A Prospective Scene*, to examine the contending factions and their motivations in postwar Tuscaloosa.

CHAPTER 3. TUSCALOOSANS RECRUIT SMOKESTACK INDUSTRIES...DOGGEDLY

The damming of the Black Warrior is the subject of Kenneth D. Willis, "Harnessing the Black Warrior River," *Alabama Heritage* 33 (Summer 1994): 19–25. Horace King, who rebuilt Tuscaloosa's bridge after its destruction by Croxton's raiders, is the subject of John S. Lupold and Thomas L. French Jr., *Bridging Deep South Rivers: The Life and Legend of Horace King* (Athens: University of Georgia Press, 2004). Paul Singleton Sr. published a reminiscence of his years working at Central Foundry in *Foundry Life: Holt, Alabama* (self-pub., 2004).

CHAPTER 4. TUSCALOOSANS TRANSFORM THEIR EVERYDAY LIVES . . . BY BUILDING A MODERN CITY

Two books—Daniel J. Boorstin's *The Americans: The Democratic Experience* (New York: Random House, 1973); and Robert J. Gordon's *The Rise and Fall of American Growth: The U.S. Standard of Living since the Civil War* (Princeton, NJ: Princeton University Press, 2016)—inspired me and suggested ways of organizing this domestic revolution by looking carefully at newspapers.

The architect who designed many important Tuscaloosa buildings in the early twentieth century is the subject of Thomas Mark Shelby's *D. O. Whilldin, Alabama Architect* (Birmingham: Birmingham Historical Society, 2009).

CHAPTER 5. TUSCALOOSANS SEE THE WORLD . . . AND VICE VERSA

The 1933 lynchings are the subject of B. J. Hollars's "'Martyrs . . . to a Mock Cause': Murder, Mayhem, and an Honorable Scrubbing in Tuscaloosa," *Alabama Heritage* 102 (Fall 2011): 28–35, which is extracted from his larger work, *Thirteen Loops: Race, Violence, and the Last Lynching in America* (Tuscaloosa: University of Alabama Press, 2011).

The confrontations surrounding the desegregation of the university in 1956 and 1963 is the subject of E. Culpepper Clark's thorough study, *The Schoolhouse Door: Segregation's Last Stand at the University of Alabama* (New York: Oxford University Press, 1963). Katie Cole looks at Buford Boone and his Pulitzer Prize–winning editorial in "Buford Boone: To Stand on Principle," *Alabama Heritage* 85 (Summer 2007): 4–7. Deputy Attorney General Nicholas Katzenbach's personal reflections on the Stand at the Schoolhouse Door can be found in "An Eyewitness Account of the Racial Integration of the University of Alabama," *Journal of Blacks in Higher Education* 61 (Autumn 2008): 60–65.

The events surrounding Bloody Tuesday are masterfully recounted in Simon Wendt, "God, Gandhi, and Guns: The African American Freedom Struggle in Tuscaloosa, Alabama, 1964–1965," *Journal of African American History* 89, no. 1 (Winter 2004): 36–56.

CHAPTER 6. TUSCALOOSANS ENDURE SIX MINUTES . . . AND EVERYONE COMES TO LEND A HAND

I found two of several books on the April 2011 tornado particularly useful. *Eye of the Storm: The Devastation, Resiliency and Restoration of Tuscaloosa, Alabama* (Tuscaloosa: *Tuscaloosa News*, 2011) is a compilation of their photographs and articles. Lars Anderson's *The Storm and the Tide: Tragedy, Hope and Triumph in Tuscaloosa* (New York: Sports Illustrated Books, 2014) recounts the Crimson Tide as both the team and individual players dealt with the tornado and ultimately brought a national championship home to Tuscaloosa. A related book by Carson Tinker, the long snapper whose girlfriend Ashley Harrison was killed, is *A Season to Remember: Faith in the Midst of the Storm* (Nashville: B&H, 2014).

Index

Page numbers in italics refer to illustration captions and sidebars.